THOMAS BEWICK

His Life and Times

BY

ROBERT ROBINSON

FRANK GRAHAM

6, Queen's Terrace, Newcastle upon Tyne NE2 2PL.

First Published 1887
Second Edition 1972
(Facsimile)
Limited to 950 Copies

SBN 902833 944

Printed by Howe Brothers (Gateshead) Limited

THOMAS BEWICK:

His Life and Times.

THOMAS BEWICK.

THOMAS BEWICK

His Life and Times

BY

ROBERT ROBINSON

With Two Hundred Illustrations

NEWCASTLE

PRINTED FOR R. ROBINSON, PILGRIM STREET

Jubilee of Queen Victoria

MDCCCLXXXVII

TO

THOMAS GOW, Esquire.

OF CAMBO, NORTHUMBERLAND,

THE FOLLOWING PAGES

ARE

𝕽espectfully 𝕴nscribed

BY

HIS GRATEFUL SERVANT,

THE AUTHOR.

PREFACE.

HOMAS BEWICK remarks that "a grace and a preface ought not to be too long,"[1] an excellent precept worthy of observance. As has been elsewhere explained, my object in this work has been mainly to relate interesting particulars heard in conversation with my dear old friends the Misses Bewick, embracing the meaning of many of the tailpieces which adorn the "History of British Birds," and little traits of Thomas Bewick's personal history and habits, believing that nothing would be considered trifling that tends in the least to illustrate the character of a man so eminent as an artist, and of known private worth. These characteristics must have a special value with all who recognise his talents and genius, when Dr. Johnson's reflection is borne in mind, that "lives can only be written from personal knowledge, which is growing every day less, and in a short time is lost for ever."

Of the many who have chosen Bewick for their theme, no one has had the friendly intercourse with his family enjoyed by myself, or been favoured so highly. My purchases of old included the Birds and Quadrupeds on imperial paper, uncut, presentation copies to his wife and children, together with

---

[1] See cut at head of Preface to "British Birds," vol. ii.

many rarities, some unique. By far the most important were Bewick's celebrated woodcuts of the Chillingham Wild Bull and the Old Horse Waiting for Death, the finest examples of wood-engraving ever produced. To these I may add that presents were made from time to time of early printed books for children, with woodcuts by the brothers, and autograph letters, specially selected to enhance the interest and value of this volume. I had also the privilege, unsolicited, to take home and use his interleaved copy of the Birds, two vols., 1821 (Lot 183 in the Bewick Sale Catalogue, February 1884), in which Mr. Bewick, agreeable to the wish of his daughter Jane, had written an explanation of a large number of the vignettes. For this valuable and interesting copy I bid at the auction one hundred pounds. E. B. Mounsey, Esq., of Darlington, became the buyer at one hundred guineas. That gentleman a few days after was offered £150 for the volumes, but declined to part with them. This lot was started at the modest sum of three pounds.

The correspondence between Mr. Bewick and Mr. Charnley, relative to his reprint of the "Select Fables," 1820, pp. 139–143, will be read with interest. The following Notes and Analysis of that work are from the pen of Miss Jane Bewick, and will be found both amusing and instructive. They are contained in an imperial 8vo copy (Lot 167 in the Bewick Sale) in the magnificent Bewick Collection at Pendower, Newcastle, the seat of J. W. Pease, Esq. At the beginning Miss Bewick gives a list of the *habitués* of that once celebrated resort of Whig politicians, Charnley's back-shop. The first name is that of the worthy bookseller himself, "Emerson Charnley, and his man, Willie Garrett;" then follow "Sarah Hodgson, the printer, and her sons, Thomas Hodgson, printer, John Hodgson, James Hodgson;

George Burnett; John Trotter Brockett, attorney; John Murray, surgeon; Rev. William Turner; William Preston, printer; John Adamson, attorney; William Nicholson, portrait-painter; Charlton Nesbit; Nat Winch; Dr. Headlam, sometimes."

Miss Bewick describes the frontispiece, or portrait of her father, by Nesbit, as "a vile caricature of T. B. The hair looks like a wig awry." Of the cut on title, "T. B. did not cut this." The cut above advertisement, "perspective bad." Ditto memoir, "Isaac Nicholson, sculpt." End of memoir, "Who was the artist here, Mr. Charnley? Where on earth was this cut produced?" Cut above contents (Tynemouth Priory), "Who did this?" Referring to the small figures in the foreground to the right, Miss Jane asks, "Are these paddocks?" Cut, end of contents. "Stag drinking; to the right, Isa. Nicholson's rock." Vignette, p. 6, "background copied from vignette in Birds." Vignette, p. 8, "Howitt's designs for Dr. Fothergill's work. This and some others were sent to him in America; what business had Mr. Nicholson with the design?" Page 10, "Tommy Trip (Thos. B.), published by Newbery;" p. 16, "Where came this from?" p. 19, "foreground cut away;" p. 20, "Gay's Fables" (1779); p. 21, "John Bewick;" p. 23, "foreground cut away;" p. 24, "sky gone;" p. 26, "bad copy, Looking Glass, p. 149, the ferns are made growing out of the tops of the trees;" p. 33, "whitened;" p. 36, "Tommy Trip;" p. 38, "Gay's Fables;" p. 40, "Uncle John;" p. 42, "The Fisherman, stolen from the Birds, bad copy;" p. 44, "from the Story-Teller, 1778, 'The Trials of Virtue';" p. 45, "foreground a little lightened;" p. 50, "Tommy Trip;" p. 52, "Select Fables" (1784); p. 54, "Tommy Trip;" p. 57, "Select Fables, no alteration here;" p. 60, "Lawrence on the Horse, bad copy;" pp. 62 and 66, "Trip;" p. 65, "Select Fables, the

b

walk whitewashed;" p. 72, "from a little story-book, Aladdin;" p. 81, "Select Fables;" p. 82, "T. B.'s Trotting Horse copied;" p. 84, "an advertisement on handbill;" p. 86, "not T. B.;" pp. 88, 92, 96, "Trip;" p. 91, "a very pretty cut;" p. 94, "Tees' Chain Bridge, copied from a cut done for Durham Agricultural Report, not by T. B.;" p. 97, "Select Fables, John Bewick, the drawing at Cherryburn;" pp. 100, 108, 116, "Trip;" the cut on p. 123 of Charnley's edition of the Select Fables, is engraved by John Bewick; p. 125, "Select Fables, beautiful design and cut;" pp. 128, 136, 138, 140, 144, 152, 166, 204, 212, 214, "from Tommy Trip;" p. 132, "reduced copy from Fisher's Spring Day, very bad;" p. 141, "by David Martin;" p. 142, "copy from Jane Hewitson's Book Cut, reduced and reversed, a marriage—see coach in background;" p. 148, "from Fisher's Spring Day, bad copy, reduced;" p. 154, "Oh! what a horse;" p. 168, "copy from a saddle-plate;" p. 178, "from Robin Hood;" p. 180, "from The Looking Glass;" p. 182, "copied from Freshfield's Book Cut;" p. 184, "engraved by David Martin;" p. 200, "very old cut;" p. 210, "Death of Jezebel;" pp. 216, 226, 244, 258, 262, 276, 284, 318, "from T. Trip;" p. 228, "from The Looking Glass;" pp. 235, 237, "from the Select Fables;" p. 241, "Gay's Fables;" pp. 243, 245, "Select Fables;" p. 247, "from the Story-Teller;" pp. 249, 251, "from the Select Fables;" p. 253, "from Pamela;" p. 257, "Story-Teller;" p. 260, Stag, copy;" pp. 265, 267, 271, "Gay's Fables;" p. 269, "Story-Teller;" pp. 273, 275, 277, 279, 281, 283, 285, 287, 293, "Select Fables;" pp. 303, 305, 307, 317, 327, "from Gay's Fables" (1779), published by Saint. Miss Jane Bewick states that ninety-eight of the cuts in Charnley's reprint of the Select Fables of 1784 are not by her father.

The following is from the office copy of the sixth edition of the Birds (1826), the last personally superintended in its passage through the press by Bewick, and to which he contributed an original and most interesting preface, omitted in subsequent re-issues of the work. This office copy abounds with marginal notes by Mr. Bewick, consisting of instructions of the most minute description to the pressmen respecting the proper printing of the cuts, affording evidence of the great care bestowed by him on this important part of the work, and his thorough knowledge and mastery of details. This will best appear from a few extracts taken at random. He goes through the cuts, marking such birds as were engraved from stuffed specimens with the word "Wycliffe;" others as drawn from "Life;" whilst the word "Nature" is pencilled to by far the largest number.

Against the Lesser White-throat, page 253, we read, "Keep the bird a little darker, or the background lighter." The Wren is marked "Wycliffe." The Swallow "Life." The Night-jar "Nature." The Partridge, p. 348, "A thin overlay here." The Stone Falcon, p. 46, "Lighten the foliage here." The Eagle-Owl, p. 52, "This has generally been printed far too pale on the back and wings." The Snowy Owl, p. 54, "Print this cut pale, but let the feathering faintly and delicately appear." The Raven, p. 79, "The legs of this bird have generally been too hard pulled." The Magpie, p. 92, "The bird might bear an overlay on the body, but the distance, though clear, is full hard enough pulled."

The originality and merits of Bewick have been set forth in past years by able writers with a felicity of language and an appreciative insight into the mind and characteristics of the great wood-engraver that leave nothing for after critics to add to their tributes of praise. John Jackson, in his "Treatise on

Wood-Engraving," and my old schoolfellow, John Gray Bell, in his excellent Catalogue of Works Illustrated by the Bewicks, gathered and combined the same with much judgment in their respective works. The Rev. Thomas Hugo, in his "Bewick Collector," likewise found it impossible to pass by the elegant and exhaustive criticism of men so eminent as Professor Wilson, Thomas Doubleday, Audubon, and others. Following their example, I have not hesitated to avail myself of such a valuable catena of matured sentiment and thought.

A marked example of the influence of Bewick's Natural Histories in diffusing a love for animated Nature among the young is instanced in the early career of the late Mr. William Proctor, Curator of the Durham University Museum. As Willoughby's Ornithology was the favourite book of Pennant when a youth, first deriving his propensity for Natural History from its perusal, so Bewick's Birds awoke a chord in the heart of young Proctor only to cease with life itself. On the occasion of a presentation made to that gentleman (December 1864) in acknowledgment of the valuable services he had rendered to Ornithology and other branches of Natural History, Canon Tristram, in the course of his address, thus alluded to Mr. Proctor's first introduction to Bewick :—

"If there ever was such a thing as a born naturalist, Mr. Proctor was undoubtedly a very favourable specimen of the class. When he was but a carpenter's apprentice he was in the habit, whenever he could get holiday, of trudging into Newcastle, a distance of sixteen miles, just to look into a bird-stuffer's window, and after gazing with wistful and curious eyes upon the treasures he saw there displayed, he would supperless and penniless trudge back again home. In the course of these rambles Mr. Proctor asked the price of a book upon birds—a book written by Thomas Bewick, the engraver. He had often looked into the window in which this work was exhibited, and he longed to become its possessor. He was but a poor carpenter's boy, but he saved up all the money he could, and one day he went into the shop and inquired the price. Old Thomas Bewick was in the shop, and he told him 13s. a volume. There were two volumes, and poor William Proctor, who had only just 13s., asked if he could have one volume, and he would call for the other afterwards, when he got sufficient money. Thomas Bewick, in his broad Northumbrian dialect, said he did not do business in that way, and at first declined the offer; but afterwards perceiving, from the blank face of the young man, the keenness of the disappointment which he felt, he handed him the two books, and told him he could take them away and pay for them when he got the 'brass.' William left the shop in transports of delight, and when he had got three or four miles from Newcastle, he sat himself down by the roadside and commenced an eager perusal of the books he had long coveted. So absorbed did he become in their contents that he did not cease reading until darkness set in and compelled him to desist. Six weeks afterwards Mr. Proctor called upon Bewick, purchased the second volume, and paid him the money, 26s. Bewick said, 'Well, my lad, I trusted thee when I did not know thee, there's thy money back,' and he made Mr. Proctor a present of the books. That begun a friendship which was only terminated by the death of Mr. Bewick. From that time the fortunes of Mr. Proctor were made—the fortune he acquired in fame, respect, and reputation."

Unostentatious and courteous in his mode of life, this humble-minded student of Nature died January 8, 1877, aged seventy-six.

On the 31st of December 1825, Bewick and his son dissolved partnership, after having been thirteen years thus connected. Newcastle was the theatre from first to last of the art life of Thomas Bewick and his son, with the exception of the year he worked in London.

There is an interesting little article in the *Newcastle Magazine* for October 1830, entitled "Three Newcastle Apprentices," signed R. P. H., *i.e.*, Robert Pollard, Holloway. Mr. Bewick's old friend and companion, then in his seventy-second year, lived at Holloway. The three apprentices were Bewick, Bulmer, and Pollard, each of whom had, by a course of probity and industry, achieved fame and independence. Mr. R. Bewick did not wish this harmless communication to appear in print, and wrote a letter to W. A. Mitchell, the publisher, to that effect; nevertheless the article, to which there could be no reasonable objection, was not withheld.

In the summer of 1828, after the lapse of fifty years, Bewick, accompanied by his daughters, visited London, to the surprise of his old friends. Mr. Bulmer sent his carriage to Bewick's lodgings, in which Pollard and he and the Misses Bewick were conveyed to Bulmer's elegant mansion in the country, where they all dined together, and after spending a delightful day, they "took their leave, and the coachman and horses were ordered out to take them back to town where taken up." Bulmer died worth £30,000. The sale of Goldsmith's and Parnell's Poems produced a profit of £1500 to Bulmer, as I was informed by Miss Bewick. The wood-engravers then in London showed every kindness and respect to the aged artist, whose days were fast drawing to a close.

The little farm of eight acres at Cherryburn, with the Land-sale Collieries on Eltringham Common and Mickley West Wantes, were rented by Thomas and William Bewick for some time after the death of their father, at £60 per annum. These might be worked with unceasing labour for many a long year without affording a tithe of the benefit derived by Mr. Bulmer from the ingenuity of the Bewicks within a few months.

The scenery on our noble river, the prime source of so much wealth and material prosperity, has changed much since the days of that pious gentlewoman, Dame Dorothy Lawson, who from the antique porch and mullioned windows of her manor-house at St. Anthony's, beheld its natural beauties and important traffic. "This seat," we are told, "was most commodious for pleasure, and pleasant for all commoditys; the rich and renown'd river Tine ebbing and flowing in such a propor-

tionable distance from the house that neither the water is inconvenient to it, nor does it want the convenience of the water.
The vast confluence of ships which it brings to Newcastle for
coles pass under the full view of the house." Such a prospect
might well gladden the heart of a lady of the seventeenth
century.

There are still resident families of position who from their
gardens on its southern shore, opposite St. Anthony's, can "sit
quietly, and, looking on the water, see some fishes sport in the
silver streams, others leaping at flies of several shapes and
colours," though the time has gone by when "looking down the
meadows," in the words of good old Izaak Walton, "I could
see here a boy gathering lilies and ladysmocks, and there a girl
cropping culverkeyes and cowslips, all to make garlands suitable
to this present month of May" ("Complete Angler," chap. xvi.)

Marvellous have been the changes for the better in the
outward aspect and social condition of society in Newcastle
since the Jubilee of good King George the Third, thanks to
the genius of Sir W. Armstrong, Richard Grainger, George and
Robert Stephenson, and other eminent engineers, and the liberality of our venerable townsman, Mr. John Clayton, without
whose aid a Grainger might have toiled in vain. Within living
memory the direct road leading from Pilgrim Street to the
Shield Field, now one of the most thronged in the town, was
deemed so unsafe after nightfall by reason of its loneliness, that
persons living in Northumberland Street, and wishful to reach
the latter place, had to go round by the Manor Chare, the Stock
Bridge, and Pandon Bank, to avoid danger to life or property.
This was before the erection of the New Bridge over Pandon
Dean in 1812.

Mr. Clayton Atkinson states that Bewick when in London

in 1776 worked "with a person of the name of Cole." Mr. W. H. D. Longstaffe informs me that the Coles were a Gates-head family. That gentleman has in his collection a "South-West Prospect of the Ancient City of York," engraved by B. Cole, 1731; it is a large sheet. At the Bewick Sale I bought (Lot 142) a fine uncut copy of "A History of Animals," by (Sir) John Hill, M.D., London, 1752. The work is in folio, and adorned with twenty-eight copperplates, signed B. Cole, sculp. This may probably be the engraver alluded to by Atkinson. In the *Gentleman's Magazine* for 1753, some of the plates in Edwards' "Natural History" are closely copied by means of woodcuts. These are well drawn and executed. The Golden Thrush in the December number is a good example. I have not been able to discover the name of the engraver.

With respect to the trade edition of Gay's Fables, published in London in 1788, I never could bring my mind to believe that the cuts were by John Bewick; some of them might be. A word to Miss Bewick would have settled the point, but with other queries this was forgot until too late. The book does not appear in Bell's Catalogue.

In the notice of Robert Johnson, p. 96, it is said that he could not engrave on wood. This is quite true, even though the cuts in the "Mirror" by R. J. should be his. At page 118 of that work, which was published by Saint, and is now very rare, there is a beautiful cut heading the Tale of Tity and Mirtillo, with others, by T. Bewick. In the seventh edition of Croxall's Æsop's Fables, published by T. Saint in 1783, p. 86, the cut above the Fable of the "Boasting Mule" is an attempt on wood by Ralph Beilby.

There are two tailpieces ("British Birds," 1847, p. 35), of which a wrong explanation has hitherto been given; both are

WILLIAM CHARNLEY,

BOOKSELLER

Newcastle upon Tyne

Born in 1727. Died in 1803.

Engraved by J. Ranson from a Miniature by Murphy taken Æ. 72.

closely connected. The true reading is this, to quote Bewick's own words:—" The attraction of an alehouse has, as usual, proved too powerful for the driver. He has left his horse and cart to refresh himself and tell news ; meantime four idle lads have got into the cart ; one unfortunately has fallen out and got killed ; consternation and dismay have taken possession of the rest."

The Sequel, p. 50.—" This is a continuation of the story so admirably depictured at p. 35. The unprofitable servant is about to reap the reward so justly due to him for leaving his cart and horse and guzzling in the alehouse. This has the same background as the previous cut."—Bewick MS.

A small view of Strawberry Hill has been christened over and over again as the Hon. Horace Walpole's Book Plate. It was engraved for the late Mr. Charnley, bookseller, to head his List of Works printed at Strawberry Hill. The receipt, in the handwriting of Mr. R. Bewick, is now before me, dated April 3, 1819. The price of the cut was £2, 2s.

The father of this gentleman, William Charnley, son of a haberdasher at Penrith, at the age of fourteen was bound apprentice in Newcastle, January 8, 1741, to Joseph Longstaffe, tinplate-worker, and afterwards turned over to Martin Bryson, who had been admitted to the freedom of the town in 1725. At the expiration of his apprenticeship in 1748 Charnley was admitted to the freedom of the town, and in 1750 his master took him into partnership, which was dissolved in 1755, when the old apprentice continued the business on his own account "at the bridge end." Mr. Charnley died August 9, 1803, aged seventy-six years (see Mr. Hodgson Hinde's " History of the Press in Newcastle").

I am indebted to my old friend, Mr. William Dodd, so well

c

versed in local and bibliographical lore, for the fine portrait of Mr. Charnley, and also for the true version of the anecdote I am about to relate. Good Mr. Charnley was very deaf, and carried an ear trumpet. Standing one Saturday at his shop door with this instrument in his hand, a pitman passed by who had just come out of Swarley's tavern, the " Black Boy." Seeing the trumpet, without knowing its use, he cried out, " Play us a tune, man, on thy trumpet." To hear what was said the bookseller put the trumpet to his ear. " What!" exclaimed the miner, " does thou want to make us believe thou can blaw a tune out of thy lug?"

Some collectors are curious to know the meaning of the letters P. V. B. B. on the beautiful cut of the Newfoundland Dog, p. 306, " History of Quadrupeds," 1790. They are the initials of Preston, printer, foreman at Hodgson's office; Vint,[1] printer and publisher; Bell, the painter, who lived in the High Bridge, and built Bell's Court in Pilgrim Street—friends who accompanied Bewick to Eslington, where the drawing was made. The monogram explains itself.

There is a vignette at p. 207 of Bewick's " Memoir," which the late Bishop Bewick, a warm admirer of the artist, thus amusingly described in an interleaved copy of the " Vignettes," octavo, 1827 :—" A countryman who kept bees, and possessed three hives, visited his treasure on a warm summer day, mounted on a donkey, with his dog. The donkey was properly secured, and his owner felt inclined to rest. Unfortunately the former began to rub his hind quarters against one of the hives, a liberty the bees at once determined to resent. Believing at first the dog to be the aggressor, one of the little creatures fastened on a

---

[1] John Vint, of the firm of Vint & Anderson, printers, in the Burnt House Entry, Side, Newcastle.

leg. The poor dog, stung with pain, made off with piteous cries ; the donkey, being tied up, could not follow, but strove to heal its torments by licking the afflicted spot. The bark of the dog and the bray of the donkey would very soon awaken its master from his pleasant nap."

On the 1st of August 1883 began that labour of love, mingled with regret, which resulted in the Catalogue of Books, Engravings, Furniture, and Silver Plate formerly belonging to Thomas Bewick, and sold by order of the Executors of Miss Isabella Bewick, deceased. Mr. J. W. Barnes of Durham, and Mr. Joseph Crawhall (the executors), called at my shop on the afternoon of that day, and empowered me to proceed at once. A most successful sale took place in the early part of February 1884. Six months afterwards the residue came to the hammer, when twenty-nine lots of "engraved wood blocks by various artists, the crude efforts of pupils, and of no art value whatever," were sold in lots of ten each, for *very small* sums.[1] Both sales were held in Newcastle.

Bewick's daughters entertained the feeling, shared by distinguished strangers when on visits to the town, that their father had been slighted, passed over, and not sufficiently appreciated by the literate part of the community of Newcastle. It must be admitted that this impression was not altogether without cause. Sometimes the pupils were put before their master when the Misses Bewick were present in company, a proceeding in very questionable taste. Other matters of a more offensive kind might be named. It is only recently that the claims of this great master to be admitted into the first rank of painters in water-colours has been recognised. In the

---

[1] "The Bewick Memento." Field & Tuer, London.

Introduction to the " Bewick Memento," the question as to who really designed the tailpieces in the Birds and Quadrupeds has been duly considered.   The testimony of Mrs. Hodgson, widow of Solomon Hodgson, Bewick's first printer and publisher, ought to have great weight.   This lady was personally acquainted with Nesbit, Clennell, and Johnson.   Yet whilst still engaged in a violent quarrel with her husband's old friend, she concludes a long and angry epistle to the editor of the *Monthly Magazine* in words which do honour to her sense of truth and justice. " I never attacked Mr. Bewick's professional abilities," continues the writer ; " on the contrary, I think him a great designer and an unrivalled wood-cutter, and I do him the justice to add further that I believe he designed and engraved all the figures and vignettes in the books above mentioned himself" (*i.e.*, the Birds and Quadrupeds).   This letter is signed " Sarah Hodgson," and dated " *Newcastle Chronicle* Office, December 23, 1805."

The recollection of the opening sentence of this Preface admonishes me to hasten to a close ; but still one fondly lingers over the past, and those scenes and sketches which " lend to loneliness delight."   For

> " Sounds which address the ear, are lost and die
> In one short hour, but that which strikes the eye,
> Lives long upon the mind."—*Watts*.

So will it ever be with the delightful and hitherto unsurpassed woodcuts of this great master.

Since this volume was first announced, some changes have been made.   To meet the wishes of friends and collectors, the size of it has been altered to imperial 8vo, so as to range with the largest paper copies of the Birds, Quadrupeds, and Fables, thus enabling gentlemen to have a uniform set of the whole. Whilst still a gallery of choice engravings by Thomas and John Bewick, the subject matter will be found amply to justify the title under which it now appears. The fine series of portraits of local celebrities, friends of Bewick, have been added at considerable cost, the price remaining the same. My grateful acknowledgments are due in the first place to the subscribers, without whose encouragement the work would never have been undertaken, and not less so to the distinguished liberality of Thomas Gow, Esq., of Cambo, for the use of his invaluable woodcuts of the Chillingham Wild Bull and the Old Horse Waiting for Death, Bewick's first and last great works; to the Natural History Society of Northumberland, Durham, and Newcastle, for permission to copy their beautiful portrait of Bewick by T. S. Good—the last portrait he sat for; to J. W. Pease, Esq., Pendower, Newcastle, for the privilege of making use of the Bewick treasures in his noble library, abounding in illuminated manuscripts by mediæval scribes, a copy of the Sacred Scriptures on thin vellum, of the fourteenth century, and early English printed books. I have reserved mention to this place of his valuable and interesting picture of the Lost Child, by Ramsay, shown at the Second Exhibition of the Northumberland Institution for the Promotion of the Fine Arts in September 1823, wherein portraits are introduced of Thomas Bewick, the Rev. W. Turner, and other Newcastle worthies, with a picturesque and faithful view of the Cathedral Church of St. Nicholas, and old buildings now pulled down. In the "Pease Collection" may be mentioned an assemblage of 1510 *proofs* of woodcuts by and after Thomas Bewick, formed for the most part by Bewick himself for his friend Mr. Vernon of Liverpool (pp. 109-114 of this volume); also the "John

Trotter Brockett Collection," sold at Sotheby's in 1823, and thus described in the catalogue—" Lot 169, Figures of British and Foreign Birds and Tailpieces, *brilliant impressions, mounted on tinted paper,* 2 vols. folio, *half Russia,* unique."

To the Rev. Edward Hussey Adamson, for the loan of woodcuts and memoranda. To James Hall, Esq., of Tynemouth, for the loan of an interesting series of woodcuts of local scenery by John Jackson, after drawings by T. M. Richardson, senior, and J. W. Carmichael. To J. W. Barnes, Esq., F.S.A., of Durham, for the loan of woodcuts and many favours. Mr. Barnes is justly proud of his Birds and Quadrupeds (presentation copies), on the largest paper, uncut; and his co-executor, Joseph Crawhall, Esq., of Newcastle, of his beautiful drawing of the White Owl. Miss Jane Bewick pronounces the plumage of this bird to be " the perfection of art."

To T. W. U. Robinson, Esq., of Houghton-le-Spring, for the loan of wood-blocks, including the admirable cut of the Bay Pony by Thomas Bewick, and a copy of that rare work, the " Ornithologia Nova." Mr. Robinson's treasures comprise uncut presentation copies of Bewick's Works of the largest size. To James Hodgson, Esq., of Newcastle, for the loan of several beautiful woodcuts. To J. G. Hodgson, Esq., of Newcastle, for the loan of the fine plate of his grandfather.

To the Rev. William Kingsley, M.A., Rector of South Kilvington, Thirsk, for his admirable criticism on Bewick's last great woodcut. To James May Fothergill, Esq., of West Jesmond, for unpublished poetry by L. Clennell. To Councillor John Dobson, Newcastle, for permission to use the late Mr. Garnett's beautiful Trade Woodcut. To Mr. George Skelly of Alnwick, for information. To John Hancock, Esq., Newcastle; to George E. Swithenbank, Esq., of Anerley Park,

Surrey; R. Y. Green, Esq., Newcastle; Mr. Thomas W. Waters, Newcastle; and to other gentlemen, for thoughtful kindness.

To Messrs. Ballantyne, Hanson & Co., my acknowledgments are due for the conscientious care and attention exercised from first to last in the printing of the illustrations; to Mr. Richard Taylor, wood-engraver, London, for his admirable rendering of Good's delightful portrait of Thomas Bewick, and others.

Newcastle, *June* 1887.

Otter Hunting—From *Somervile's Chase.*

Dean BUCKLAND, towards the conclusion of his speech at the Anniversary Dinner of the Natural History Society, Newcastle, on the 27th of August 1838, the Duke of Northumberland presiding, said—

"Before he sat down, he (Dean Buckland) begged to observe that he should never enter the town nor the Museum of Newcastle without a joyful recollection of one whose name he had heard but once feebly uttered since he came here on this occasion, but whose name would never be forgotten by any friend of Natural History; and when he uttered the name of Bewick—(loud applause)—and associated with it the progress of Natural History in this town, he uttered the name of an individual who, he believed, had done as much by his works, published at a time when Natural History was unknown as a popular science but only to a few profound individuals,—who had done as much as White of Selborne, even at a distance of a quarter of a century; when, he said, he uttered the name of Bewick, he had a pride and pleasure in stating that he believed the whole world would never forget that Bewick was a native of Newcastle. (Loud applause.)"—*Local Paper*.

The following is from a valuable contribution on the subject of the Fine Arts Section of the Newcastle Jubilee Exhibition, specially composed for the *Newcastle Daily Chronicle* newspaper (11th May 1887). The writer, Mr. John Evan Hodgson, R.A. (Professor of Painting at the Royal Academy), is a grandson of Mr. Solomon Hodgson, to whose memory Bewick engraved the beautiful cut given at p. 219 of this work.

"By a complicated but not unnatural association of ideas, my thoughts are brought round to Thomas Bewick, whose portrait, by Good, is certainly both one of the most interesting and one of the best pictures in the collection. An artist of great eminence once told me that he could discern little merit in Bewick's work. After much puzzling over that confession, I have been forced to relegate it to the domain of insoluble problems, with the square circle and the perpetual motion; and with humble submission to superior genius and power, I must respectfully protest that Bewick has sounded every keynote of landscape art. Almost every incident of rural life seems to have been noticed and portrayed; and were I seeking for some irrefragable proof of the Englishman's innate love of Nature and delight in her for her own sake, I would instance the lives of Thomas Bewick and Gilbert White of Selborne. Good's portrait is undoubtedly a lifelike portrait of the grand old artist and naturalist, and it is a fortunate circumstance that the city of Newcastle has been able to secure for her Jubilee Exhibition an authentic portrait of one of her worthiest and most distinguished citizens."

LIST OF SUBSCRIBERS.

*The names of Subscribers who have died since the commencement of the
Work are printed in Italics.*

The Reverend EDWARD H. ADAMSON, Vicar of St. Alban's, Felling.

RALPH ATKINSON, Esq., Newcastle.

L. W. ADAMSON, Esq., Whitley House, Whitley.

HORATIO ADAMSON, Esq., Tynemouth.

Mr. WILLIAM ANDERSON, Newcastle.

Mr. THOMAS ARKLE, Highlaws.

The Rev. JOHN F. BIGGE, Vicarage, Stamfordham.

Sir WILLIAM BOWMAN, LL.D., F.R.S., London, *two copies.*

EDWARD BOYD, Esq., Moor House, Durham.

MATTHEW BOWMAN, Esq., Newcastle.

WILLIAM BRIGGS, Esq., Bristol.

FREDERICK BLOOMER, Esq., London, *two copies.*

The Rev. Dr. J. C. BRUCE, Newcastle.

GAINSFORD BRUCE, Esq., Q.C., Yewhurst, Kent.

ALDERMAN BARKAS & SON, Newcastle, *four copies.*

The Rev. J. R. BOYLE, Newcastle.

ROBERT BLAIR, Esq., South Shields.

WILLIAM BEER, Esq., Newcastle.

Mr. RICHARD BROWN, Toronto, Canada.

The Rev. J. E. ELLIOT BATES, Milbourne Hall, Northumberland.

THOMAS J. BEWICK, Esq., Haydon Bridge.

The Right Rev. Dr. BEWICK, Lord Bishop of Hexham and Newcastle.

Miss ISABELLA BEWICK, Cherryburn.

d

* J. W. BARNES, Esq., F.S.A., Durham.

CHARLES WILLIAM BIGGE, Esq., Newcastle.

M. W. BIDDULPH, Esq., Newcastle (Major, Northumberland Fusiliers).

* JOSEPH CRAWHALL, Newcastle, *two copies.*

MATTHEW T. CULLEY, Esq., Coupland Castle, Wooler.

The Rev. HENRY B. CARR, Rectory, Whickham.

The Rev. CHARLES B. CARR, Berwick-on-Tweed.

Captain H. J. CARR, R.N., Whickham.

The Rev. C. R. CARR, Exmouth.

HENRY CLAPHAM, Esq., Sheriff of Newcastle.

Councillor ADAM CARSE, Newcastle.

Councillor JOHN CUTTER, Newcastle.

JOHN CURRY, Esq., Bishop Oak, Wolsingham.

Mr. J. E. CORNISH, Bookseller, Manchester, *two copies.*

NATHANIEL GEORGE CLAYTON, Esq., Denton Burn.

JOSEPH CLARKE, Esq., The Roos, Saffron Walden.

GEORGE J. COOKSON, Esq., Newbrough, Fourstones.

NORMAN C. COOKSON, Esq., Oakwood, Wylam.

J. BLENCOWE COOKSON, Esq., Meldon Park, Morpeth.

G. D. ATKINSON CLARK, Esq., Belford Hall, Northumberland.

W. D. CRUDDAS, Esq., Elswick.

JOSEPH CRAGGS, Esq., Newcastle.

GEORGE W. T. COVENTRY, Esq., Upton-on-Severn.

The Rev. OWEN CARR, Newcastle.

Colonel CARR, Dunston Hill.

JAMES PATTERSON CASSELLS, Esq., M.D., Glasgow.

WALTER CHARLES CARR, Esq., Gateshead.

JOHN COPPIN, Esq., Bingfield, Corbridge.

JOHN A. COWEN, Esq., Blaydon Burn.

JOSEPH COWEN, Esq., Stella House.

Mr. W. DREWETT, Bookseller, Kingston-on-Thames.

MARTIN DUNN, Esq., Newcastle.

Miss EASTON, Nest House, Gateshead, and Layton Manor, Yorks, *two copies.*

T. W. EMBLETON, Esq., The Cedars, Leeds.

---

* Executors of the late Miss Isabella Bewick, of Gateshead.

ALFRED EMLEY, Esq., Newcastle.

RALPH CARR ELLISON, Esq., Dunston Hill.

The Rev. HENRY ELLISON, Rector of Melsonby.

GEORGE A. FENWICK, Esq., Bywell Hall.

JAMES MAY FOTHERGILL, Esq., West Jesmond.

JOHN GEORGE FENWICK, Esq., Moorlands, Gosforth.

GEORGE BAKER FORSTER, Esq., Lesbury House.

EDWARD FISHER, Esq., Newton Abbot, Devon.

GEORGE FREEMAN, Esq., Newcastle.

THOMAS C. GRAINGER, Esq., Newcastle.

ROBERT Y. GREEN, Esq., Newcastle.

Mr. JAMES GARLAND, Grey Street, Newcastle.

GEORGE CLEMENTSON GREENWELL, Esq., Duffield, Derby.

GEORGE GREEN, Esq., Jarrow.

THOMAS GOW, Esq., Cambo, *six copies.*

CHARLES M. GOYDER, Esq., M.D., Newcastle.

W. P. GARRISON, Esq., *The Nation,* New York.

WILLIAM GRIMSHAW, Esq., The Cedars, Sunderland.

MAJOR GENERAL GORDON, Guernsey.

CAPTAIN J. B. GASKELL, Liverpool.

EDWARD GREEN, Esq., Cullercoats.

THOMAS HOOD HENDERSON, Esq., Newcastle.

Mr. F. HAY, Grainger Street, Newcastle.

ALFRED HOLMES, Esq., Newcastle.

ALDERMAN THOMAS HEDLEY, Newcastle.

J. G. HODGSON, Esq., Newcastle.

Mr. P. HALL, Grey Street, Newcastle.

HENRY HEWITT, Esq., Newcastle.

JOHN HUTTON, Esq., Castle Eden.

Mr. THOMAS HUTCHINSON, Pegswood.

MATTHEW HECKELS, Esq., F.G.S., Heaton.

Mr. ADAM HOLDEN, Bookseller, Liverpool.

Messrs. HODGES, FIGGIS, & Co., Booksellers, Dublin, *three copies.*

GEORGE HOWARD. Esq., Naworth Castle, Cumberland.

THOS. GEO. HUTTON, Esq., The Cedars, Sunderland.

JOHN HANCOCK, Esq., Newcastle.

JAMES HALL, Esq., Tynemouth.

HUBERT E. H. JERNINGHAM, Esq., Longridge Towers.

Mr. A. JACKSON, Bookseller, London, *three copies.*

The Rev. OCTAVIUS JAMES, Clarghyll Hall, Cumberland.

Mrs. B. H. JOBLING, Newcastle.

MASON JACKSON, Esq., Earl's Court, London.

JAMES LEATHART, Esq., Bracken Dene, Low Fell.

The Rev. JOHN LOW LOW, M.A., Rector of Whittonstall.

JOHN LORD, Esq., Brighouse, Yorks.

CHARLES LILBURN, Esq., Sunderland.

F. G. LAWRENCE, Esq., Sutton, Surrey.

JOHN LANGLEY, Esq., Exmouth, Devon.

WILLIAM LAW, Esq., Littleborough, Manchester.

ANDREW LESLIE, Esq., Coxlodge Hall, Newcastle.

W. H. D. LONGSTAFFE, Esq., Gateshead.

The Honourable CLAUD LAMBTON, Lambton Castle, *two copies.*

EDWARD B. MOUNSEY, Esq., Darlington.

A. B. FREEMAN-MITFORD, Esq., C.B., Batsford Park, Gloucestershire.

Sir JOHN MAJORIBANKS, Lees, Coldstream.

Mr. R. JEFFERY MACKENZIE, Newcastle.

ROBERT MURAS, Esq., Wolverhampton.

HENRY M. MATHER, Esq., Newcastle.

HENRY CLAYTON MANISTY, Esq., Newcastle.

Messrs. MAWSON, SWAN, & MORGAN, Booksellers, Newcastle, *four copies.*

THOMAS MURRAY & SON, Publishers, Glasgow.

JOHN WADDON MARTYN, Esq., Croydon.

FREDERICK MORRICE, Esq., Ditchingham Hall, Suffolk.

Mr. MATTHEW MACKEY, Newcastle.

NEWCASTLE PUBLIC LIBRARY.

The Right Hon. Lord NORTHBOURNE, Betteshanger, Kent.

JOHN H. B. NOBLE, Esq., Jesmond Dene House.

Mr. GEORGE NESHAM, Durham.

The Rev. GEORGE ORNSBY, M.A., Vicar of Fishlake, Yorks.

Mrs. ANNIE C. PULLEINE, Clifton Castle, Bedale.

CHARLES PERKINS, Esq., Kirkley, Newcastle.

HENRY POWER, Esq., Hyde Park, London.

John Philipson, Esq., Newcastle.

Mr. Henry Piper, Gateshead.

James Price, Esq., Jarrow.

J. W. Pease, Esq., Pendower, *two copies.*

M. J. Pelegrin, Esq., Newbrough Park.

John Pattinson, Esq., Shipcote House, Gateshead.

N. K. Punshon, Esq., Killingworth.

Rev. John Quick, Bawden, Halifax.

Sir Matthew White Ridley, Bart., M.P., Blagdon, Northumberland.

Robert Norman Redmayne, Esq., Newcastle.

Adam Robertson, Esq., Alnwick.

Thomas W. U. Robinson, Esq., Hardwick Hall, Durham.

Mr. Edwin Robson, Gateshead.

Sir John Swinburne, Bart., M.P., Capheaton, Northumberland.

Captain Shawe Storey, Arcot Hall, Northumberland.

William Strangeways, Esq., Newcastle.

Thomas Taylor Smith, Esq., Greencroft Park, Durham.

George E. Swithenbank, Esq., Anerley Park, Surrey.

John Straker, Esq., Stagshaw House, Corbridge.

Mr. George Skelly, Alnwick.

John Storey, Esq., Newcastle.

Mr. W. J. Smith, Bookseller, Brighton, *two copies.*

The Rev. Henry Slater, Rectory, Riding Mill-on-Tyne.

Mr. John Sampson, Bookseller, York, *three copies.*

Alexander S. Stevenson, Esq., Tynemouth.

B. F. Stevens, Esq., Trafalgar Square, London.

Robert Spence, Esq., North Shields.

The Rev. W. J. Townsend, Newcastle.

John Taylor, Esq., Glenbuck House, Surbiton.

The Rev. R. Tilbury, Brignall, Rokeby.

Arthur Tite, Esq., Ware, Herts.

W. G. Tacey, Esq., Bradford.

G. H. Thompson, Esq., Alnwick.

Mr. J. Teal, Bookseller, Halifax.

Thomas Tate, Esq., Allerburn, Alnwick.

W. G. Woods, Esq., Pigdon, Morpeth.

John A. Woods, Esq., Benton Hall, Newcastle.

Mr. John Wilson, Newcastle.

Mr. Edward Wilson, Newcastle.

E. J. Walker, Esq., Low Elswick.

The Rev. S. R. Wigram, Ingle Dene, Oxford.

F. White, Esq., Birmingham, *three copies.*

H. A. Wedgwood, Esq., Erlscote, Cheltenham.

Mr. John Waller, Newcastle.

Mr. Thomas Carrick Watson, Gateshead.

Mr. Thomas F. Ward, Newcastle.

Mr. John Wheldon, Bookseller, London.

LIST OF ILLUSTRATIONS.

PAGE

Thomas Bewick.   After Portrait by T. S. Good   .   .   *Frontispiece*
(Engraved on Wood by Rich. Taylor.)

Ball Ticket.   Newcastle Assembly Rooms, 1795   .   .   .   *Title*

Portrait of William Charnley.   By T. Ranson   .   .   .   xvii

The Home of the Otter.   (From " Somervile's Chase," 1796)   .   xxiii

Title to Book I.   (From " Somervile's Chase," 1796)   .   .   xxxix

" Sweet Auburn."   (" Poems by Goldsmith and Parnell ")   .   1

Queen Anne.   (Goldsmith's " History of England ")   .   .   1

Vignette.   (" The Hive," 1806.)   By Luke Clennell   .   .   2

Portrait of the Earl of Derwentwater.   After Kneller   .   .   5

Albert Bane.   (" The Hive," 1806.)   By Thomas Bewick   .   6

Fox Hunting.   (" Somervile's Chase," 1796.)   By T. Bewick   .   9

The Boasting Trout.   (" Tales for Youth," 1794.)   By J. Bewick   13

Portrait, Rev. C. Gregson.   After Bewick   15

Waiting for Death, 1785.   Engraved on copper by T. Bewick, 1786   16

Newgate, Newcastle   17

Monastery of Grey Friars   18

Heads of English Monarchs.   By Thomas Bewick   .   25, 27, 29, 31

Portrait, Gilbert Gray   32

Portrait, Thomas Spence   34

Portrait, John Cunningham.   After Thomas Bewick   .   .   39

Beilby, Ralph, Memorial Plate   44

Bar Bill Cuts, &c.   By Thomas Bewick   46

Portrait, Sir M. W. Ridley, Bart.   47

PAGE

Nancy Collins. ("The Hive," 1806.) By Thomas Bewick . 51

The Ant and the Wasp. ("Tales for Youth," 1794.) By J. Bewick 56

Little Jack. ("The Looking Glass for the Mind," 1794.) By J. Bewick 61

Ruins of Tynemouth Monastery. Engraved by J. Jackson . 65
(From a Drawing by T. M. Richardson, sen.)

Tailpiece. ("The Looking Glass for the Mind.") By J. Bewick 68

Liberty and Slavery. ("The Hive," 1806.) By T. Bewick . 74

The Slave Trade. ("The Hive," 1812.) By Thomas Bewick . 76

Valentine and Unnion. ("The Hive.") By Luke Clennell . 77

The Chillingham Wild Bull, 1789. By Thomas Bewick . . 79

Old Oak Tree. ("Goldsmith's Poems," 1795.) By T. Bewick . 85

Frontispiece to "Elmina," 1800 86

Title to Book II. ("Somervile's Chase," 1796.) By T. Bewick 87

Hare Hunting. ("Somervile's Chase.") By Thomas Bewick . 89

Ballad Singer. Rough copy of Sketch by T. Bewick, 1788 . 91

The Traveller. ("Goldsmith's Poems," 1796) . . . 92
(Engraved by Thomas Bewick after R. Westall.)

The Hermit, Angel, and Guide. R. Johnson, del. T. Bewick, sculp. 97

The Conceited Magpie. By John Bewick, 1794 . . . 100

The Wilful Boy and the Hornets. By John Bewick . . 101

Vignette. ("Goldsmith's Poems.") By John Bewick . . 110

Northumberland Bank Note 113

From "The Adventures of a Fly," 1790. By John Bewick . 115

Autograph Letter of Thomas Bewick, in fac-simile . . . 115

St. Augustine preaching before King Ethelbert . . . 116
(Used on the title-page of Lingard's "Anglo-Saxon Church," vol. i., 1806.)

"The Hive." By Thomas Bewick, 1806 118

"The Siege of Calais." By Luke Clennell, 1806 . . . 119

Portrait of George Gray. From a painting by H. P. Parker . 122

The History of Joseph. By Thomas Bewick . . . 124

The Story of a Disabled Soldier. By Luke Clennell . . 125

	PAGE
Cut from "The History of a Fly." By John Bewick	128
Portrait of John Trotter Brockett	129
Ingratitude Punished. By John Bewick	132
Alcestes and Prætus. By John Bewick	133
Shepherd Lubin. ("The Repository of Literature," 1808.)	134
The Cuckoo and the Swallow. By John Bewick	135
The Wounded Soldier. By Thomas Bewick	138
The Perfidious Duck and the Stork. By John Bewick	144
The Envious Dog and the Ermine. By John Bewick	146
Portrait, Rev. John Hodgson	146
The Peacock and the Blackbird. By John Bewick	147
Filial Piety. By Thomas Bewick	148
Celadon and Amelia. By Thomas Bewick	149
Tailpiece. ("The Looking Glass for the Mind.") By J. Bewick	152
Tailpiece. ("The Looking Glass for the Mind.") By J. Bewick	156
Portrait of the Rev. William Turner	156
Tailpiece. ("Somervile's Chase," 1796.) By Thomas Bewick	160
Waiting for Death, 1828. By Thomas Bewick	161
Robert Bewick's Bookcut	162
Race Cut. ("Sporting Magazine," 1793.) By John Bewick	168
Returning Good for Evil. By John Bewick	169
Stephen Geo. Kemble as Sir John Falstaff. By Thomas Bewick	170
Meditation. From Hodgson's Office	172
Caroline; a Lesson to Cure Vanity. 1792. By John Bewick	173
From "Harrison's Picture Book," 1792. By John Bewick	174
Rosina. ("The Looking Glass for the Mind.") By J. Bewick	175
The Story of Le Fevre. By Thomas Bewick	176
From "Youthful Recreations." Newbery, London	178
Armorial Bearings of Thos. Hodgson, Esq. By T. Bewick, 1819	180

(In the distance St. Nicholas Church, the old Castle, Windmills, a Staith with Coal Keels.)

PAGE

Marsden Rock.   By John Jackson   183

Italian Ruins.   Drawn and engraved by John Bewick   .   .   184

History of the Empress Catherine.   By Luke Clennell   .   188

North Shields.   By Jackson   188

From Hodgson's ed. of "The History of a Fly."   By J. Bewick   189

From Hodgson's ed. of "The History of a Fly."   By J. Bewick   190

A Pleasant Story.   From Hodgson's Office   191

The Modest Man.   ("The Hive," 1806.)   By Thomas Bewick .   192

From "The Life of a Fly" (Hodgson's ed.)   By John Bewick .   195

The Beggar's Petition.   ("The Hive," 1806.)   By T. Bewick .   196

From Harrison's "Nursery Picture Book"   198

The Village.   ("Poems by Goldsmith and Parnell," 1795)   .   200

Title to Book III.   ("Somervile's Chase," 1796)   .   .   .   201

Huntsman and Hounds.   ("Somervile's Chase")   .   .   .   203
        (Drawn by John and engraved by Thomas Bewick.)

The Wanderer Destroyed, 1794.   By John Bewick .   .   .   205

From "The Life of a Fly."   By John Bewick   .   .   .   208

From "The Oracles."   By John Bewick   209

The Story of Obidah.   ("The Hive," 1806.)   By T. Bewick .   211

The Story of Melissa.   By Luke Clennell   .   .   .   213

The Story of Maria.   By Thomas Bewick   .   .   .   214

Portrait of Robert Roxby   215

The Battle of Blenheim.   ("The Hive," 1812)   .   .   .   217

Cut in memory of Solomon Hodgson, 1800.   T. Bewick, sculp. .   219

Morning of the Chase, 1796.   By Thomas Bewick .   .   .   220

The Envious Shepherd.   ("Tales for Youth," 1794.)   By J. Bewick   222

The Moth and the Water Fly.   ("Tales for Youth," 1794.)   By
     John Bewick   223

The History of Jonathan.   ("The Looking Glass for the Mind")   225

The Rival Dogs—Nancy and her Canary Bird.   ("The Looking
     Glass for the Mind.")   By John Bewick   226

PAGE

The Silly Lamb—The Cat and the Fish.　By John Bewick　.　227

The Destruction of Envy.　("Harrison's Picture Book ")　.　.　228

The Ungrateful Fox—The Timorous Boy—The Contemplative Hero.　(" Tales for Youth," 1794.)　By John Bewick　.　229

The Turkey-Cock and Turtle-Dove—Avarice Punished.　("Tales for Youth," 1794.)　By John Bewick　.　.　.　.　230

The Sad Historian.　John Bewick, del. et sculp.　.　.　.　231

Memorial Pillar.　(" Poems by Goldsmith and Parnell ")　.　.　233

King George III. Hunting in Windsor Park.　("Somervile's Chase")　234

Otter Hunting.　(" The Chase ")　.　.　.　.　.　.　235

The Tomb.　From Newbery's Office.　By John Bewick　.　.　236

Cut from " The History of a Fly "　.　.　.　.　.　240

The Earth Worm.　("Tales for Youth," 1794.).　By J. Bewick .　241

The Benighted Traveller.　By John Bewick　.　.　.　.　242

Hedworth Wind and Water Mills .　.　.　.　.　.　242
(This village is in the parish of Jarrow, near Hebburn.　The pretty little view is engraved on copper by Robert E. Bewick.)

Bookcut of John Adamson, Esq.　By Thomas Bewick　.　.　243

Oak Tree .　.　.　.　.　.　.　.　.　244

Title to Book IV.　(" Somervile's Chase," 1796)　.　.　.　245

Headpiece to " The Hermit," by Parnell, 1795.　By J. Bewick .　247

The Departure.　Drawn by R. Johnson.　T. Bewick, sculp.　.　248

The Vain Sparrow and Cruel Judge.　By John Bewick, 1794　.　250

The Spider and the Chieftain.　(" Tales for Youth ")　.　.　251

Memorial Cut to Robert Johnson .　.　.　.　.　.　255
(From a drawing by himself.　Engraved by Charlton Nesbit, 1796.)

Memorial Cut from " Goldsmith and Parnell's Poems," 1795.　By John Bewick　.　.　.　.　.　.　.　.　256

The Hermit at his Morning Devotion.　(" The Hermit," by Parnell.)　John Johnson, del.　Thomas Bewick, sculp. .　.　256

Dionysius the Tyrant.　By Luke Clennell (L.C.)　.　.　.　260

Alexander and Septimus.　By Luke Clennell (L.C.) .　.　.　261

PAGE

The Northumberland Lifeboat.　By Luke Clennell (L.C.) .　　.　262

The Grateful Turk.　By Luke Clennell (signed L.C.)　　.　.　265

The Turf Hotel, Newcastle　　.　　.　　.　　.　　.　267, 269

St. Mary's Chapel, Tynemouth.　By J. Jackson　　.　　.　　.　268

Tynemouth Priory and Lighthouse.　By J. Jackson .　　.　　.　272

Storm at Sea.　("Tales for Youth," 1794.)　By J. Bewick　　.　286

Tiger Hunting.　("The Chase," 1796.)　By T. Bewick　.　　.　289

The Bay Pony.　(Reay's "Sportsman's Friend," 1801)　.　　.　299

(This beautiful cut was drawn and engraved by Thomas Bewick.)

Tailpieces from "Ferguson's Poems," 1814　.　　.　　.　　.　300

Portraits of King George I., II., and III.　("Goldsmith's History

　　of England," 1807)　.　　.　　.　　.　　.　　.　　.　301

Robert Earl of Salisbury.　A fac-simile portrait by T. Bewick .　302

Camoens, Bust of.　By Thomas Bewick　.　　.　　.　　.　303

Armorial Bearings of John Murray, Esq.　　.　　.　　.　　.　307

Coulson's Business Card.　By Thomas Bewick　　.　　.　　.　308

Garnett's Business Card.　By Thomas Bewick　　.　　.　　.　310

Cut from "The History of a Foundling"　　.　　.　　.　　.　314

Note.—The tailpiece on p. 2 is one of sixteen engraved by Clennell, representing youthful sports.　The entire number is given.

CHERRYBURN.—Old English names of places in Northumberland sound sweetly compared with many modern appellations in the same county. A scattered plantation of cherry trees had for generations skirted the margin of a burn or rivulet on the south bank of the Tyne, opposite Ovingham, and gave name to the locality.

On the upland hard by stood, in 1752, a retired little homestead, with its garden, stackyard, and out-offices, the home of John Bewick, whose father had farmed lands at Bywell and other places on Tyneside from about the year 1700. He also rented Mickley Bank Colliery. His descendants still hold the estate under the Wrightson family, work the same mine, and plough the same fields their forefathers tilled in the days of Queen Anne. Here Thomas Bewick was born on August 12, 1753, his father having three sons, of which he was the eldest, and five daughters.

QUEEN ANNE.

John, the second son, became a wood engraver, of whom more hereafter, and William, the youngest, continued the business of the farm and colliery after the death of his father in 1785. To

A

William Bewick was born two daughters and six sons, Thomas, John, William, Ralph, Joseph, and Matthew. Of these Ralph only was married, and had a family.

His offspring, Mr. John Bewick, and his sisters Isabella and Agnes, now reside at Cherryburn. "Long may the name of Bewick flourish there in prosperity and peace," was the remark of my old and honoured friend, the Rev. John F. Bigge, Vicar of Stamfordham, on the occasion of the burial of the last child of Thomas Bewick.

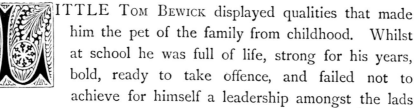

ITTLE Tom Bewick displayed qualities that made him the pet of the family from childhood. Whilst at school he was full of life, strong for his years, bold, ready to take offence, and failed not to achieve for himself a leadership amongst the lads of the village. His wild and headstrong spirit delighted in active field amusements and country sports and pastimes —pursuits that did not favour a very rapid advance in his studies. Small progress was made in grammar or arithmetic, and still less in acquiring the rudiments of the Latin tongue, to the regret of his friendly tutor, the Rev. Christopher Gregson, then Vicar of Ovingham. For the

wayward stripling he entertained a sincere regard, and many were the efforts made to reclaim him, that he might be brought to observe the rules of the school, and become more regular in his attendance. He was urged to emulate and follow the example of other boys, who, though younger than himself, were becoming

good scholars, and an honour to their preceptor. By kindly
words of persuasion a reformation was at length effected that
severe discipline and punishments had failed to accomplish.
He soon made up for misspent time, and by dint of application
acquired a good, plain, useful English education, sufficient to
enable him to pass through life with credit and respect. The
yeoman of that period received but an ordinary education; the
tenant-farmer had to rest content with still less. Each had to
work hard early and late to support their families and maintain
a decent position. Nothing was left in those days for servants
to do that the gaffer and his wife, assisted by their sturdy sons
and active daughters, could manage themselves. Chap books,
broadsides, and ballads adorned with rude woodcuts, supplied
by hawkers, or bought when at Newcastle on market-days,
sufficed to amuse both old and young through the long winter
nights. These largely partook of indecent jest and ribald song.
The tone of society in town and country was then coarse
and licentious, nor were even some of the clergy free from its
degrading influence.

The domestic annals of Northumberland from the outbreak
of the great civil war in the seventeenth century to the unhappy
risings in 1715 and '45, the latter only eight years before the
birth of Thomas Bewick, afforded ample material for conversation in the baronial hall, the old manor-house, and the cottage
of the peasant. Events of stirring interest rapidly followed
each other, the gravity of which all classes could understand.
So much of stern reality had passed before the eyes of the
dwellers on Tyneside between Hexham and Newcastle, a distance of only twenty-one miles, that they did not need to be
informed by " News Sheets " of what they themselves had seen
and their fathers had told them. In the ale-houses at Ovingham

and Corbridge, old men might still be found in the days of
Bewick's grandfather who had seen the Scots army under
Leslie cross the Tyne by the fords at Ovingham, Bywell, and
Eltringham, and heard the boom of their artillery, hooped with
cords and wet raw hides, as they played upon the English
breastworks from Newburn Church tower. They could tell
also of the siege of Newcastle, and the gallant defence made by
the townsmen under their patriotic mayor, Sir John Marley; of
the imprisonment of King Charles I. in our ancient town, and
how his Majesty used to pass from the grand old residence in
which he lodged in Pilgrim Street to play at golf in the Shield
Field.

Northumberland, at that time harried and impoverished by
exactions and forced loans by Royalist and Roundhead alike,
was in a truly miserable condition, particularly the poorer class
of farmers and husbandmen. The wealthy and prosperous
town of Newcastle suffered but little. Feudal feeling was still
strong in the North, resentment deep though secret was widely
felt, when news came that Sir John Fenwick of Wallington had
been arrested on a charge of high treason and committed to the
Tower, and after the farce of a trial had been gone through,
beheaded on Tower Hill. This talented gentleman of long
descent was condemned, upon suspicion of treason only, by a
law made after the crime was done, at the instance of a guilty
approver. His legal murder long rankled in the hearts of the
people, and contributed to foster dislike to the reigning dynasty
and the principles of the Revolution. From this time to the
ill-fated attempt in 1715 to restore the eldest son of James
II. to the throne of his ancestors, only nineteen years had
elapsed.

G. Kneller pinxit.

THE RIGHT HON.ᵇˡᵉ JAMES RADCLIFFE.

EARL OF DERWENTWATER.

Beheaded 24ᵗʰ February 1716.

THE melancholy end of the young EARL OF DERWENT-
WATER and his heroic brother sank deep in the popular
mind, and found expression in the then well-known
" Lament," so full of pathos : [1]—

> " Farewell to pleasant Dilston Hall,
>   My father's ancient seat,
> A stranger now must call thee his,
>   Which makes my heart to greet.
> Farewell each kindly well-known face
>   My heart has held so dear ;
> My tenants now must leave their lands,
>   Or hold their lives in fear.
>
> " No more along the banks of Tyne
>   I'll rove in autumn grey ;
> No more I'll hear at early dawn
>   The lav'rocks wake the day.
> And who shall deck the hawthorn bower
>   Where my fond childhood strayed ?
> And who, when spring shall bid it flower,
>   Shall sit beneath the shade ? "

[1] The Right Hon. James Radcliffe, third Earl of Derwentwater, a martyr in the rebellion of 1715, was born on the 28th June 1689, his mother being the Lady Mary Tudor, youngest natural daughter of King Charles II. Through her influence, together with the friendship formed whilst a boy at St. Germains with the little Prince, afterwards called the " Pretender," he was led to join this ill-fated enterprise in favour of the Stuart dynasty. Early on the morning of the 6th of October 1715, the Earl, with his brother Charles, and many friends, left Dilston Hall, never to see it again. On the 13th of November, seventy-five noblemen and gentlemen, mostly Northumbrians, with one hundred and forty-three of the same rank from Scotland, surrendered after a heroic fight to the army of King George at Preston. Lord Derwentwater with the other noblemen were conveyed to London and lodged in the Tower, tried, found guilty, and sentenced to death. On the fatal 24th of February 1716, the Earl of Derwentwater and Lord Kenmure were beheaded on Tower Hill, faithful to the last, and true to the Prince for whom they sacrificed all they held most dear.

Charles Radcliffe, the youngest son of the second Earl of Derwentwater, and brother of Earl James, was born in England on the 3rd of September 1693 ; married in 1724 Charlotte Mary, Countess of Newburgh. Accompanied by his son, he was captured on board of a French privateer, laden with military stores, bound to Montrose, in Scotland, for the service of Prince Charles. He was committed to the same gloomy fortress which had received his beloved brother thirty years before, from whence he was led to execution on the 8th of December 1746. He was the more bold and resolute, and met death with becoming fortitude and constancy.

HE late WILLIAM LAWS, Esq. of Prudhoe Castle, agent for the Duke of Northumberland, was a gentleman well known to Mr. Bewick, and out-lived him many years.

His grandfather was a youth at school at the time of the execution of King Charles I., and lived to hear of the beheading of the last Earl of Derwentwater and his gallant brother, Charles Radcliffe, Esq., thirty years afterwards. From an unpublished letter in the collection of William Oswald Charlton, Esq. of Hesleyside, it appears that Charles Radcliffe, under the assumed name of Thompson, revisited the North of England and the home of his forefathers in July 1721.

He travelled from Durham in company with Mr. Widder-ington, and called at Lumley Castle, where he was kindly received, and from thence proceeded to Newcastle, where he

put up at the Bull and Crown in the Groat Market. From this tavern he addressed a letter to the housekeeper at Dilston, the good and faithful Mrs. Busby; in it he requests the loan of five guineas.

Whilst at Durham he had only five or six shillings, two shirts, and a pocket-handkerchief. He desires that the money should be sent him by Lady Swinburne, or some other faithful hand, as he could not trust the lad who brought the note. He promises to see her at Dilston before leaving England, to arrange some matters; he was obliged to leave Durham "for very good reasons." This loan was repaid by Mr. Errington of Capheaton.

To such straits the scion of a noble house was too often reduced in those troublous days.

 GENERATION later witnessed the last effort made by the Jacobite gentry of the North to upset the House of Hanover in favour of Prince Charles Edward Stuart.

Ill-judged and unwise might be the enterprise, still there was something generous and unselfish in risking life and fortune for the sake of a principle they deemed it to be their duty to uphold. The confiscation by the Government of the estates of so many old families was for the time a misfortune. The loss of that profuse hospitality and kindness to the poor, for which they had been distinguished, was severely felt by the needy and dependent. But as Bewick has it, "Good times and bad times, and all times get over." Society at length righted itself under the blessing of a settled and strong government; private philanthropy and public spirit effected changes in the manners, mode of life, and habits of the people, which have proved as beneficial as they have been lasting.

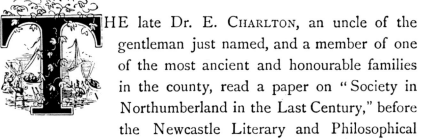

HE late Dr. E. CHARLTON, an uncle of the gentleman just named, and a member of one of the most ancient and honourable families in the county, read a paper on "Society in Northumberland in the Last Century," before the Newcastle Literary and Philosophical Society, in 1874. A few copies only were printed for private circulation. The following extracts cannot fail to amuse, as they vividly illustrate the habits of the gentry during the early manhood of Thomas Bewick :—" Many, and indeed most, of the Hanoverian gentry," he remarks, "spent their winters in Newcastle, and retained their town-houses there till far into the present century. The majority of the Jacobites and Catholics kept apart. Of the lives they led we obtain much insight from some correspondence of about the middle of the last century. As to Newcastle, its gaiety far surpassed that of the present day. They seem, about 1755, to have had balls or masquerades

twice a week during the winter. The races were then, as now, a great season of festivity. About the year 1750 the races seem to have lasted three days, and during all that time the gentlemen did not go to bed, but sat up all night carousing in Debord's, the fashionable tavern in the Cloth Market, still passing under its ancient name of the White Hart."

"We have been amused by the letter of a Jacobite squire, writing to Sir Francis Delaval, and begging him to make up a quarrel that had taken place there, and excusing himself from being mixed up with it by saying that he was 'much in liquor at the time.' The old squires took plenty of time in returning home from the races. 'My husband has not yet got home,' writes a lady from the west country, 'but he wrote the other day for his horses to be sent to Hexham, so he will be on his way.' As they went back to their dreary homes, they loved to stop at some Jacobite friend's who had not been able to join in the dissipation of the week, and whose anxiety to learn the news of the day formed a good excuse for a prolonged drinking bout.

In the absence of intellectual amusements and of a good supply of books time must have hung heavily enough on their hands. . . . They rose early, and were often in the saddle before daybreak in winter to hunt up their fox. Going out to the chase seems to have been at times conducted with as much parade as is usual in France or Germany at the present day. 'On the first day of the season, the gentlemen of the Newcastle Hunt met at Debord's with great parade, and with French horns, and much music and smacking of whips.'[1] . . . Among the Delaval papers we find an amusing letter from a country squire in Northumberland to his friend, Sir Francis, in London, begging him to procure for him in London 'a hand-organ to play a dozen tunes or so, with a handle on ye outside to turn it about with; it is a thing I have a great longing for.' . . . The study of music or painting seems to have been hardly thought of in the family circle. One lady's husband stays long at Newcastle, whither he had gone to see Domenico, the fire-eater, and at last returns, bringing with him four fiddlers and a drummer, and the house has now no rest. 'I like music, especially the " White Cockade,"' says the sly little Jacobite writer, 'but this is rather too much.'"

HAT an immense advance do we not behold at the present day in all that tends to refine and cultivate the understanding,—the cruel and barbarous sports of bull-baiting and cock fights banished for ever from the number of popular amusements, whilst deep drinking and swearing are now only to be found amongst the lowest class of artisans! The colliers are not the degraded body they once were, but attach themselves with success to scientific and philosophical research, a love for plants and flowers, and the study of botany and ornithology, being very widely diffused.

---

[1] In looking through a file of the *Newcastle Chronicle* for 1768, I find the following most extraordinary account of a fox hunt:—" A fox being closely pursued by Lord Strathmore's hounds, threw himself in at the dayhole of a colliery near Gibside, where several of the hounds followed with some of the hunters, and after a chase of an hour and a half through all the turnings and windings of the colliery, he was at last taken under a heap of rubbish where he had crept for safety. The hunters were obliged to get lanthorns and candles, and had a very fine diversion in the subterraneous caverns, about 300 feet under the surface, having the fox several times in view during the chase."—13th February 1768.

Every pit village can boast of at least one bird or animal preserver. Bewick's "History of British Birds," and Goldsmith's "Natural History," have done much to create and foster a taste for such pursuits. The possession of a good pianoforte is far from uncommon, whilst a violin or a flute is seldom wanting in the house of a miner.

Mr. Bewick, in his graphic and instructive Memoir of himself, thus speaks of his early essays in art whilst a schoolboy at Ovingham :—

"I was for some time kept at reading, writing, and figures—how long I know not; but I know that as soon as my question was done upon my slate, I spent as much time as I could find in filling with my pencil all the unoccupied spaces with representations of such objects as struck my fancy, and these were rubbed out, for fear of a beating, before my question was given in. As soon as I reached Fractions, Decimals, &c., I was put to learn Latin; and in this I was for some time complimented by my master for the great progress I was making; but, as I never knew for what purpose I had to learn it, and was wearied out with getting off long tasks, I rather flagged in this department of my education, and the margin of my books, and every space of spare and blank paper, became filled with various kinds of devices or scenes I had met with, and these were accompanied with wretched rhymes explanatory of them. As soon as I filled all the blank spaces in my books, I had recourse, at all spare times, to the gravestones and the floor of the church porch, with a bit of chalk, to give vent to this propensity of mind of figuring whatever I had seen. At that time I had never heard of the word 'drawing;' nor did I know of any other paintings besides the king's arms in the church, and the signs in Ovingham of the Black Bull, the White Horse, the Salmon, and the Hounds and Hare. I always thought I could make a far better hunting scene than the latter: the others were beyond my hand. I remember once of my master overlooking me while I was very busy with my chalk in the porch, and of his putting me very greatly to the blush by ridiculing and calling me a conjuror. My father also found a deal of fault for 'misspending my time in such idle pursuits;' but my propensity for drawing was so rooted that nothing could deter me from persevering in it, and many of my evenings at home were spent in filling the flags of the floor and the hearthstone with my chalky designs.

"After I had long scorched my face in this way, a friend, in compassion, furnished me with some paper upon which to execute my designs. Here I had more scope. Pen and ink, and the juice of the brambleberry, made a grand change. These were succeeded by a camel-hair pencil and shells of colours, and, thus supplied, I became completely set up; but of patterns or drawings I had none. The beasts and birds which enlivened the beautiful scenery of woods and wilds surrounding my native hamlet furnished me with an endless supply of subjects. I now, in the estimation of my rustic neighbours, became an eminent painter, and the walls of their houses were ornamented with an abundance of my rude productions *at a very cheap rate.* These chiefly consisted of particular hunting scenes, in which the portraits of the hunters, the horses, and of every dog in the pack, were, in their opinion, *as well as my own,* faithfully delineated."

IS recollections of home, and the round of duty he performed whilst a boy, is remembered and dwelt upon with pleasure. His ardent love of Nature is always apparent.

"In the vermin-hunting excursions in the depth of winter, while the whole face of Nature was bound in frost and covered with deep snow, in traversing through bogs, amidst reeds and rushes, I have often felt charmed with the sight of birds—flushed and sometimes caught by the terrier dogs—which I had never seen or heard of before; and I am still in doubt whether some of them have not escaped being noticed as British birds.

"These were the diversions of the winter months, which I enjoyed in an extreme degree amidst the storm and the tempest. In that season I was also sometimes better employed in looking after a small flock of sheep on the fell, a part of which was my own. The extremity of the weather had taught them to seek a place of shelter under a steep but low 'brae,' overhung with whins, under which, in such weather, I was almost certain to find them and their associates all huddled together. To this place, through wreaths of snow, I early bent my way, with a bundle of hay on my back, and my pockets sometimes filled with oats, which I distributed amongst them. Upon these occasions, though at other times extremely wild, they were quite tame, and seemed to know me. . . .

"At that time of life every season had its charms; and I recollect well of listening with delight, from a little window at my bed-head, to the murmuring of the flooded burn which passed my father's house, and sometimes roused me from my bed to see what it was like. After this my first and common employment was to 'muck' the byre; and when the servant girl did not come soon enough, I frequently tried my hand at milking the cows; and I was always particularly keen of being there in snowstorms. When this was the case, within the byre door I snugly watched the appearance of various birds which passed the little dean below, and which the severity of the weather drove from place to place in search of shelter. With the sight of my intimate acquaintances, the robins, wrens, blackbirds, sparrows, a solitary crow, and some others, I was not much attracted, but always felt an extreme pleasure and curiosity in seeing the more rare visitants—such as the woodcock, the snipe, and other waders, with the redwings, fieldfares, &c.—make their appearance. . . .

"From the little window at my bed-head I noticed all the varying seasons of the year; and, when the spring put in, I felt charmed with the music of birds, which strained their little throats to proclaim it. . . .

"As soon as the bushes and trees began to put forth their buds, and make the face of Nature look gay, this was the signal for the angler to prepare his fishing-tackle. In doing this I was not behindhand. Fishing-rods, set-gads,

The Boasting Trout.—*Tales for Youth*, 1794.

and night-lines were all soon made fit for use, and with them, late and early, I had a busy time of it during the summer months, until the frosts of autumn forbade me to proceed. The uneasiness which my late evening wadings by the waterside gave to my father and mother, I have often since reflected upon with regret. They could not go to bed with the hopes of getting to sleep while haunted with the apprehension of my being drowned; and well do I remember to this day my father's well-known whistle which called me home. He went to a little distance from the house, where nothing obstructed the sound, and whistled so loud, through his finger and thumb, that in the still hours of evening it might be heard echoing up the vale of the Tyne to a very great distance. This whistle I learned to imitate, and answered as well as I could, and then posted home."

The little window at his bed-head is pictured in John Bewick's view of Cherryburn house, just below the gable. To the left beneath the hedge-row is the burn or rivulet, and below it the dene, which is continued along the bottom of the cut.

T length the time came when boyish pastimes must be parted with, and the companionship of schoolfellows cease; when preparation for an entry upon the battle of life, and that discipline on which so much will depend, can be delayed no longer. Mr. Bewick thus narrates the first step in the story of his apprenticeship :—

"Being now nearly fourteen years of age, and a stout boy, it was thought time to set me off to business; and my father and mother had long been planning and consulting, and were greatly at a loss what it would be best to fix upon. During the summer of 1767, William Beilby and his brother Ralph took a ride to Bywell to see their intimate acquaintance, Mrs. Simons, who was my godmother, and the widow of the late vicar there. She gave them a most flattering account of me: so much so, that they, along with her and her daughter, set off that same afternoon to Cherryburn to visit us, and to drink tea. When the Newcastle visitors had given an account of their enamellings, drawings, and engravings, with which I felt much pleased, I was asked which of them I should like to be bound to; and, liking the look and deportment of Ralph the best, I gave the preference to him. Matters bearing upon this business were slightly talked over; and my grandmother having left me twenty pounds for an apprentice fee, it was not long till a good understanding between parties took place, and I soon afterwards went to R. Beilby upon trial.

"The first of October was the day fixed upon for the binding. The eventful day arrived at last, and a most grievous one it was to me. I liked my master; I liked the business; but to part from the country, and to leave all its beauties behind me, with which I had been all my life charmed in an extreme degree— and in a way I cannot describe—I can only say my heart was like to break; and, as we passed away, I inwardly bade farewell to the whinny wilds, to Mickley Bank, to the Stobcross Hill, to the water banks, the woods, and to particular

trees, and even to the large hollow old elm, which had lain perhaps for centuries past on the haugh near the ford we were about to pass, and which had sheltered the salmon fishers, while at work there, from many a bitter blast. We called upon my much esteemed schoolfellow, Christopher Gregson,[1] of Ovingham, where he and his father were waiting to accompany us to Newcastle—all on the same

[1] The Rev. Christopher Gregson, born in 1738, held the living of Ovingham for upwards of forty-three years. Bewick states, in his delightful Memoir, that the stipend was only thirty pounds per annum, till the "lay rector, Thomas Charles Bigge, Esq. of Benton, added some land to the glebe, by way of bettering his condition." After a time he began to keep pupils, and was considered a successful teacher of the young. He died, universally respected, on the 26th December 1809, aged 71 years, and lies interred at Ovingham.

errand—(we were both bound on that day). While we were condoling, comforting each other—I know not what to call it—at the parsonage gates, many of the old neighbours assembled at the churchyard wall to see us set off, and to express their good wishes; and amongst the rest was a good, sensible old woman of the village, named Betty Kell, who gave us her blessing, and each a penny for good luck. This being done, our horses were mounted, and we commenced our journey. The parties kept a little distance from each other. I suppose our late preceptor was lecturing his son, and my father was equally busied in the same way with me."

When they reached Newcastle the indenture, after some demur, was drawn up and duly signed. Young Bewick now entered upon his seven years' servitude, a period found to be in most cases one of singular hardship and endurance.

The late Miss Bewick informed me that at the time the lad left home he had in his pocket a small drawing representing an old horse standing by a bank-side, near to the withered trunk of an aged oak tree, Cherryburn in the distance. This, his earliest known design, he many years afterwards engraved. I obtained the little copperplate from the Misses Bewick, and have now, by favour of the owner, Thomas Gow, Esq. of Cambo, much pleasure in bringing it under the notice of my readers.

WHEN young Bewick began his apprenticeship the halo of antiquity rested upon Newcastle. Everywhere the good town was intersected by pleasant gardens. Its famed old wall, flanked by towers at short distances, then existed almost entire. Ponderous gates of massive masonry, which had protected the inhabitants through many centuries of turbulence and domestic anarchy, frowned stern and gloomy as they stretched across the main streets from Westgate to Pilgrim Street. The river Tyne was spanned by a bridge of mediæval architecture, whilst stately mansions and

NEWGATE, NEWCASTLE.

quaint old houses with carved enrichments added much in those days to impress strangers with an idea of the wealth and dignity of its merchants and gentry. Delightful it then was, and long after, to wander by the Maiden's Walk on a summer morning, through the fields and meadows of Elswick and Benwell, and Newburn and Denton Burn, and at eventide, after the turmoil of the day, to note the cry of the corncrake, or

C

the lark's evening hymn, or how, as when "light thickens, and
the crow makes wing to the rooky wood" far over the Tyne to
Axwell and Ravensworth and the distant shades of Gibside, to
witness the gradual approach of night and Nature's silent reign!

One princely residence, built about 1580, was the pride, not
of Pilgrim Street only, but of Newcastle, the air of antiquity
which clung about it disposing the mind to thoughts of serenity
and peace.

In the olden time, when faith was strong, a Monastery of
Grey Friars flourished here, and the monastic gardens in all
their quiet beauty existed till within little more than fifty years
ago, though six hundred years had passed since Duns Scotus,
the glory of the Franciscans, and Hugh of Newcastle, studied
within its walls.

 EVOTION, aided by fancy, might still conjure
up the form of the Subtle Doctor, as wrapt
in meditation he paced its cheerful walks,
clad in the long grey habit of the Order,
with girdle of rope, his soul fixed on God
and things divine. Now and then, whilst at school, I used to
pass a leisure hour under the pleasant shade of the fine old
trees that grew around, and on one occasion, not to be forgotten,
had the happiness to experience something of the supernatural.

In the early days of my apprenticeship I went through the
house just before its demolition, and viewed the apartments
occupied by King Charles I. whilst a prisoner in the hands of
the Scotch. In summer time the peacocks might be seen
proudly treading the spacious lawn, in keeping with the lordly
aspect of the place; and on stormy winter nights the western

THE MONASTRY of GREY FRIARS, NEWCASTLE UPON TYNE.

wind swept through the trees with loud and weird-like sound, inspiring feelings of awe.

This house was built by Robert Anderson, merchant. In Speed's map of the town, 1610, it is called the "Newe House." Sir Francis Anderson, Knt., in 1675 conveyed it to Sir William Blackett, Bart., who added the two wings in a modern style. It came into the possession of Sir Walter Blackett, Bart., by his marriage with Sir William's granddaughter. In 1782 it was sold to Mr. Geo. Anderson, an opulent architect, whose son, Major Anderson, lived in it at the time the annexed view was taken. The heir of this gentleman sold the estate, about twelve acres, to the late Richard Grainger, Esq., in 1832, for £50,000.

Whatever time Bewick had at his disposal in the morning, or after shop hours in the evening, or could spare from his dinner-hour, was spent in the enjoyment of the open country air. Nor had he to travel far that he might revel amid green fields and pleasant gardens. In the first days of his apprenticeship, as I have been told by the late Miss Jane Bewick, he would run without a cap from the workshop, through Denton Chare, to the Spital Field and the Forth. Many of the shops in that ancient thoroughfare were then occupied by fruiterers and confectioners, who used to remark as he passed their doors, "There goes Beilby's wild lad." It was in passing along this "Chare" in after years with his friend Richard Wingate that he sketched the little owl ("Brit. Birds," vol. i. p. 55, 1797); and it was here Mr. Bewick once offered to set up his daughter Isabella as a bookseller, but she declined—"the responsibility was too great," she remarked in conversation one evening.

Bewick would occasionally change his route, and vary the scene. Entering the Castle Garth by the Black Gate, a gloomy structure of the time of Henry III., he would then, by the low Norman postern on the Castle stairs, soon reach Tyne Bridge. Both those venerable remains are still in existence. To a youth born and bred in the country, the novelty of such a scene as would then present itself must have been striking and picturesque in the extreme. The bridge, of mediæval architecture, a study in itself, stood on the site of the Pons Ælii of Hadrian. Narrow and inconvenient, by reason of the projecting old timber houses, with shops below, by which it was crowded, it was rendered still more so by three strong towers. What was called the Magazine Gate, built in the reign of Charles I., stood at the north end. A fine marble statue of his royal successor, clad in a Roman toga, graced the south front; in the middle there was another tower, which served as a prison; whilst a third stood near the Gateshead end of the bridge. Beneath their antique portals a stream of horsemen and pedestrians, carriages of the gentry, royal grenadiers in quaint uniform, and regiments of local militia changing quarters, was no uncommon sight; whilst carriers' carts from neighbouring villages, heavily laden waggons from Leeds, Sheffield, Manchester, York, London, and Nottingham were passing along almost daily. Here were the shops of saddlers, hardwaremen, hatters, drapers, grocers, cheesemongers, and other traders, but especially booksellers. To the latter the attention of young Bewick would be mainly directed; portions of the literary stores they contained (and some were very considerable indeed) were openly exposed to view.

> "Volumes on shelter'd stalls expanded lie,
> And various science lures the learned eye;
> The bending shelves with pond'rous scholiasts groan,
> And deep divines, to modern shops unknown;
> Here sauntering 'prentices o'er Otway weep,
> O'er Congreve smile, or over Dyer sleep."

HEN on an errand, our young apprentice would no doubt be tempted to linger now and then for a few minutes and examine with pleasure such books as the "Nuremberg Chronicle," so full of wonders, "Holinshed's Chronicles," the learned Conrad Gesner's "History of Birds, Beasts, and Fishes," adorned with thousands of fine woodcuts, or the plates in Edwards' recently published "History of Birds"—little dreaming that centuries hence, when that bridge should have long passed away, and the "famous town of Newcastle" had become a city, his woodcuts, the offspring of his genius, would be held in universal admiration. About the middle of the seventeenth century the principal booksellers had their shops on Tyne Bridge and the Sandhill. Robert Barker, who in 1639 came to Newcastle in the train of King Charles I.; had his shop on the Sandhill, and his office in St. Nicholas Churchyard. He was succeeded by Stephen Bulkley (who brought his type and press with him from York), so well known as the printer of "Gray's Chorographia" in 1649. The almost mythical William London, a contemporary, with his marvellous catalogue of books in ancient and modern languages, and on almost every branch of learning, probably resided in this much-coveted locality. Richard Randell and Peter Maplisden dwelt upon the Sandhill, near the bridge, where you could have "Books bound after what manner you please." Joseph Hall in 1693 used to have sales of books by auction on the bridge, and at the beginning of the eighteenth century lived here Sarah and afterwards Joseph Button, the friend and correspondent of Daniel Defoe. Thomas Bewick used to study Reay Sabourn's Latin Grammar, published by Button in 1733.

HERE was JOHN LINN, bookbinder, at the sign of Locke's Head, on the middle of Tyne Bridge, and JOHN FLEMING, and his widow after him, who published the *Newcastle General Magazine* at his "shop under the Magazine Gate," safe and snug from those driving showers of sleet and rain, and boisterous gusts of wind, that so often sweep down the valley of the Tyne in the autumn and winter months. There also flourished MARTIN BRYSON, an eminent bookseller, who once received a letter from Allan Ramsay, addressed to

> "MARTIN BRYSON,
> Dwelling on Tyne Brigg,
> An upright, downright, honest Whig."

The poet had a son who was an assistant with Bryson.

The best of the old houses at the south end of the bridge let for £21, and consisted mostly of a shop on the basements, with a cellar below, to which access was gained by a winding stair. In the cellar was a door in two parts, secured by iron bolts; the upper part was used as a window to let in light, and by the lower half goods were let down, to be conveyed away by boats on the river, immediately below, which at high water reached nearly to the cellar floor. Above the shop were a kitchen and parlour, opposite each other, whilst another staircase led to the bedrooms.

HEN Joseph Hall or Sarah Button first opened their windows in the morning and sat down to breakfast whilst the clock on the Exchange was striking seven, it must have been a pleasurable sight to behold the broad and silvery river flowing silently beneath. The rural quiet pervading the fair valley, the sheep feeding on its southern slopes amid trees and woodlands, in an atmosphere pure and untainted, would form a charming prospect. Tyne Bridge and its traditions, Roman and mediæval, occupy an important page in local history.

One remarkable event in its annals, chronicled by Leland, is dear to all natives of the Northern Metropolis who cherish a love for the venerable past. On a bright sunny day in the month of July 1503, the Princess Margaret, daughter of Henry VII., then in her fourteenth year, passed through Newcastle on her road to Scotland, the affianced bride of King James IV. The passage itself is too long for insertion. "Upon the bryge," we are told, "cam in processyon rychly revested the college of the said towne. . . . At the bryge end, upon the gatt, war many children, revested of surpeliz, syngyng mellodiously hympnes, and playing on instruments of many sortes." Alas! the domestic happiness of this young and illustrious lady was but short-lived. In less than ten years she was a widow, and her royal husband, the gay and chivalrous James, lay a bloody corse on Flodden Field.

𝕽𝖔𝖞𝖆𝖑 𝖁𝖎𝖘𝖎𝖙𝖘 𝖙𝖔 𝕹𝖊𝖜𝖈𝖆𝖘𝖙𝖑𝖊.

 OBERT CURTHOSE, eldest son of William the Conqueror, on his return in 1080 from an unsuccessful enterprise against Malcolm, King of Scotland, erected a fortress which was called the New Castle. The *old castle* is supposed to have been the Roman fortress Pons Ælii. From this *new castle* the adjoining town derives its name.

KING HENRY I., Beauclerc, is supposed by Bourne to have built St. Nicholas' Church between the years 1115 and 1128. He gave the Church of Newcastle, with that of Newburn and others, to the See of Carlisle.

KING STEPHEN, being at Durham, invaded Northumberland. David, King of Scotland, at this time commonly resided in Newcastle. Peace was made between the two kings in 1139.

KING HENRY II. had a mint at Newcastle. KING JOHN in 1209 had a conference with William, King of Scotland, in this town, and made it his residence for a lengthened period.

KING HENRY III., in 1255, accompanied by his Queen, were in Newcastle, which they left for Werk Castle, to have an interview with their daughter, the Queen of Scotland, and her husband.

WILLIAM THE CONQUEROR.

KING HENRY I.

KING STEPHEN.

KING HENRY II.

KING JOHN.

KING HENRY III.

D

KING EDWARD I. was in Newcastle in 1292, to whom John Baliol did homage in the hall of his palace within the castle. This monarch by charter (1299) united the ancient Vill of Pampedon to Newcastle, the two places henceforth to constitute one town and borough.

KING EDWARD II., with his minion Gaveston, fled from York to Newcastle, pursued by the incensed barons, headed by the Earl of Lancaster: retiring to Tinmouth, they took ship for Scarborough.

KING EDWARD III., the victor of Crecy and Poictiers, kept his Whitsuntide here in 1334, soon after which Edward Baliol, King of Scotland, did him homage in the Church of the Black Friars amid great solemnity.

KING HENRY IV. was at Newcastle in 1400. By charter dated May 23d in that year it was the royal pleasure to separate the town of Newcastle-upon-Tyne from the county of North-umberland, and make it a distinct county of itself, with the title of "the county of the town of Newcastle-upon-Tyne."

KING HENRY VI., with his heroic Queen and many of the nobility who fled with him from Yorkshire after the fatal battle of Towton, took refuge in this town. Amongst the gentlemen who fell on the side of the house of Lancaster, history makes mention of John Carlele, Knight, a member of the family of which Leland speaks when he says, "The Gray Freres in Newcastle of the Cairluelles foundation, originally marchauntes of the same town, and after men of lande."

KING EDWARD I.

KING EDWARD II.

KING EDWARD III.

KING HENRY IV.

KING HENRY V.

KING HENRY VI.

KING EDWARD IV., after his great victory, marched north-wards as far as Newcastle, but soon afterwards returned to the South.

KING RICHARD III., in the year 1483, confirmed the grant of former charters to the town. His death at Bosworth was fol-lowed by the peaceable accession of KING HENRY VII., who made Newcastle his residence for some time. In 1490 he made a grant of the fair called St. Luke's Fair to the town.

KING HENRY VIII. granted in 1544 the Black Friars, with the houses, orchards, and gardens thereto belonging, to the Corporation of Newcastle, reserving to himself the bells, lead, and timber of the Church.

KING EDWARD VI., 1549, granted to the Corporation of Newcastle the Chapel of the Blessed Mary at Jesmond; also the Chapel of St. Laurence, which stood near the margin of the Tyne, a little below Ouse burn.

QUEEN MARY, 1554, confirmed to the town several royal charters granted by her ancestors.

KING JAMES I., on his way to Scotland, 1617, arrived at Newcastle from Durham on St. George's Day, where he was met upon the Sandhill by the mayor (Lionel Maddison), alder-men, and sheriff; and, after an oration by the town-clerk, was presented by the mayor, in the name of the Corporation, with

KING EDWARD IV.

KING RICHARD III.

KING HENRY VII.

KING HENRY VIII.

KING EDWARD VI.

QUEEN MARY.

a great standing bowl, to the value of an hundred jacobuses and an hundred merks in gold; the mayor carrying the sword before him, accompanied by his brethren on their foot-cloths.

KING CHARLES I. This unhappy monarch visited Newcastle on several occasions. After the disastrous battle of Marston Moor, on July 2, 1644, Newcastle was the last bulwark of the Royal cause in the North. After offering a very spirited resistance of about ten weeks, it finally surrendered on October 22d of that year. As a reward for the gallant defence made by the inhabitants during the siege, his majesty bestowed upon it the proud motto, "FORTITER DEFENDIT TRIUMPHANS."

KING CHARLES II. confirmed previous charters to the town, and granted others. A fine statue of the Merry Monarch, in a Roman habit, which formerly stood over the Magazine Gate, at the north end of Tyne Bridge, is now placed near to the entrance of the Merchants' Court, adjoining the Guildhall, Newcastle.

KING JAMES II. A magnificent equestrian statue of King James, cast in copper, was erected a little before the Revolution in the midst of the Sandhill, Newcastle. The statue was raised upon a pedestal of white Italian marble, 14 feet from the base, which was of black polished marble. This fine work of art was approved by Sir Christopher Wren, and cost the town £800 sterling. In November 1688 it was pulled down by a hot-headed Protestant mob from Sandgate, provided with ropes for the purpose, and thrown into the river. Bourne says, "It was confessed the most beautiful and curious of its kind that was in the whole kingdom. Certainly it was a great ornament to the town, and 'tis therefore great pity it is not still in being, though it was the statue of an unfortunate king."

KING JAMES I.

KING CHARLES I.

KING CHARLES II.

KING JAMES II.

HILST an apprentice, and catering for himself on four shillings and sixpence per week, young Bewick became acquainted with GILBERT GRAY, an eccentric but most worthy and intelligent bookbinder, who had been shopman to Allan Ramsay at the time he composed the "Gentle Shepherd." Originally intended for the Kirk, he received a liberal education at the College of

GILBERT GRAY.

Aberdeen. Having somehow imbibed a rooted dislike for priests and priest-craft, he gave up all thoughts of enter-ing the ministry, for, as he told his friend, "of a 'trouth,' Thomas, I did not like their ways." After leaving Scotland he directed his steps to New-castle, and first entered the employ of Messrs. Bryson & Charnley, whom he afterwards left for that of Mr. Slack and his successor, Mr. Solomon Hodgson, publishers of the *New-castle Chronicle*. In the workshop of this worthy tradesman the youthful wood-engraver spent his winter evenings, a docile and attentive disciple of this sage in humble life. Many of the books sent to bind he was allowed to read, and encouraged to converse freely on such passages as interested him most. These obligations Bewick never forgot in after life, but remem-bered with gratitude when his own course was nearly run.

We may be sure the familiar objects in that old workshop would also linger long in his memory. The strong shelf at the back that held Gilbert's stock of milled boards, the well-worn grindstone on which he was wont to sharpen his plough-knives, the cumbrous standing press and long iron pin, the clumsy pasteboard shears, the closet in which he kept his supply of leather and Dutch marbled papers, Bewick would require no effort to recall to his fancy.

Gray "rose early to work, lay down when he felt weary, and rose again when refreshed. His diet was of the simplest kind, and he ate when hungry, and drank when dry, without paying regard to meal-times." To instruct the ignorant, to visit poor debtors in prison, and by paying what they owed, if proved deserving, restore them to liberty and their families, was a duty he loved to discharge. To objects such as these Gray devoted his little savings and the profits of his small but useful publications. "He varied his favourite dish of hasty-pudding with pease, which usually stood in a bowl near him while at work, and which, with water, satisfied the wants of nature." Animal food he rarely tasted, and once on being presented with a goose, had it salted, hung up, and cut into slices and broiled as wanted. The time at length came when the old man, full of days and good works, must cease from his honest toil, and receive the reward due to his life of self-denial and perseverance in well-doing. His weary frame, exhausted by long watching and attending the sick-bed of his aged wife, with whom he had lived most happily, sank under the burden, and, strong in Christian hope, he departed this life, 12th February 1794, aged 85 years, though intimate friends believed that 95 was nearer the truth. Mr. Bewick, with others who respected his character, attended the funeral.

EWICK relates in his Memoirs, p. 71, that it was through his frequent visits to the workshops of Gilbert Gray and his son William that he first became acquainted with Thomas Spence, who was born on the Quayside, Newcastle, on the 21st of June 1750. From it we learn that

"He was one of the warmest philanthropists in the world. The happiness of mankind seemed with him to absorb every other consideration. He was of a cheerful disposition, warm in his attachment to his friends and in his patriotism to his country; but he was violent against people whom he considered of an opposite character. With such he kept no bounds. For the purpose chiefly of making converts to his opinion 'that property in land is everybody's right,' he got a number of young men gathered together and formed into a debating society, which was held in the evenings in his schoolroom in the Broad Garth. One night, when his favourite question was to be debated, he reckoned upon me as one of his 'backers.' In this, however, he was mistaken; for, notwithstanding my tacitly assenting in a certain degree to his plan,—viz., as to the probability of its succeeding in some uninhabited country or island,—I could not at all agree with him in thinking it right to upset the present state of society, by taking from people what is their own, and then launching out upon his speculations. I considered that property ought to be held sacred, and, besides, that the honestly obtaining of it was the great stimulant to industry, which kept all things in order, and society in full health and vigour. The question having been given against him without my having said a word in its defence, he became swollen with indignation, which, after the company was gone, he vented upon me. To reason with him was useless. He began by calling me, from my silence, 'a Sir Walter Blackett,' adding, 'If I had been as stout as you are, I would have thrashed you, but there is another way in which I can do the business and have at you.' He then produced a pair of cudgels, and to work we fell. He did not know that I was a proficient in cudgel-playing, and I soon found that he was very defective. After I had blackened the insides of his thighs and arms he became quite outrageous, and acted very unfairly, which obliged me to give him a severe beating."

The rough usage this political theorist and dreamer received at the hands of young Bewick did not dissolve their old friendship, for, as we afterwards find, he called upon Mr. Spence at Haydon Bridge on his journey to Scotland, where he was a

Tho.ˢ Spence
April 2ᵈ 1810

"welcome guest," and stopped two days. In "The Spensonian Commonwealth" every fifth day was to be a Sabbath, or day of rest. The Established Church was to be maintained at the public cost; Dissenters, if they set up any other religon, were to bear the cost of it themselves. Spence set himself not only to remodel the British Constitution, but to reform the English language. In 1775 he invented a New Alphabet, consisting of forty letters, each of which represented a different sound. A stanza from his version of Gray's Elegy may be given as a specimen :—

AN ELIJE, RITIN IN A KUNTRE CHURCH-YARD. GRA.

> " Thi Kurfu tolz thi Nel ov parting Da,
> Thi louing Herd Windz slole o'r thi Le,
> Thi Plomin homwurd plodz his wereid Wa,
> And livz thi Wurld too darknis and too me."

Mr. Spence died in London, 8th September 1814. We are told that he was of a sanguine and open countenance, cheerful disposition, and winning manners. However erroneous his views, his honesty and sincerity were never doubted.

N Sunday morning the 17th November 1771, when Thomas Bewick had just entered the fifth year of his servitude, an event took place which was re-membered and spoken of on Tyneside for genera-tions afterwards. This was no other than the fall of Tyne Bridge. Five hundred and twenty-three years before, the greater part of the town, together with its bridge, was destroyed by fire; and in 1339 part of the bridge was carried away by a sudden inundation, when no less than 120 persons were drowned. Having weathered many a storm and tempest during

five centuries, the end came at last. In consequence of heavy
and long-continued rains in the west, the Tyne and her tribu-
tary streams became swollen beyond all previous floods the
records of which have been preserved. The first alarm was
given about two o'clock. The dreadful noise made by the rush
of waters through the arches of the bridge aroused the inhabitants from their sleep to a sense of their danger. All was dark,
and the cold excessive. The middle arch of the bridge, and
two other arches near to Gateshead, were carried away, and
seven houses, with shops standing thereon, together with several
of the inmates, were overwhelmed with immediate destruction.
One house was carried away entire as far as Jarrow Slake. A
family of five persons, including two children, remained for six
hours, perishing with cold, on a portion of the bridge only six
feet square, until George Woodward, a heroic bricklayer in
Gateshead, accomplished their rescue. The arches and houses
on each side of them had fallen into the gulf below. Boats
plied on the Sandhill for some hours, the water being six feet
deep. Thomas Bewick, then strong and active, rowed about
in one of them, endeavouring, with others, to make himself
useful in helping to save property. Three sloops and a brig
were driven upon the Quay, and left there when the flood
abated. A wooden cradle was picked up at sea by a vessel,
in which was a child, alive and well. Ralph Beilby engraved
on copper a view of the ruins of the bridge, from a drawing by
his brother William. It is curious, but without any merit as an
engraving. At Bywell the catastrophe was severely felt; ten
houses were swept away, and six persons perished. The whole
village was under water; and in the dining-room and other
rooms on the first floor of Mr. Fenwick's house it was eight
feet deep. Most of the valuable stud of horses belonging to

that gentleman were got inside of the Black Church, and saved themselves by holding by the tops of the pews, which were allowed to continue in their gnawed state for several years. I have heard Miss Bewick say that her grandfather, Robert Elliot, who farmed lands under the Ellison family at Woodgate, near Bill Quay, was on a visit to Mr. Hall of Bywell at the time. There was to have been a turkey for supper. A relative came in and mentioned the alarming rise of the tide. He was told that, whenever they promised themselves to be more than usually comfortable and happy, he was sure to come in with some story or another and damp their joy. The words were scarcely uttered when the waters rushed into the room and put out the fire. It is needless to say that the turkey was soon forgot in their endeavour to secure the safety of themselves and their property. A mare belonging to Mr. Elliot was saved in the same church by getting upon the altar-table. An old-fashioned press which stood in Miss Bewick's kitchen in West Street came from Bywell, where it floated about the room on that memorable night. Nowhere was the flood more disastrous than at Ovingham, where the boat-house was carried away, together with the boatman, his wife, and two children, his mother and his brother, his man and maid servant, with two young men. Those ten persons all perished, except the boatman and his brother, who were carried down the river for 250 yards, together with the thatch of their house, until their headlong course was fortunately stayed by a wood. Here they remained upon the trees for ten hours, drenched with water and almost starved with cold and hunger, before they could be rescued. Not the least interesting of the "Newcastle Reprints" is "An Account of the Great Floods in the Rivers Tyne, Wear, &c., in 1771 and 1815, and of the Eruption of Solway Moss."

EWICK'S apprenticeship was now drawing to a close. Few forms were more familiar to the people of Newcastle at this time than that of JOHN CUNNINGHAM, the pastoral poet. Shortly before the poor player breathed his last, Bewick took his portrait. "He walked after the poet in the streets of Newcastle, stopped, loitered behind, repassed him, and in this manner, unobserved by the dying bard," sketched his likeness. Cunningham died at his lodgings in the Groat Market on the 18th September 1773, aged forty-four, respected not only for his talents, but on account of his private character, many gentlemen of the town attending his funeral.[1] The organist played a solemn dirge. His friend and patron, Mr. Slack, publisher of the *Newcastle Chronicle*, erected a table-monument over

[1] John Cunningham was born at Dublin in the year 1729, his parents having some time before migrated from Scotland. At the early age of seventeen he produced a drama, entitled "Love in a Mist." From inclination and the pressure of family circumstances he was led to attach himself to theatrical pursuits, though destitute of some personal attractions always considered needful to insure success as an actor. York, Sunderland, Durham, Northallerton, and other towns in the North of England, appear to have been regularly visited by the company of which he was not an unimportant member. Newcastle he ever esteemed his home. In 1766 he published a collected edition of his fugitive pieces, which he was strongly recommended to dedicate to Mrs. Elizabeth Montagu of Denton Hall, whose beauty and elegant acquirements were recognised in the first literary circles of the day. David Garrick, then in the zenith of his fame, was idolised by the poor player, who not only dedicated his work, but actually walked up to London to present the English Roscius with a copy, expectant and hopeful. His reception was chill in the extreme. Garrick put two guineas into the poet's hand, with the remark, " Players, sir, as well as poets, are always poor !" Mortified beyond expression, he left the presence of the brilliant actor sad and dejected. From this time Cunningham declined in health, and from some cause unknown left the kindly shelter of Mr. Slack's roof for lodgings a few doors off. Here he died. His excellence as a pastoral poet, and his kindly heart, endeared him to a large circle of friends. For many years young ladies belonging to some of the best families in the town were wont to meet and scatter flowers over his grave. In our own day, Joseph Cowen, Esq., whose true liberality, eloquence, and ability will, irrespective of party, long be remembered by the people of Newcastle, has placed in the venerable church where the poet rests in peace a rich stained-glass window to his memory. He has also headed a subscription to restore the monument, now fallen into decay, and the inscription almost obliterated, set up by the first proprietor of the *Newcastle Chronicle*.

his remains in St. John's Churchyard. If it be a vile thing
to libel a man's character whilst living, it is surely not
less reprehensible and cruel to caricature his features and
gait after death. This has unwittingly been the fate of
Cunningham. The first transgressor, I believe, was Richard-

son, in the "Local Historians' Table Book," who represents
the bard as an ill-looking, poverty-stricken mendicant, whereas
his features were pleasing, and himself always decently ap-
parelled. His form, indeed, was then attenuated by sickness.
The portraits profess to be copied from a miniature by Bewick,
which is not the case; his drawing being three-quarters length

and oval, 2½ inches by 2 inches, including the margin, which bears the following inscription : " Mr. Jno. Cunningham, Pastoral Poet. Drawn a few days before his death by Bewick." Above the head is a laurel crown, omitted in the engraving. This miniature formerly belonged to the late Miss Hornby of Newcastle, and was bought by me when in London at the sale of the Jupp Collection, and afterwards sold to William Law, Esq. of Littleborough. Thurston enlarged this portrait most admirably ; his drawing, which has been beautifully engraved by Worthington, forms part of my " Bewickiana."

The following is from the pen of Cunningham (Poems, p. 80, 1766) :—

THE SHEEP AND THE BRAMBLE-BUSH.[1]

A FABLE.

A thick-twisted brake in the time of a storm,
  Seem'd kindly to cover a sheep ;
So snug, for awhile, he lay shelter'd and warm,
  It quietly sooth'd him asleep.

The clouds are now scatter'd, the winds are at peace,
  The sheep's to his pasture inclined ;
But ah ! the fell thicket lays hold of his fleece,
  His coat is left forfeit behind.

My friend, who the thicket of law never try'd,
  Consider before you get in ;
Tho' judgment and sentence are pass'd on your side,
  By Jove, you'll be fleeced to your skin.

---

[1] Poems, chiefly Pastoral, by John Cunningham. These lines will also be found in " Bewick's Select Fables," 1784, p. 303, but without the poet's name. Isaac Taylor designed and engraved the frontispiece to the second edition of Cunningham's Poems, which Bewick and his friend Pollard when young men " thought was the best thing that ever was done."—Memoir, p. 103.

T this period of his life, when the work of the day was finished, soon after seven o'clock, Bewick would leave his lodgings, and set out to visit his parents at Cherryburn. Leaving the town by Westgate Tower, wherein his friend William Bulmer dwelt, along with his mother and sisters, it was a long walk, and usually took him three hours. Beyond the dark and time-worn archway of the Tower were a few red-brick houses with small dormer windows, old-fashioned thatched cottages, a cartwright's shop, and a smithy—Summerhill being then almost a continuous garden up to the toll-bar at the top of the hill. Here began a wild and open country, extending over the lands of Fenham, Kenton, and the Nun's Moor, far eastward to the sea.

Benwell, with its solitary farms and quiet roadside inn, was soon passed. On reaching Wallbottle the way became more lonesome. It was a relief in these journeys, when undertaken at night during the autumn and winter months, to hear in the distance the rumbling of a carrier's cart or waggon bound for Newcastle, laden with fruit, eggs, butter, or poultry. The sound would gradually become more audible, until at length a covered, shapeless waggon appeared, having a lamp attached, which often proved to be old Corbett's, the Hexham carrier. He put up at the Pack Horse in the Side, and now and then brought jobs to Beilby's. After a friendly salutation, with a crack of the whip the horse moved on with quickened pace, and soon was lost to view. The next village was Heddon-on-the-Wall. Here the youthful traveller turned off from the main road in the direction of Horsley. If the long miles he had already trod were cheerless, the dark path he was now

F

about to enter was more so, and required some courage. This was Horsley Lane, which led direct to Ovingham after passing Mount Hooley. Whilst threading his course along this narrow road, deeply ploughed with cart ruts, the village clock might be heard to strike ten, and as the sound died away the stillness and gloom seemed to increase.

The moon, breaking from behind a cloud, would for awhile illumine the grey Saxon tower of Ovingham Church and the ruins of Prudhoe Castle, the ancient seat of the Umfrevilles, on the opposite bank of the Tyne, and then again all would be wrapt in darkness. Ovingham reached at last, it sometimes happened that his further progress was stayed, if the night proved stormy, or the ferry-boat could not be had. He would then remain with his friend Mr. Dobson till the following morning, when, rising early, he crossed the river, and took breakfast with his father and mother at Cherry-burn.

Only one born and bred amid the hardships of a country life, and accustomed from boyhood to travel in the night, could undertake such pedestrian "flights up the Tyne" as Bewick religiously performed. The season of the year, or the state of the weather, was never considered. He learned that to be placed in the "midst of a wood in a winter night, amid whirlwinds of snow, when the tempest howled above him, was sublimity itself." The rigour of winter in due time gave way to the brightness of spring and all the glories and fulness of summer. The pencil of the artist and the song of the poet would alike fail to picture the charms of Tyneside, such as Bewick beheld one hundred years ago. In pastoral loveliness its scenery could not be surpassed. He well describes his own impressions in the following words :—

" As soon as the days began to lengthen and the sprouting herbage had covered the ground, I often stopped with delight by the sides of woods to admire the dangling woodbine and roses, and the grasses powdered or spangled with pearly drops of dew, and also, week after week, the continued succession of plants and wild flowers. The primrose, the wild hyacinth, the harebell, the daisy, the cowslip, &c., these, altogether, I thought no painter ever could imitate. I had not at that time ever heard the name of the great and good Linnæus, and knew plants only by their common English names. While admiring these beautifully enamelled spots on my way, I was also charmed with the equally beautiful little songsters which were constantly pouring out their various notes to proclaim the spring. While this exhilarating season glided on by imperceptible degrees, unfolding its blossoms until they faded into summer, and as the days lengthened, my hours of rising became more and more early. I have often thought that not one-half of mankind knew anything of the beauty, the serenity, and the stillness of the summer mornings in the country, nor have ever witnessed the rising sun's shining forth upon the new day."

These weekly visits, dictated by filial piety, continued until the death of his parents in 1785.

HE first employment the young apprentice was put to, was copying "Copeland's Ornaments" and blocking out the wood about the lines on the diagrams (which Mr. Beilby finished) for Dr. Charles Hutton's Diaries and "Treatise on Mensuration," one of them being a view of the steeple of St. Nicholas' Church, under the shadow of which his life may be said to have been passed.[1] In a letter in the *Newcastle Magazine* for June 1822, Dr. Hutton gives interesting particulars relative to the Beilby family, and his connection with Bewick :—

" Between the years 1760–1770, two brothers, William and

---

[1] This view, Bewick's first known attempt on wood, is almost identical with a little cut of the steeple which appeared more than once in the *Newcastle Courant* newspaper for 1745, heading an advertisement of Joseph Barber, bookseller, in Amen Corner.

Ralph Beilby, rendered themselves famous in the arts of drawing and seal-engraving, lettering on plate and other metals,
and painting or lettering on glass and burning it in, &c.   The
elder brother, William, settled as a teacher of drawing in schools
and to individuals, while Ralph adopted the profession of a
seal-engraver.   Having passed several years in his native town,
William migrated to the metropolis, and set up a boarding-
school at Chelsea, which, it would seem, was not successful,
as we find him afterwards residing somewhere about Nottingham, in the same way, where he died many years ago.   Ralph
continued as a seal-engraver till his death in 1817."

About 1760, Dr. Hutton began making preparations for his
work on Mensuration, the first edition of which was put to press

in 1768, employing Ralph Beilby to
execute the necessary diagrams.   He
procured the blocks of boxwood from
London, with the tools for cutting
them, instructing Mr. Beilby and
Thomas Bewick how to cut and
square the blocks, and to cut or
engrave lines upon them.   "Thus then," observes Hutton,
"I was the instructor of the very ingenious Mr. Bewick in
this branch of engraving, which he has since carried to such
a high state of perfection."   On the completion of this job,
young Bewick addressed himself with uncommon ardour and
perseverance to the task of obtaining a complete insight into
and mastery of the art of wood-engraving.   The study of its
resources and capability from henceforth became the pleasure
and business of his life.   If tools were wanting, his inventive
genius and mechanical skill soon supplied the deficiency.

HE first book with pictorial woodcuts by Bewick, entitled "The Youth's Instructor and Entertaining Story-Teller," was published by Thomas Saint in 1774. Many of the cuts in this work are beautiful, and testify to the advance the young artist had already made in his profession. At a very early period of his apprenticeship, two or three bar bills, from the correct drawing and neatness of execution displayed in the cuts with which they were headed, attracted much notice. The first was a "George and Dragon," done for W. Howe, of the George Inn, Penrith. It has no border. Miss Bewick gives 1767 as the date of this cut. About the same time another with a similar design (varied) was cut for Richard Dungett, who kept an inn in the Bottle Bank, Gateshead; and a third for the Cock Tavern at the head of the Side, then one of the best in the town.

The first mail coach from Newcastle to London started from this inn in 1786. The landlord, Matthew Hall, died in 1804. The examples on next page were engraved for public-houses in Newcastle and other towns.

"The 1st of October 1774 arrived at last; and, for the first time in my life, I felt myself at liberty," is Bewick's remark on looking back on this interesting day, which ended his servitude and made him his own master.

In the last month of Bewick's apprenticeship a contested parliamentary election for Newcastle took place. The poll continued open for eight days. The candidates were Sir Walter Blackett, Bart. (whom Bewick calls the "silent member"); Sir Matthew White Ridley, of Blagdon, co. Northumberland, Bart.; the Hon. Constantine John Phipps, afterwards Lord Mulgrave;

THE BLACK BULL.

THE COCK.

THE GEORGE AND DRAGON.

YOUNG NORTHUMBERLAND.

THE HALF MOON.

THE HAT AND FEATHER.

THE KING'S HEAD.

THE QUEEN'S HEAD.

LAMBERT SCULP.ᵗ

SIR M.W. RIDLEY BARᵗ. M.P.

Died 16 April 1813 Aged 68.

and Thomas Delaval, Esq. The two baronets were elected.
Sir Matthew Ridley, who succeeded his father, represented the
town during eight successive Parliaments. He was born in
1746, and died April 16, 1813, in the sixty-seventh year of his
age, and was interred in the family vault in St. Nicholas'
Church, Newcastle, where a most beautiful monument to
his memory, by Flaxman, was erected in 1819. From the
twentieth year of the reign of King George II. (1747) till
within a few months of the accession of her Majesty Queen
Victoria, the much-respected house of Ridley served our dear
country in the British Senate with patriotic faithfulness and
honour.

The most popular of local songs ends—

"REET Star o' Heaton,
  You're aye wor darling sweet-on';
  May heaven's blessings leet-on
  Your lyedy, bairns, and ye !
        Weel may the keel row," &c.

REVIOUS to 1775 Bewick had engraved some
cuts of Fables for Thomas Saint, of which Mr.
Beilby thought so highly that he had impressions taken of five of the best, and sent them to
the Society for the Promotion of the Fine Arts.
The cut of the "Huntsman and Old Hound," in particular,
was deemed by that body so meritorious and worthy of reward,
that the artist was offered the choice of a gold medal or the
sum of seven guineas. He elected to have the latter. Had
preference been given to the medal, it would have been
treasured by his family through many long years with much

pride, and, it is to be hoped, would have found a home at Cherryburn when the last daughter of Thomas Bewick should have passed away. But then he would have lost that un-alloyed pleasure of the heart he felt in presenting the guineas to a beloved mother. This event took place in February 1775.

On this occasion Bewick remarks, "Amongst the several congratulations of kind neighbours, those of Mr. Gregson, my old master, stood pre-eminent. He flew from Ovingham, where the news first arrived, over to Eltringham, to congratulate my father and mother; and the feelings and overflowings of his heart can be better imagined than described."

After the expiration of his apprenticeship, Bewick worked for a few weeks with Mr. Beilby as a journeyman, at a guinea a week, and then went to spend Christmas at Cherryburn. Here he joined in hunting parties with the Nimrods of the country-side, and accompanied his father, as in former days, in collect-ing what money was due for coals from the farmers and other customers, as well as executing a large number of cuts for Thomas Angus, the famous Newcastle printer of Chapbooks and Garlands. He was thus employed throughout the year 1775 and for some months of 1776. He still pursued with ardour his favourite amusement of angling. This was a re-creation of which he believed he could never tire. It happened on a hot summer afternoon in June, whilst thus engaged, that all of a sudden he fell into a meditative mood; he pon-dered awhile, then tied up his rod and walked home. He told his mother that he had resolved to see more of the world, and would begin by visiting his relations in Cumberland. He requested her to put up some shirts for him; three guineas were sewn into the waistband of his breeches, and then, with a good

stick in his hand, he began his travels, followed by his favourite
and faithful companion "Witch." For nearly two months he
traversed on foot a considerable part of Cumberland and the
Highlands of Scotland. After visiting Penrith and Carlisle, he
crossed the Border, and saw Selkirk, Dalkeith, and Edinburgh;
thence to Glasgow and Dumbarton, and onwards to the Highlands by the western side of Loch Lomond; returning by
Stirling, Falkirk, and Linlithgow to Edinburgh.

Through all his lonely wanderings—by the mountain's misty
side, the dreary waste, or solitary heath, as well as in the brighter
landscape of sunny fields and woodlands—Witch clung to her
master. She would run for a considerable distance before him,
and then lie down and wait until he came up, when off she
would start again. I have a pencil sketch of this dog by
Bewick, under which he has written: "'Witch,' ob. 9th February 1784, æt. 9½, accompanied T. B. in his journey to Scotland." This I obtained from Miss Bewick, together with a few
portraits of Highlanders, men, women, and children, ministers
and soldiers, some only thumb-nail size, sketched during this
tour. Having seen this much, he now set his face homeward.
A Leith sloop, bound for Newcastle, received him on board just
as she was moving from the pier. After encountering a violent
storm off the Firth of Forth, during which he suffered much
from want of rest, repose was sought in a wretched bed, in which
he could neither lie on his side nor easily turn over. The kindness and compassion of his nature in such a trying situation
was now brought out, for to complete his distress a little infant
was put in bed beside him; this child he tenderly nursed until
its sick mother relieved him on her recovery. After resting a
day or two at South Shields he set off to Newcastle, where he
arrived on the 12th August 1776. Here he did not propose to

G

remain long.   As all artists, actors, and men of genius in every
profession aspire after metropolitan fame, that they may in time
acquire fortune and reputation, Bewick made up his mind to go
to London, where so many of his old friends were now located.
Funds only were wanting.   After working for a few weeks in
Newcastle, he earned sufficient to enable him to carry out his
intention.   Having paid for his passage by a collier, after a
voyage of about three weeks, he arrived in London on the 1st
of October 1776.   His schoolfellows, Christopher and Philip
Gregson ; his former companion, William Gray, then a bookbinder in Chancery Lane; and his friend Robert Pollard, received him with gladness.   The first two provided a lodging, and
the last, through the kindness and influence of his master, Isaac
Taylor, with plenty of work.   Thomas Hodgson, printer, George
Court, Clerkenwell, who served his apprenticeship with John
White, the printer of the *Newcastle Courant*, had a taste for
wood-engraving, and embellished with rude and curious cuts
many of the old ballads and histories printed by his master.   He
too, in anticipation of his arrival, had in readiness a store of little
jobs.   These, along with Mr. Carnan, and Newbery of St. Paul's
Churchyard, kept him busily employed during the nine months
he spent in London.   In the streets of that vast city, he looked
with grief and sorrow on the sad fate of so many young and
handsome women, following the paths of sin and misery,
who might have lived happily and respected.   He deplored
their wretchedness, and, when needed, relieved their poverty.
London life and manners proved distasteful to one of such
simple habits and mode of living.

The usage Bewick met with from his fellow-workmen, and
other causes, combined to create such a feeling of dislike, that
he determined to leave the Metropolis and never set foot in it

again. He would rather, he said, "enlist for a soldier, or go and herd sheep at five shillings per week as long as he lived, than be tied to live in it."

The "Hole-in-the-Wall," Fleet Street,[1] was a tavern much frequented by people from Newcastle, and there every Monday night he used to repair to meet friends from the North and see the Newcastle newspapers. Many a pleasant evening, after the labour and confinement of the day was over, was spent in this harmless and agreeable manner.

NANCY COLLINS—*The Hive*, 1806.

The announcement that he was about to leave London and "never return" was received with surprise and astonishment. Isaac Taylor and Thomas Hodgson could not conceal their feelings of chagrin and disappointment. His last night in London was passed with a few friends at the "George" in

---

[1] Had Bewick tarried a few weeks longer in London he would no doubt have joined in celebrating the victory obtained by the free burgesses over the Corporation, held at the "Hole-in-the-Wall." There an elegant dinner was provided by Newcastle men then in London, on the 11th of August 1777. Amongst the toasts and sentiments were the following: "The coal trade and our friends at Newcastle;" "Long life and good health to Mother Willis," the respected landlady.

Brook Street; and, as might have been expected, they did not separate till a late hour. In the morning, after taking leave of his landlord and family, he got on board a collier, and arrived in sight of St. Nicholas' Church steeple about the 22d of June 1777. No sooner did Bewick reach Newcastle than he called upon his old master, his mind filled with thoughts regarding his future prospects and the best mode of profitably employing his talents. He felt a delicacy in commencing business on his own account, which did him much honour, as it arose from a fear lest Mr. Beilby should consider it as done in opposition to himself. His London friends had supplied him with plenty of work, which would take a considerable time to finish; he therefore fitted up a bench at his old lodgings at Hatfield's.

About this time an election took place in Newcastle, occa-sioned by the death of Sir Walter Blackett. The candidates were Sir John Trevelyan, who sought to occupy the seat held by his uncle, Sir Walter, for the long period of forty-three years. There was a severe contest, his opponent being the notorious Andrew Robinson Bowes, Esq., who had recently married Lady Strathmore. Mrs. Elizabeth Montagu of Denton Hall[1] describes in a letter her ladyship's extraordinary conduct at Newcastle. She was accustomed "to sit all day in the window at a public-house, from whence she sometimes lets fall some jewels or trinkets, which voters pick up, and then she gives them money for restoring them—a new kind of offering bribes." The town is described as being "in a wild uproar." Mr. Bowes

---

[1] This lady, who was the eldest daughter of Matthew Robinson, Esq., of West Layton, in Yorkshire, married in 1742 Edward Montagu, Esq., of East Denton, in Northumberland. She survived her husband twenty-five years, and died 25th August 1800, in the eightieth year of her age.

lost the election, although he "sold £5000 a year of his lady's income for life, to procure himself £40,000" ("A Lady of the Last Century," by Dr. Doran). A truly extraordinary picture of the times!

Mr. Beilby was no doubt apprehensive that his former apprentice would commence business in the town sooner or later. Bewick's thorough knowledge of the trade connection and requirements of the office in St. Nicholas' Churchyard would give him many advantages. Proposals for a partnership were at once made through a mutual friend. The idea did not at first recommend itself to Mr. Bewick, but on consideration he consented, and acted wisely in doing so. Although without capital, he thereby acquired an excellent position in a highly respectable and established business. In the light of subsequent success, consequent on the development of his genius, he might regret the step, but at the time he did well to entertain the suggestion. Thus the firm of Beilby & Bewick, destined to become so famous, began its commercial career.

N the partnership being legally completed, Mr. Bewick took his younger brother John, then in his seventeenth year, as an apprentice, whose amiable and cheerful disposition won the esteem of Mr. Beilby, and endeared him to all who had the pleasure of his acquaintance. Of him and his works an extended notice will be given hereafter. "While my brother was my apprentice," Bewick remarks in his Memoir, "he frequently accompanied me on my weekly visits to Cherryburn. He was then a clever, springy youth, and our bounding along together was often compared to the

scamperings of a pair of wild colts. These journeys commenced
while I was an apprentice. I then mostly went and returned
on the same day ; but when I became my own master, for many
years, in summer's heat and winter's freezing cold, I did not
miss a single week." These visits continued regularly from
1777 till 1785. The route taken by the brothers in these
weekly wanderings, frequently by night, is worthy of mention.
In the course of conversation one evening, I inquired of Miss
Bewick what road her father generally took. She said that
occasionally, but only seldom, he would cross over to Gateshead,
and then go along the south bank of the Tyne by Swalwell
and Winlaton. But this way he disliked, mainly on account
of Crowley's Crew,[1] a fighting and violent set of men whom it
was difficult to avoid, as they were always to be found standing
in groups along the road and about the doors of public-houses
he was obliged to pass in going through these villages. He
commonly used the high or military road, constructed by
General Wade after the rebellion of 1745. In summer-time,
when the days were long and the nights light, the footpath by
the waterside by way of Elswick, Scotswood, and Newburn
was both short and pleasant, and often travelled by the family
in going to and returning from Ovingham when the tide
permitted, but was attended with considerable danger on
dark, wet, and winter nights, particularly that part which lay
between Wylam and Ovingham, where the road was narrow,
the river being on one side and thick bushes which obscured
the footpath on the other. In those long walks, whether by
himself whilst an apprentice, or afterwards in company with his
brother, they were never molested, though at that time daring

---

[1] Crowley's Crew—Sons of Vulcan—employed at the ironworks at Swalwell and Winlaton,
near Newcastle, established by the estimable Sir Ambrose Crowley about two hundred years ago.

attempts by well-mounted gentlemen of the road against peaceful travellers were frequent, who, whilst a pistol was held to
their head, were compelled to yield up purse, watch, and
whatever valuables they had.

A few extracts from the *Newcastle Chronicle* for 1770
afford a striking picture of the times :—On March 3, we read
that as the steward of Mrs. Ord of Fenham was returning home
from Newcastle, he was attacked by two footpads, who knocked
him off his horse, and robbed him of his watch and money. In
August, the postman carrying the mail between this town and
Durham was robbed of the bags on Gateshead Fell, and on
another occasion on Chester Moor. On a Saturday night in
October, a blacksmith was stopped by two footpads near
Elswick Mill, and robbed of his marketing and money ; whilst
Alderman Peareth's servant was robbed by two men on
horseback near the gibbet on Gateshead Fell on the 1st of
November. Only three days after this, two gentlemen were
robbed near Birtley by two mounted highwaymen armed with
pistols. A gentleman on horseback was stopped by a footpad
near Chester bar, who presented a pistol, but did not fire ; and a
farmer near Kenton was stopped near the gallows on the Town
Moor, and robbed by two men on horseback, armed with
pistols. Mr. Liddle of Newton, son of Sir Thomas Liddle, of
Ravensworth, had a desperate encounter with armed footpads
on the Durham Road. Pistols were fired on both sides ; Mr.
Liddle happily escaped unhurt. Much blood was found on the
ground afterwards, but the robbers escaped in the darkness of
a December night. Lumley Thicks was a famous resort for
robbers, and avoided by all travellers as much as possible.
The perpetual occurrence of such crimes, and the alarm they
occasioned, explain what some consider the too frequent intro-

duction of the gallows in so many of Bewick's little land-scapes.

In the *Gentleman's Magazine* for the year 1785 we read: "This morning a shocking spectacle was exhibited before the debtor's door of Newgate, where twenty miserable wretches were in one moment plunged into eternity." Robbery and burglary were the crimes for which they suffered—not one was even charged with murder. Capital punishment was common in those days for offences which now would only meet with imprisonment with hard labour.

Whilst an apprentice, and during the year 1775, Bewick

The Ant and the Wasp—*Tales for Youth*, 1794.

drew and engraved a portion of the cuts which embellish the "Select Fables," published in 1776, as well as by far the larger number executed for an edition of "Gay's Fables," which came from the press of Thomas Saint in 1779, after being delayed about five years. The *editio princeps* of this important little volume is indispensable to the Bewick collector, embracing as it does the cuts submitted by Mr. Beilby to the Fine Art Society, and for which Thomas Bewick was awarded a premium.

It has been said that Bewick had the assistance of his brother in the execution of many of the cuts. Having gone through the book carefully, with the hope of being able to identify any such from my knowledge of his style, the conclusion I have come to is, that not more than half-a-dozen are entirely the work of his hand, though he might possibly have rendered some help with others.

It must be remembered that John Bewick had only been an apprentice for about two years. In the cut heading the first Fable, p. 13, we have an example of cross-hatching in the cloak of the Traveller: this process never found favour with Bewick. I am persuaded that the first ten cuts, having their angles ornamented with agricultural implements, anything but graceful, were never engraved by him. The pleasing tailpiece at p. 19, a youth amusing himself with his dog under a tree, is Bewick all over, and in striking contrast, both in drawing and execution, to the cuts which precede and follow.

These may be attributed without hesitation to David Martin. Miss Isabella Bewick told me that she had often heard her father speak of him. He was an apprentice with Beilby when Bewick first entered his service. It will be shown hereafter, from a long and valuable statement of Bewick's, now published for the first time, that David Martin executed some of the cuts for the "Select Fables" of 1784, hitherto thought to be the exclusive work of Thomas and his brother.

We now come to "Tommy Trip's History of Birds and Beasts, with the History of Little Tom Trip himself and his Dog Jouler, and of Woglog, the Great Giant. Newcastle, 1779." Mr. George Clayton Atkinson observes that it is to this little book that we are indebted for Bewick's more finished and celebrated productions, the Histories of Quadrupeds and British

H

Birds. The frontispiece, with the following cuts, are neatly
engraved, the natural attitude of the animals and birds being
well preserved in most cases, indicating the future excellence
of the artist—viz., the Student, the Lion and the Jackal, the
Horse, the Chameleon, the Roebuck, the Angler, the Wild Boar,
the Eagle, the Vulture, the Falcon, the Cuckoo, the Nightingale, &c. From the introductory account of Tommy Trip,
Miss Bewick was led to believe that the author of this tiny
volume was no other than Oliver Goldsmith. Of this I think
there can be little doubt. The amusing production is worthy
of insertion :—

"Tommy Trip, the author of the following sheets, is the only son of Mr.
William Trip, of Spittle Fields, London. He is but short in stature, and not
much bigger than Tom Thumb, but a great deal better, for he is a good scholar,
and whenever you see him, you will always find him with a book in his hand,
and his faithful dog Jouler by his side. Jouler serves him for a horse as well as
a dog ; and Tommy, when he has a mind to ride, pulls a little bridle out of his
pocket, whips it upon honest Jouler, and away he gallops tantivy. As he rides
through the town, he frequently stops to know how the little children do, and
if they are good and learn their books, he then leaves an apple, an orange, or a
plumcake at the door, and away he gallops again tantivy. You have heard
how he beat Woglog, the great giant. But lest you should not, I will tell you :—
As Tommy was walking through a meadow on a moonlight night, he heard a
little boy cry, upon which he called Jouler, saddled him, and rode away. He
found Woglog with a little boy under his arm, whom he was going to throw into
the water. Little boys should never loiter about in the fields, nor even in the
streets after it is dark. However, as he had been a good boy in other respects,
little Trip was determined the giant should not hurt him, and called out, 'Here,
you great giant, you Woglog, set down the little boy,' or I'll make you dance
like a pea on a tobacco pipe. Are you not ashamed to set your wits to a
child?' Woglog tried to seize little Trip between his finger and thumb, and
thought to have cracked him as one does a walnut ; but just as his hand reached
him, Jouler snapped at it, and bit a piece off his thumb, which put the giant in
so much pain that he let fall the little boy, who ran away. Then Trip up with
his whip, and lashed Woglog till he lay down and roared like a town bull, and

promised never to meddle with any little boys or girls again. Then Trip put the child upon Jouler and carried him home, charging him to be a good boy, and to say his prayers and learn his book, and do as his papa and mamma bid him, which this little boy has done ever since, and so must all other little boys and girls, or nobody will love them. Little Trip is not only an agreeable companion and a great scholar, but one of the best poets of the age, which is owned by the poets themselves, which I think an incontestable proof of his abilities. He has by him several dramatic pieces, not culled from other authors, as the custom is, but all originals. The following song, composed by him when he was very young, will prove his superiority in lyric poetry :—

> ' Three children sliding on the ice
> Upon a summer's day,
> As it fell out they all fell in,
> The rest they ran away.

> ' Now, had these children been at school,
> Or sliding on dry ground,
> Ten thousand pounds to one penny
> They had not all been drown d.

> ' You parents who have children dear,
> And eke you that have none,
> If you would have them safe abroad,
> Pray keep them all at home.' "

The next production of Saint's Press that claims attention is a 12mo volume of "Select Fables," published in 1784. It is described on the title as "A New Edition, Improved," having reference to the earlier impression, printed by him in 1776, with an inferior set of cuts. The illustrations in this rare little tome are very considerably in advance of those contained in "Gay's Fables," 1779. Bewick in the interval had improved in his drawing, and acquired greater freedom in the use of his tools. In design and execution the best of these cuts may fairly compare with many contained in the "Fables of Æsop," his last work. For true, genuine, deep wood-cutting, so characteristic of Bewick's unequalled style, they are far superior. Many of the cuts were undoubtedly the work of John Bewick, others the work of David Martin.

N 1778 there was a Society in Newcastle, composed of respectable tradesmen, who met together for friendly conversation and to discuss the politics of the day. The meetings were held at Richard Swarley's, the Black Boy Inn, in the Groat Market. Mr. Bewick was elected a member on 17th October 1778, the ticket of admission being engraved by Ralph Beilby, and bore the motto, " Honi soit qui mal y pense "—" The Newcastle House of Lords." Members on entering the room paid their *shot :* this was the small sum of fourpence, which was spent in refreshment. A chairman was elected for the evening to keep order, and when not otherwise engaged, Bewick seldom allowed a week to pass without more than once enjoying such pleasant intercourse. At ten o'clock the meeting broke up, according to rule, and members left for their several homes. One cannot sufficiently admire the moderation, simplicity, and true temperance displayed in those old-world doings.

Of another social club which he entered afterward, the card of admission reads thus : " Brotherly Society, held at Whitfield's Golden Lion, Newcastle. Mr. Thomas Bewick admitted a brother, 18th December 1782 (No. 32). Jno. F. Dixon, President. Jos. Gory, Secretary."

This card has a beautiful border of flowers cut by Bewick. The Golden Lion stood on the west side of the Bigg Market, a few doors above the Pudding Chare ; it was an Elizabethan tavern, two stories high, and entered by a low stone arch with one step down.

The parlour was panelled with oak, the ceiling low. On a winter night, when the outer shutters were closed, and a good fire burning, it appeared the picture of comfort.

A long yard, extending to the rear of Rosemary Lane, provided ample stabling for the many carriers who used to put up at the house, and whose carts and waggons stood in the street in front. At the entrance was a well-worn stone mount

LITTLE JACK—From the *Looking Glass for the Mind,* 1794.

(an object now rarely seen even at old country inns), to enable farmers' wives to get easily on the pillion behind their husbands in riding home.

This old inn has just been pulled down, together with its neighbour, the Unicorn. Built about the same time, they have at last succumbed before the march of improvement. In former days, before long bars and gin palaces had any exist- ence, its respected landlady, Mrs. Elliott, famed for her beauty, realised a handsome fortune by honest trading. Eighty years have changed for the worse the liquor traffic in Newcastle.

BRIEF retrospect of what Newcastle has done in the past in relation to the Fine Arts may not be out of place, or an unfitting introduction to a more extended notice of the Bewicks, and the school of which the elder brother was the admitted founder.

In the formation of that British School of Painters of which England is so justly proud, these northern parts have borne no inconsiderable share. Northumberland and Durham have produced artists, architects, and engineers whose genius has shed a lasting lustre on our country. Though we may not have given birth to a Claude, a Berghem, or a Cuyp, or to an engraver whose work could vie with the unapproachable excellence of that of Durer or Marc Antonio, few provincial towns in England have attained to a higher position, or rendered more important services in promoting a taste for the Fine Arts. Though much remains to be done to educate the popular mind, Newcastle has at all times, as might have been expected, attracted to herself the most promising amongst the youth of the neighbouring villages. Here native talent has ever found, when needed, patrons ready to foster and aid the ingenious in their struggles with adversity, and afford that early and kindly help without which they might have lived and died unknown.[1] In 1778 the gold pallet was

---

[1] John Charlton, the distinguished animal-painter, was, when a boy, for some time in my service. He employed his leisure in sketching with an ordinary steel or quill pen admirable little rural scenes without premeditation or forethought, afterwards using water-colours or Indian ink for more finished productions. These were bought by customers for one shilling each, which served for pocket-money on a rather liberal scale. I asked him once who taught him drawing. He replied, "No one ; I could always draw." The late Miss Jane Bewick observed, on my showing her some of his sketches, "Now, that lad has genius." At that time few were more capable of expressing themselves better, or had a keener perception of the merits of original talent, than that venerable lady. Afterwards, through the interest of Mr. John Hancock, the well-known naturalist, and last surviving friend of Thomas Bewick, Charlton obtained employment in the office of Sir Isaac Lowthian Bell, who fostered and encouraged his studies.

TYNEMOUTH PRIORY,

FROM THE ENTRANCE ARCH.

given by the Society for the Encouragement of the Fine Arts to Robert Watson for the best historical drawing. Three years before this, Thomas Bewick received a premium from the same Society. Earlier still, William Bell was presented by Sir Joshua Reynolds with the gold medal accorded by the Royal Academy. George Gray, so well known by his fruit-pieces and knowledge of natural science, and John Martin, whose original and sublime conceptions so vividly bring before us the awful events of sacred history, and illustrate with such power the scenes depicted in Milton's grand epic, "Paradise Lost," were men of whom our good town may justly boast; whilst the exquisite enamels of Charles Muss, a pupil of Martin's, will ever be admired for their marvellous delicacy and beauty. In the foremost rank of English landscape-painters the name of Thomas Miles Richardson and his talented family stands pre-eminent, coupled with those of Ewbank and Carmichael and George Balmer, many of their works being worthy of the pencil of Turner, Stanfield, and David Cox.

Robert Watson, artist and engineer, was the son of Joseph Watson, a member of the Free Porters' Company in Newcastle. His mother made sausages in the Flesh Market. Robert was born on April 20, 1755, about two years after Thomas Bewick. At an early age, we are told, he evinced such a fondness for drawing, that, after his education was finished, his parents apprenticed him to a coach-painter. In this situation he did not long continue. Leaving his native town, he went to London, and became a student in the Royal Academy. His artistic skill and literary ability as an art critic obtained for him the patronage and friendship of Dr. Johnson, Sir Joshua Reynolds, and other eminent men. He obtained an appointment in India as engineer, where, after displaying on many occasions a masterly knowledge of his profession, he was unfortunately seized with a fever, from the effects of which he died, in the twenty-eighth year of his age.

William Bell was a native of Newcastle, where his father was an ingenious bookbinder. Mr. Bell went to London about the year 1768, and was amongst the first of those who entered as students in the Royal Academy. For his picture of " Venus Soliciting Vulcan to Forge the Armour of Æneas" he obtained the gold medal. The figures were all portraits. William Carr, the herculean smith of Blyth, fitly represented Vulcan. Bell was much patronised by Sir John Delaval (afterwards Lord Delaval), and died about 1800.

The Chevalier Sir John Martin, K.L., was born on July 19, 1787, at Low Land Ends, Haydon Bridge, near Hexham. He was one of twelve children, and when very young was sent to the Free Grammar School at that place. One day, whilst the three masters of this establishment were standing together, he took a burnt stick and sketched the group on the wall near the fireplace, to the surprise and admiration of both teachers and scholars. When he was about fourteen years of age his parents settled in Newcastle, and resided near the White Cross. They apprenticed John to Mr. Wilson, coachmaker. Quarrelling with his master, his indentures were cancelled, and at the age of seventeen he ventured to London, where, within a few years, by dint of great application, careful study, and the untiring exercise of his extraordinary talents, he acquired a great name and the blessing of independence. His well-known pictures of " Zadoc in Search of the Waters of Oblivion," "Joshua Commanding the Sun to Stand Still," " The Fall of Nineveh," and " Belshazzar's Feast," have justly merited praise in every art centre both in Europe and America. From

RUINS OF TYNEMOUTH PRIORY,

FROM THE NORTH-WEST.

foreign courts he received many marks of honour and distinction. Belgium conferred the Order of Leopold (knighthood) and the large medal of the Exhibition; he was elected a member of the Academy of Antwerp; and the King of the French presented him with a gold medal and a splendid present of Sèvres china. He died 17th February 1854.

Whilst an apprentice, the elder Richardson, Carmichael, Woodhouse, famous for his lifelike portraits on glass (in black), and other artists, together with Ewbank, were frequent visitors at the shop of my master in the Royal Arcade.[1]

Thomas Miles Richardson was born at the Ballast Hills, Newcastle, May 15, 1784. At the age of fifteen he was apprenticed to Messrs. Gibson & Usher, joiners and cabinet-makers, who soon afterwards dissolved partnership. He served out his time with one Gibson, a dissipated fellow, whose favourite job was the annual erection of tents and booths on the Town Moor on the occasion of the races. Richardson's father, who was master of St. Andrew's Free School, died in 1806, when his son Thomas was chosen his successor. Whilst in this position, having confidence in himself, he began to give lessons in drawing, and continued to do so for about seven years. He then resigned his post as schoolmaster, and followed with ardour the bent of his inclinations. Posterity has done that justice to his talents which in this instance was but sparingly meted out whilst living. During my apprentice-

---

[1] Thomas Brown, bookbinder, removed from the Nun's Gate to the Royal Arcade soon after it was built, where he commenced business as a bookseller in connection with binding. He afterwards removed to Mozley Street, and about 1842 migrated to Toronto, Dominion of Canada. His father, who was admitted a member of the Stationers' Company, Newcastle, by servitude in 1774, was the father of the trade in the North of England.

I

ship fifty years ago many of his best pictures and drawings sold for very small sums. In 1836 a selection of his works were disposed of by lottery. My master, who was an old friend of Richardson's, strove hard to promote the success of the scheme, and obtained a goodly number of subscribers at one guinea each. I remember several of the pictures which were then exhibited in the shop; they would now be greedily purchased by eager buyers at ten times the price at which they were put into the lottery.

Mr. Richardson's children inherited the genius of their father and his love for the Fine Arts. His eldest son settled early in life as an artist in London, where he has continued to reside, carrying the art of painting in water colours to the highest perfection. His works are generally purchased privately as soon as exhibited. At the dispersion of Mr. Ismay's collection at Strawberry House, Newcastle, in 1872, I gave £514, 10s. for two very large and magnificent examples of this artist, being views of Borrowdale in Cumberland and Monaco in Italy. Both are now at Longridge Towers, near Berwick.

John Wilson Ewbank, the son of Michael Ewbank of Gateshead, innkeeper, was born at Darlington, 4th May 1799. His parents removing to the banks of the Tyne in 1804, in course of time he was bound an apprentice to Mr. Thomas Coulson of Newcastle, an eminent house-painter, whom he accompanied to Edinburgh about the year 1816. By the advice of his master, Mr. Ewbank took lessons of Mr. Nasmyth of that city. Endowed with rare talents, and a keen appreciation of the beauties of nature, he rapidly advanced in the knowledge of the true principles of painting. Flushed with success, and the achievement of unlooked-for fame and fortune, which, unhappily for himself, he was destined to enjoy but for a brief period, the position he had won was no sooner gained than lost. His fall carried with it the abandonment of every feeling of self-respect, and ended in poverty and wretchedness, his artistic efforts displaying more and more the moral wreck of the man. Drunkenness became habitual. Whilst we were engaged in the office posting the ledger, about twelve o'clock one cold winter night in December 1836, some one began to rattle at the door, which was locked. No notice was taken of this at first, thinking that whoever it might be they would soon tire. As the annoyance continued, my master told me to go and see who it was. On the door being opened, in came Mrs. Ewbank, thinly clad, and shivering with cold. She begged for a shilling, as they were starving; I was told to give her one and let her go.

Ewbank had a daughter who was very beautiful, with long dark eyelashes, her complexion being as the bloom of the damask rose. She had her portrait taken, I believe, by Simms of Edinburgh, when quite young. She was represented in a white dress, seated under a tree in a garden, arranging a wreath of wild flowers, herself the fairest and most lovely, adorned with all the graces and charms of childlike innocence. Alas! long before twenty summers had flown, every trace of her former beauty had disappeared, and she and her brother might be seen, borne down with want, selling their oil sketches in the streets and taverns of Newcastle and Shields.

> " A budding rose,
> Blasted before its bloom,
> Whose innocence did sweets disclose
> Beyond that flower's perfume."
>
> —*Shenstone.*

The family at last took up their abode in a dark and unwholesome cellar in Sunderland—a single chair its only furniture, with a pallet of straw for a bed. There, struck down with fever in its deadliest form, poor Ewbank lay until he was removed to the Infirmary, where, on the 28th of November 1847, at the early age of forty-eight, he breathed his last. Such was the sad end of this senior member of the Royal Scottish Academy.

I have sold this victim of intemperance many a sheet of cardboard, which he was wont to divide into four or more parts, rapidly sketching on each with one of Airey's pencils an admirable view of some Highland loch or Border homestead, castle, or tower. These he sold for ninepence or a shilling, whenever he could find a buyer. An old friend of his, who was also an artist, and clever in copying Morland, told me that once whilst he and Ewbank were at Shields, and too poor to buy cardboard, they drew on the back of a pack of cards they carried with them whatever their fancy suggested. These they sold for a few pence.

N Christmas week, 1784, Bewick, whilst sliding on the ice at Ovingham, was seized with a mysterious presentiment of coming ill, at which he felt surprised. There was to be a family dinner. Every one seemed cheerful; his father told his best jokes and drollest stories, and nothing appeared more likely than that for many years to come all present would meet again in health and happiness. But this was not to be. The year 1785, whilst still young, was one of sorrow for Mr. Bewick. On the 20th of February, at the age of fifty-eight, his mother, whom he loved so well, succumbed to a chill received whilst on an errand of mercy to a sick girl. This was his first and heaviest grief. But sorrows seldom come alone. His eldest sister, who had so carefully nursed her mother in her last brief illness, became the object of his anxious solicitude. The fatigue she had undergone told on a rather delicate constitution, enfeebled by constant watching and other duties attendant on a sick-room. She died on the 24th of June 1785, at the residence of her brother at the Forth, and was buried at Ovingham.

On Tuesday, the 15th day of November in the same year, Bewick began to engrave the first wood-block for his " History of Quadrupeds" with the figure of the Dromedary. Whilst engaged on this cut, news was brought of the death of his father. This event, which took place on his seventieth birthday, broke the spell that had for so many years governed Bewick's filial round of visits to Cherryburn.

Those attentions hitherto paid to his parents were soon to be transferred to another object. The void left by their loss required filling up, for the sense of being alone weighed on his spirits. He had no longer the companionship of his brother John.

Of a social disposition, and formed for a domestic life, he longed for the society of one to whom he might impart his confidence and share his joys and troubles.

On the 20th of April 1786, being then in his thirty-third year, Bewick married Isabella Elliot, the daughter of Robert Elliot, a farmer then living at Ovingham.

Their ages nearly corresponded, and what was better still, they were of a kindred temper and disposition. The attachment was of old standing. Dovaston relates that on one occasion when a lad, at church with Miss Elliot, in consequence of some juvenile prank of his, the young lady jumped up and cried out to the parson, "O sir, guide Thomas Bewick"—an interruption which obtained for the delinquent a sound flogging on the following day. After twenty years had rolled away she became his wife.

Miss Elliot was born at Woodgate, above Bill Quay, and opposite to Bill Point. The latter place is represented, "Brit. Birds," vol. ii. p. 144 (ed. 1826). On the recommendation of Mr. Rennie, the eminent engineer, it has since been removed by the Corporation of Newcastle.

LLUSION is made in the Memoir, p. 142, to the "woodcuts of Roman altars and arms of the Bishops of Durham," done for Hutchinson's History of that county, as the first job of any importance he had been called upon to execute. The following letter to Mr. Hutchinson (enclosing a sketch of Nevill's Cross restored) is interesting. Beilby's design was not adopted, but Bewick's good taste and judgment is very observable in his recommendation as to the background and accessories, if any. His obligation to Geo.

Allan, Esq., of the Grange, for the loan of works on ornithology is acknowledged at p. 153 of the same work. This letter is now published for the first time, from the original holograph in my collection. From what is there said, it appears certain that Bewick entertained the idea of publishing an illustrated "History of British Birds" from the very time he began to engrave the cuts for the "Quadrupeds," though its final carrying out was made to depend on the success of the first venture.

"NEWCASTLE, 21*st March* 1786.

"DEAR SIR,

"Enclosed is the sketch of Nevill's Cross, as requested in your last, different from both Bailey's and Lambert's, and is a medium between the two; also it is done as near the description of it in the book as we could make it. The following is the height, &c. :—Seven steps, 6 inches each, 3 ft. 6 in.; sole-stone, 12 ft. 1 in.; socket, 27 inches, 2 ft. 3 in.; pillar, 3½ yards, 10 ft. 6 in.; boss, 4 ft. 6 in.; cross, 7 ft. 9 in.; in all, or the whole height, 29 ft. 6 in. Mr. Beilby drew it by a scale from this measurement, and took some pains to make it exact. If it meet with your approbation, please to return it, and I will do the cut in time, so as not to stop the press: any little alteration which you may think necessary may be added. I think it would be improper to put in a battle scene in the background, but it would not be amiss to give a pretty exact view of the country around it, as described in your book, with a few monks praying, &c., at the foot of the wood cross which was erected afterwards for that purpose. We are much obliged to Mr. Allan for the many favours conferred on us. It would take up a deal of room to particularise each, so we must be content to return our sincere thanks for the whole, and endeavour in future to make every return in our power. The impressions by Gardner are excellent things of their kind indeed. The two curious old books are not of any immediate use to me, as it will be some time before I can work through the 'Quadrupeds.' They may be of service if I was begun with the 'Birds,' but that will entirely depend upon the encouragement in the sale that the first meets with. Mr. Beilby means to call upon you on his return from a journey to the South, about three weeks or a month hence.

"I am, Dear Sir,

Yours, &c.,

"THOMAS BEWICK."

I have little doubt but that the "two curious old books" here referred to was a copy of the "Ornithologia Nova," a History of Birds, illustrated with 350 woodcuts, published in two volumes 12mo, at Birmingham, in 1743–5, ten years before Bewick was born, and fifty-four years before the publication of his " Land Birds." Though the figures admit of no comparison with the latter, they are still very remarkable, and superior to any English woodcuts of the period. The work is rare, which may account for its not being mentioned by Chatto in Jackson's " Treatise on Wood-Engraving." Had he known of its existence, it would have been much to his purpose, showing that a " History of Birds " adorned with cuts had so long ante-dated Bewick's masterly performance—proving also that the art of wood-engraving was no secret in this country, but practised not only in London, but also in the provinces.

ON Tuesday, September 19, 1786, a most deplorable accident occurred in Newcastle, by which an amiable young gentleman, the hope of a much-respected family, came to a sad end. The day was bright and pleasant ; crowds of people from all parts of the town streamed towards the Spital-field and its approaches. The tower of St. John's Church and the steeple of St. Nicholas were filled with spectators to witness the first ascent in Newcastle of Mr. Lunardi's far-famed balloon. The field lay close to the Royal Grammar School, the ancient Chapel of St. Mary the Virgin. The master (Rev. Hugh Moises) had given the scholars a holiday. All was pleasurable excitement, and business for the time was suspended. Mr. Bewick and his newly-married wife awaited the event from the

garden behind their own house. Mr. Lunardi having occasion
to draw the plug from the funnel of his machine, the sudden
noise and emission of gas created an unnecessary alarm to
several gentlemen on one side of the balloon, who rushed from
their respective stations. In the panic which ensued most of
the ropes which held the balloon were set free. The remaining
cords proved inadequate to secure it, and it ascended with great
velocity. One of the ropes fastened to the top of the aerial
transport was held by Mr. Ralph Heron, the son of an eminent
solicitor, who had inadvertently coiled it round his hand and
arm. He was by this means carried up far above the height
of St. Nicholas' Church steeple. His weight having turned the
balloon, its top, to which the rope was tied, tore off, and the

unhappy gentleman fell into a garden adjoining. Terror and dismay
filled every heart, whilst the cries
and anguish of the assembled multi-
titude were most distressing. His
father, mother, and sisters were on
one of the stands in an agony of

grief. He fell, partly erect, upon a tree, and thence upon a
flower-bed of soft mould, into which he sank nearly knee-deep
and stuck fast.

Mr. Heron, though found to have sustained no external
injury from the fall, expired in a few hours. His aged sisters,
who lived in Eldon Square, I knew very well, particularly Miss
Charlotte, who was gifted with charming conversational powers.
These ladies invariably left the town whenever similar exhibi-
tions took place in after years.[1]

---

[1] Vincenzo Lunardi made his first balloon ascent in England on September 15, 1784.

OHN HOWARD, the philanthropist, was in Newcastle in 1787 on his truly Christian mission of
visiting the prisons in England and Scotland, with
the design of softening the rigour to which their unhappy
inmates were subjected by brutal gaolers and turnkeys, the
cells being in many towns a disgrace to humanity. The
horrors he was the means of disclosing were not even suspected by those who had both the power and will to provide
a remedy. In the eloquent language of Burke, the labours

Liberty and Slavery—*The Hive*, 1806.

of Howard led him " to dive into the depths of dungeons, to
plunge into the infection of hospitals, to survey the mansions
of sorrow and pain, to take the gauge and dimensions of misery,
depression, and contempt." Such was this great benefactor
to those who had not the power to help themselves. He trod
in the footsteps of his Divine Master; and in that day when
He shall make up His jewels, the spirit of this great Englishman will "shine as the brightness of the firmament, and as the
stars for ever and ever." The prison for the county of North-

umberland was on the lower floor of the Old Castle, and was described so late as 1801 [1] to be " a fearful sight to humanity." How far we have advanced in true civilisation will be apparent if we look back to the state of prison accommodation in Newcastle as then pictured by a local historian :—" The unhappy and not infrequently *innocent* prisoners, brought from their homes, were immured in this hideous dungeon, to take their trials at the assizes, the prisoners before trial being manacled, conveyed through the public streets in a cart, thrown into this den of filth, covered only with a little straw, chained to the wall, and shown like wild beasts to the gaping mob by a rapacious gaoler at twopence a piece." Mr. Bewick, with all right-minded persons, viewed with indignation such acts of wanton cruelty, and lived to see the barbarity done away.

A more truthful or saddening picture the artist never drew than that represented here. A reduced sketch of this cut, so full of pathos, will be found in the " History of Quadrupeds," ed. 1824, p. 403. For thirty years the wretched man thus depicted had been confined in prison, the hapless victim of an unfeeling and obdurate creditor—

" Meagre were his locks,
Sharp misery had worn him to the bones."

" He was sitting upon the ground, upon a little straw, in the farthest corner of his dungeon, which was alternately his chair and bed. A little calendar of small sticks was laid at the head, notched all over with dismal days and nights he had passed there. He had one of those little sticks in his hand, and, with a rusty nail, was etching another day of misery, to add to the heap."— *The Hive.*

In the great political and social questions of the day

---

[1] Baillie's " History of Newcastle," pp. 194–196.

Bewick took a warm interest; his generous sympathy was always enlisted in the cause of justice and humanity. The admiration he entertained for the noble and patriotic efforts of William Wilberforce, in striving for the abolition of the iniquitous slave trade, knew no bounds. Mrs. Bewick used to say, "Why, what can you do to help him?" and he would reply by saying that he considered it to be the duty of every honest man to afford Wilberforce all the support in his power.

The Slave Trade—*The Hive*, 1812.

No town in the kingdom was more earnest than Newcastle in appealing to the Legislature for the emancipation of the poor blacks. Mr. Bewick would have rejoiced, had he lived, to witness the triumph of Christian effort and disinterested perseverance in giving freedom to the slave in our distant colonies.

The American War was highly unpopular with the great body of the English people, and created a strong feeling against all but defensive warfare. This was a primary article in the Liberal creed. Mr. Bewick had, as all good men must have, an abhorrence of war and bloodshed: the foreign policy of Mr. Pitt was his special detestation, and was a theme on which he dwelt with zest and relish, and he never tired of enforcing his views against all gainsayers. He made no allowance for the immense difficulties which beset that great Minister in a European crisis of so extraordinary and tremendous import.

When Bewick left home in a morning for his place of

VALENTINE and UNNION—*The Hive*, 1806.

business he was frequently accompanied by his little daughter Isabella. They were wont to pass along the Forth Lane into Westgate Street, and through St. John's Lane to the Bigg Market, then down into the Groat Market. He used to make calls on his road to hear the news of the morning; but there was one shop in particular, that of Mr. Leadbitter, a saddler, next to the Crown and Thistle Inn, where his stay used to be so prolonged in talking over the politics of the day, that Miss Bewick said "she was wearied and tired out in listening to them."

N interval of five years had elapsed since the
publication of the "Select Fables," published by
Saint in 1784, Bewick being now in the thirty-
sixth year of his age. Though he had not
produced anything deserving of special notice since that
time, he had been most diligent in acquiring a perfect
mastery of the technique of his art. For the last four years
he had laboured incessantly, mostly in the evenings at home
after shop hours, in drawing the figures of the animals, designing the vignettes, and engraving both on the wood for
the proposed "History of Quadrupeds," now drawing near to
completion. Many were the interruptions that disturbed the
prosecution of his task, and necessitated its being laid aside
for a time, in order that the jobs which came in from day
to day might be got through. These could not be put off,
but required immediate attention; being ready-money transactions, they supplied the needful to meet current expenses.

An important commission, which would not only add to his
immediate fame as an artist and student of nature, but be remembered to his praise and honour ever after, was about being
received. In the autumn of 1788, Mr. Bewick was in correspondence with Marmaduke Tunstall, Esq., of Wycliffe-on-the-
Tees, in Yorkshire, respecting an engraving of the Chillingham
Wild Bull which that gentleman wished to have done. Mr.
Tunstall was an ardent naturalist and true Christian philosopher.
In his Memoir Mr. Bewick relates how at Easter-tide, 1789,
he set out for Chillingham for the purpose of obtaining a sketch
of one of those remarkable animals, and the difficulty he experienced in accomplishing his object, from the continual change
of position and restless habits distinctive of those aborigines of

THE WILD BULL

OF THE ANCIENT CALEDONIAN BREED, NOW IN THE PARK AT CHILLINGHAM CASTLE, NORTHUMBERLAND.

Bewick NEWCASTLE 1789

our Northumbrian moors and forests. Bewick's first idea was to engrave the Chillingham Bull and Cow on one copperplate. He afterwards saw reason to change his plan, and adopt wood instead, confining himself to a figure of the Bull alone. On wood, Bewick was a master without a rival. To this fortunate preference for the material best fitted for the display of his genius and wonderful talent as a wood-engraver we are indebted for the most accurate representation of the Chillingham Wild Bull in existence, and unquestionably the finest example of animal portraiture ever cut on wood. The skill displayed in this cut exhibits a perfect knowledge of the resources and capability of wood-engraving for the faithful rendering of foliage and of the natural texture of this noble animal, as well as for the display of those tints and gradations of light and shade observable in nature, and required to give finish and colour to the composition. The undisputed merits of this fine work amply justify the judgment of connoisseurs and art critics in pronouncing it to be the *chef-d'œuvre* of the artist. Mr. Bewick himself always considered it his masterpiece. The ancient breed of cattle, of which this bull is a member, has become nearly extinct. They were supposed by Sir Walter Scott to have inhabited, from pre-historic times, the vast primeval forest extending from the Tweed to Glasgow, at the two extremities of which—namely, Chillingham and Hamilton—they are still found.

Impressions of the Chillingham Bull on parchment, in the first state—*i.e.*, with the ornamental border, and before the name and date—are of extreme rarity, and, when they do occur for sale, command long prices, from twenty to thirty pounds not being considered too much. Fifty pounds, it is said, were paid for the one now in the South Kensington Museum. The impression given in this work will be found on comparison to be equal in brilliancy and richness of tone with any hitherto printed, except some few special copies. The late Miss Bewick's fine proof on vellum, in the first state, has, by the liberality of her executors, Jos. Crawhall, Esq., Newcastle, and J. W. Barnes, Esq., F.S.A., Durham, been presented to the Museum of the Natural History Society in Newcastle.

But few copperplates were executed by Bewick, and what he did in this way yielded neither profit nor fame. In the summer of 1786, Sir Henry George Liddle, Bart., of Ravensworth Castle, County Durham, in company with two other gentlemen—viz., Mr. Bowes and Matt. Consett, Esq.—determined on making a tour through Sweden, Lapland, and Denmark, and on their return bring over to England two female Laplanders, with five reindeer, in which they were successful. The popular belief has always been that this adventure was the result of a wager made after dinner. An account of this expedition was drawn up by Mr. Consett, and published, in 1789, in a thin quarto volume.

The frontispiece, engraved by Mr. Bewick, contains portraits of the tourists. Sir Henry stands in front, attired in the rich garb of an English gentleman of the period, conversing with Mr. Bowes, who has a watch in his hand. Behind him is Mr. Consett. They are viewing the midnight sun at Tornao, in Lapland. At page 67 there is an exceedingly beautiful representation of a reindeer, admirably drawn and engraved by Mr. Bewick "from the living animal." The cheerless landscape is most truthfully expressed. The three plates of birds are the exclusive work of Bewick himself, although signed " B. & B., sculpt., Newcastle." Mr. Beilby, as a partner, insisted on having his name introduced. About 1808, on the occasion of a sale of old furniture and lumber at Ravensworth, before the old castle was pulled down, Bewick, who was present, bought the horns of the identical reindeer he had drawn and engraved some twenty years before. Until lately they adorned the kitchen wall at Bewick's house in Gateshead. They are now owned by Edward B. Mounsey, Esq., Darlington.

About this time Newcastle had not only very clever artists and musicians, but a club of wits, whose harmless pleasantries have not as yet passed out of remembrance.

This memorable tour was the occasion of a famous and most amusing literary hoax. Messrs. John and Thomas Davidson, then eminent attorneys in Newcastle, the former being Clerk of the Peace for Northumberland, and his brother presiding over the Stamp Office, had in their employ as clerks three young gentlemen of considerable literary ability. These were George Pickering, Thomas Bedingfeld, and James Ellis. In the *Newcastle Courant* of the 2nd September 1786 appeared a letter, signed T. S., together with what professed to be a *Lapland Song,* with a translation; and on the 21st of October an elaborate criticism on the same, with a new and more accurate translation, which the writer assures the reader " is as literal as the idioms of the two languages will admit."

The song was afterwards set to music, and, with the first translation, published, as having been sung by the female Laplanders at Ravensworth Castle; it was afterwards inserted *as genuine* by Mr. Consett in his account of the tour, and copied from thence into several of the London magazines. These truly original compositions sprung from the lively imagination of two of those gentlemen. Mr. Pickering wrote the first letter containing the Lapland Song, and Mr. Bedingfeld the exquisite criticism which followed.[1]

---

[1] Poetry, Fugitive and Original. By Thomas Bedingfield, Esq., and Mr. George Pickering. By a Friend (James Ellis, Esq., Otterburn). Newcastle. 8vo. 1815.

L

In addition to the plates contained in this work, Mr. Bewick engraved about this time two large copperplates, representing the Whitley Large Ox (Mr. Hall's), and Mr. Spearman's Kyloe Ox. The former was published in 1789, and the latter in 1790.

In the "Memoir," pp. 144, 145, the author supplies the following brief narrative concerning the origin of the "History of Quadrupeds:"—

"Having, from the time that I was a schoolboy, been displeased with most of the figures in children's books, and particularly with those of the 'Three Hundred Animals,' the figures in which, even at that time, I thought I could depicture much better, and having afterwards very often turned the matter over in my mind of making improvements in that publication, I at last came to the determination of making the attempt. The extreme interest I had always felt in the hope of administering to the pleasure and amusement of youth, and judging from the feelings I had experienced myself that they would be affected in the same way as I had been, whetted me up and stimulated me to proceed. In this, my only reward besides was the great pleasure I felt in imitating Nature. That I should ever do anything to attract the notice of the world, in the manner that has been done, was the farthest thing in my thoughts, and so far as I was concerned myself at that time, I minded little about any self-interested considerations. These intentions I communicated to my partner; and, though he did not doubt of my being able to succeed, yet, being a cautious and thinking man, he wished to be more satisfied as to the probability of such a publication paying for the labour. On this occasion, being little acquainted with the nature of such undertakings, we consulted Mr. Solomon Hodgson, bookseller, and editor of the *Newcastle Chronicle*, as to the probability of its success, &c., when he warmly encouraged us to proceed.

"Such animals as I knew I drew from memory on the wood; others which I did not know were copied from 'Dr. Smellie's Abridgment of Buffon' and other naturalists, and also from the animals which were from time to time exhibited in itinerant collections. Of these last I made sketches first from memory, and then corrected and finished the drawings upon the wood from a second examination of the different animals. I began this business of cutting the blocks with the figure of the dromedary on the 15th November 1785, the day on which my father died. I then proceeded in copying such figures as above named as I did not hope to see alive. While I was busied in drawing and cutting the figures of animals, and also in designing and engraving the vignettes, Mr. Beilby, being of a bookish or reading turn, proposed, in his evenings at home, to write or compile the descriptions. With this I had little more to do than furnishing him, in many conversations and by written memoranda, with what I knew of animals, and blotting out in his manuscript what was not truth. In this way we proceeded till the book was published in 1790.

"The greater part of these woodcuts were drawn and engraved at night, after the day's work of the shop was over."

Apropos to the above is the following letter written by Bewick in 1788, which appeared in the *Bibliographer* for December 1881. Mr. H. Trueman Wood, of the Society of Arts, in introducing the letter, says nothing was known of its existence until he, in company with Mr. Wheatley, was recently turning over a mass of papers in one of the garrets of the Society. Mr. Wood adds :—

"We had each worked away at our respective bundles without making any discovery of importance, when suddenly I came on Bewick's name at the bottom of a letter. 'Here,' said I, 'is something worth keeping; it is a letter of Bewick, asking the Society to help him with his "British Quadrupeds." He says he encloses some specimens of it.' 'Yes,' said Mr. Wheatley, making a dive into his box, 'and here they are !' How long the letter and its enclosure had been separated—why they were separated—is more than I can say, but it is certainly not a little curious that they should then have seen the light simultaneously. Bewick, as indeed may be inferred from the letter, was one of the many artists whose youthful talents were rewarded by the Society of Arts. In 1775 he received a premium of seven guineas for an allegorical vignette on wood. As he was born in 1753, he must have been twenty-two when he took this prize. It is pleasant to find that he, like Flaxman and others, was not insensible to the help he had received, since he shows in the letter the truest gratitude—a lively sense of favours to come."

The letter is as follows :—

"NEWCASTLE, *22nd May* 1788.

"SIR,—I have herewith, by favour of Mr. Gregson, transmitted to your care some Specimens of Wood Cuts, with Proposals for Publishing, by subscription, a History of Quadrupeds; which I hope you will be so obliging as to lay before the Society for the Encouragement of Arts, &c., of which Society I understand you are yet Secretary. The favourable Reception which some of my Juvenile

Performances have met with from that Honourable Body, and their request to me at that time 'That I would not rest satisfied with one attempt, but subject my future Performance to their inspection,' have again emboldened me to submit my Labours to their View. I know not that there is at this Time any Reward offered by the Society, or any competition in the way, but if I should be so happy as to find that the work now in hand meets with their Approbation and Patronage, it might silence the clamour of ill-natured criticism, and tend to promote its sale. When the curious are served with the best Impressions, a second and inferior Edition will be done for the use of youth at Schools, with a view more widely to diffuse a better Knowledge of this Branch of Natural History, and also to awaken in the contemplative mind an admiration of the wonderful works of Nature. If you think it worth your notice, I will send you the rest of the prints to complete the Set as soon as they are done.

> " I am, Sir,
>
> With the greatest Respect,
>
> Your most obedient and humble Servant,
>
> (Signed)   " THOMAS BEWICK."

The following is a copy of the prospectus referred to in Bewick's letter. It is printed on a broadside, with specimens of the illustrations :—

" NEWCASTLE, 28*th January* 1788.

" Proposals | for publishing by subscription | A General History of Quadrupeds, | containing a Concise Account of every Animal of that Kind | hitherto known or described. | With | observations on the Habits, Faculties, and Propensities | of each Creature | intended as | A Complete Display of that Part of Animated Nature, | At once Useful, Instructive, and Entertaining. | Embellished with | Accurate Engravings on Wood | of each Animal. | Drawn from the Life, or Copied from the Productions of the best Authors | on that subject. |

" TO THE PUBLIC.

" To add to the number of Publications already extant on this Branch of Natural History, may seem at first View both presumptuous and unnecessary ; but when it is considered that the great expense of the more voluminous Works confines them chiefly to the Libraries of the Wealthy, and that the smaller Publications of this sort are such mean and pitiful Productions as must disgust every Reader of Common Observation, the propriety and usefulness of this undertaking will appear sufficiently obvious.

" The great care that has been taken to give the true Portrait and Character of each Creature, and the masterly execution of the Wood Engravings, will, it is hoped, strongly recommend this Work to every Admirer of that part of Nature's Productions. Many of the animals have been accurately drawn from Nature; and in this respect the Editor has been peculiarly fortunate in being enabled to offer to the Public more faithful Representations of some rare Quadrupeds than have hitherto appeared.

"**** The work will be neatly printed, in One Volume Octavo, on a good Paper, with entire new Types.

" §†§ Price to Subscribers 8 Shillings in Boards. To be paid on Delivery. Printed for, and sold by S. Hodgson, by whom Subscriptions are taken in; also by Beilby and Bewick, Engravers, W. Charnley, R. Fisher, D. Akenhead, J. Atkinson, E. Humble, and T. Whitfield, Newcastle; L. Pennington, Durham; J. Graham and J. Reed, Sunderland; R. Christopher, Stockton; W. Grey, Nottingham; W. Tesseyman and J. Todd, York; and W. Creech and C. Elliott, Edinburgh."

HE author is indebted to J. W. Pease, Esq. of Pendower, Newcastle, for permission to print the following most interesting letter from Thomas Bewick to his brother John, then a resident in London, together with the accompanying local song. Pleasure is expressed by the writer of the letter with the execution of the cuts for the "Emblems of Mortality," after Holbein's designs. This work was published in 1789.

"Our 'Natural History'" refers to the "History of Quadrupeds," then in progress, the first edition of which was published in 1790. The twenty-six impressions of animals already sent off were *proofs* printed at the office of Thomas Angus. Of these I possess a set coloured by Bewick himself, and presented to his daughter Isabella on the 1st of January 1800. Robert Pollard's engraving of the Hermitage at Warkworth, published in 1787, is a fine large print; the landscape is engraved by J. Peltro, the figures by Pollard.

M

"NEWCASTLE, *9th Jan.* 1788.

"DEAR BROTHER,

"I have your letter of the 1st Nov. last now before me. I find it came per Capt. Carr. I am much pleased with the Cuts for 'Death's Dance,' and wish much to have the book when it is done. I am surprised you would undertake to do them for 6s. each. You have been spending your time and grinding out your eyes to little purpose indeed. I would not have done them for a farthing less than double that sum. I showed them to Mr. Edwards, a very capital and eminent painter, as well as a very worthy man, now here, painting the scenes in the new play-house. He approved much of them, but was surprised when I told him the price which you had for them. He, I expect, will be your friend after this, when he returns to London. I am glad to find that you have begun on your own bottom, and I would earnestly recommend it to you to establish your character by taking uncommon pains with what work you do. I hope it will, in the end, turn better out than doing it slightly.—I suppose your next will be an answer to one which I sent with 26 impressions per Matthew Williamson. I have wished for your answer to it for some time past. If Mylock's print be the same as the one which you so obligingly sent to me, I think nothing of it. It is not worth (in my opinion) one of the two Tigers which I long since sent to you, in order to exchange with him. I am obliged to you for the drawing of the Lion; Mr. Edwards says it is a faithful representation. I wish I had as good a one of the Wolf, the form and shape of which is so variously and contradictorily represented to me by different people that I am quite puzzled as to its real appearance. I am glad to find that a large collection of animals is now on its way to this Town. They are expected here on the latter end of this month. They consist of varied kinds of the Ape tribe, Porcupine, Tiger-Cat and Tiger, Greenland Bear, and one of the finest Lions (very lately brought over) that ever made its appearance on this Island; so that I expect to have the opportunity of doing such of them as I want, from the Life. Our 'Natural History' will be put to press in a little time. The first Edition will be done by subscription. You may perhaps, in the course of a month, see it advertised in the N'Castle papers, at the Hole in the Wall, Fleet Street. T. Dobson and I was at our little niece's Christning on Christmas Day: I was Godfather, and Nancy and another the Godmothers. It is a fine little girl. Brother William and his family are very well; he is going on very prosperously with his Colliery. I spent one night at Ovingham, one at Eltringham, and one at Hedley, and then returned to Town, and found all very well at home. I wish you would send your account of what you have paid and recd. on my acct. in London. It is best to keep all square once a year at least. I paid for 'Gay's Fables' £ s. d. (I told you at the time, but have forgot). Aunt Nanny and Tommy do not seem to hit it so well as I could wish: she is queer, and he can make no allowance for a poor old woman. I shall conclude with wishing you the compls. of the season. My Bell also desires her best respects. Give my thanks and compls. to Mr. Pollard. I am much obliged to him for the

Hermitage at Warkworth, and am sorry for the loss he has met with in the death of his Brother, and my old Friend.

"I am, Dear Brother, yours, &c.,

"THOMAS BEWICK.

"MR. JOHN BEWICK, ENGRAVER,
No. 7, CLERKENWELL GREEN, LONDON."

" Thou's aw candied, maw bonny Hinney,
Thou's double japandied, ay-u-a, Hinney ;
Thou's aw candied, maw bonny Hinney,
Thou's double japandied, ay-u-a.

" Gan up the Toun, maw bonny Hinney,
An' riyde on the Brum, a-u-a, Hinney ;
Gan up an' doun, maw bonny Hinney,
Thou's th' Flower of the toun, ay-u-a.

" Fir shep and for culler, thou's leyke th' mother,
A-u-a, hey-u-a, maw bonny Hinney ;
Fir shep and for culler, thou's leyke the mother,
A-u-a, hey-u-a, maw bonny Bairn.

" Fir Heyde and fir Hue, maw bonny Hinney,
There's nane leyke thou, a-u-ay, Hinney ;
Fir Heyde an' Hue, maw bonny Hinney,
There's nane leyke thou, ay-u-a.

" Gan up the Raw, maw bonny Hinney,
Thou bangs thim aw, ay-u-a, Hinney ;
Gan up the Raw, maw bonny Hinney,
An' clash thir jaw, ay-u-a.

" If you have not the above, it will add one more to your collection."

Newcastle can boast of many capital songs in the *vulgar tongue*, remarkable for their genuine wit and humour. These are still enjoyed even by the educated and refined gentry of Northumberland and Durham with a relish as keen as that felt by the humbler classes of society. John Bewick and his friends—Pollard, Bulmer, Gregson, and William Gray—would often entertain themselves with such ditties on an evening, when the work of the day was over. Though resident in London, Newcastle would ever be fondly remembered.

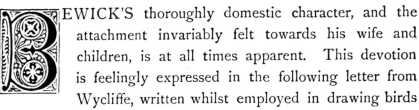

EWICK'S thoroughly domestic character, and the attachment invariably felt towards his wife and children, is at all times apparent. This devotion is feelingly expressed in the following letter from Wycliffe, written whilst employed in drawing birds from stuffed specimens in Mr. Tunstall's Museum. It was in his family that he placed his chief happiness, being ever a faithful husband; he had his reward in the affection of a dutiful wife and an obedient son and daughters. Beyond home pleasures he desired nothing; in this he showed true wisdom.

"WYCLIFFE, *Aug. 8th*, 1791.

"MY DEAR BELL,

"I never opened a letter with more anxiety, nor read one with more pleasure in my life, than I did my Bell's last week. To hear of you being all well gave me the greatest of pleasures. How desirous am I to hear of your still continuing so.—My dear little Boy is hardly ever out of my mind. I hope the Sea will mend him. If upon my return I find him recovered I think I shall be frantic with joy.—Indeed, if upon my return I find you all well, I shall look upon my fireside at the Forth like a little Heaven.—I hope I shall, when I return, but I think it will be about 3 weeks yet before I have that pleasure. The young Gentleman has sent Mr. Collier notice that he will not be at this place till the latter end of the month. I have plenty of work before me to keep me closely employed a much longer time, but I am tired out

T. Bewick, sculp.

THE TRAVELLER.

*Published, March 1887, by Robert Robinson, 21 Pilgrim Street,
Newcastle-upon-Tyne.*

To face page 96.

*

already, and wish it was over. I have dulled myself with sticking to it so closely. In short, I lose no time in order to get through with the business. When you write again tell me when you will be at the Forth, lest I should be at a loss where to direct to you. Also tell me how you all are, for that is everything with me. Take care when you return to the Forth lest the beds should be damp by your long absence. Tell Jane and Robert that if they behave well I will let them see a vast of little pictures of Birds when I come home; and I hope my little Bell will be able to say more than *dadda* when I see her again.

"I am, with compls. to all,

My Bell's loving husband,

"THOMAS BEWICK."

Miss Isabella Bewick kindly presented me with the next letter I have the pleasure to bring before the notice of my readers. It is addressed to her father by her uncle John, and was selected by that lady for me, as being more than usually interesting. From it we learn the fact that a "History of British Birds," to correspond with the "Quadrupeds," was at that early period well  known even in London. A dissolution of partnership with Mr. Beilby was, as might be expected, a subject for discussion in the family immediately after the publication of the first edition of that work. The pecuniary advantages of such a step, in view of the brothers combining their talents, and pulling together in business, was obvious, yet the elder held back, afraid to commit himself by such an act. Many times Miss Bewick and myself have talked the matter over, and speculated on the results, but the early death of John would, in my opinion, have considerably lessened much of the promise held out by a union of interests. It is clear that Bewick did not gain what he had a right to expect by the exercise of such rare gifts and indefatigable industry.

"DEAR BROTHER,

"Your last letter came just in time to prevent me writing to you in a very Ill Humor, it being much longer than your usual time of writing, and I being told by Mr. Dilly and others that you were busy with the 'History of Birds,' and frequently asked questions respecting it, and I knowing nothing of the matter, vext me not a little, but I am glad to find it is not the case, as I hope if ever it be done, 'twill be on your own account. A great deal might be said respecting a Dissolution of Partnership both *pro* and *con*, but at present all I shall say is, that I am pretty certain not a Friend you have that sincerely wishes well to you and Family, but will strongly recommend it. As to its appearing to you like beginning the world again, it might be so, tho' not without some knowledge of it. In my opinion you have had the most favourable beginning that possibly man could have, particularly that branch of Business which I hope 'tis your wish ever to pursue, both for your Honor and advantage (*i.e.*, publishing your own works) : it is but just that every man should reap the benefits of his own ingenious industry. You are sensible that every day, and week, the intricate matrimonial accounts of partnership must increase, so that if you have, or ever had, any wish to part, now is the time ; if on the contrary, be not persuaded by me. It may be thought arrogance in me to dictate to you respecting this Business, therefore shall only say that I am ready and willing to exert and strain every nerve to assist with whatever may be in my power. I cannot help admiring the intrepid proposal of your faithful Helpmate : she seems to have enter'd on the Business with some degree of spirit. I am perfectly of her way of thinking, and should do the same myself on such an occasion, tho', to be sure, *Crowdy* here wou'd be esteemed a dish of some novelty, but I could live in a hollow Tree on Bread and Cheese, which might be equally cheap. I am still in my Country Lodgings, and perfectly recovered, thank God. I may, if nothing particular happens to prevent me, take a trip to Newcastle in the spring, just to ask how you all do, and away again. Mr. Dilly wou'd be glad to know how you mean to dispose of your 2nd Edition ; he wishes much to have a hand in the Pye. I have not seen Dickinson these some months past. I have wished much for my Gun ever since I have been at Mount Pleasant. Shou'd be glad if you could send her, and an old favourite tinn Powder flask with my name upon it, the first opportunity. With these sets of Animals you'd please to mention the price. I shou'd likewise be glad to have an account of what I am in your debt. You never gave any answer to that business of Mr. William Bulmer's ; I dined with him last Sunday at Mr. Pollard's. If to-morrow be fine I expect Mr. Stothard and Mr. Pollard at

Mount Pleasant. My compliments to George Gray, and if he has any wish to see London I could procure him Employ at a Guinea and half per week Fruit-Painting, &c., in the Jappanning line. . . . .

" I am, Dr. Brother,

" Mr. Bewick,   " JNO. BEWICK.
    Forth,
      Newcastle-upon-Tyne." [1]

" That business of Mr. William Bulmer's," alluded to at the close of this letter, I take to be an interchange of ideas and opinions between Bulmer and Mr. Bewick, which eventually resulted in the fine edition of Goldsmith's Poems, published by the former in 1795. The selection consisted of " The Traveller," " The Deserted Village," and " The Hermit," by Parnell, forming one handsome quarto volume. The excellence of the typography, printing, and paper was only exceeded by the extraordinary beauty and novelty of the illustrations. The part that John Bewick had in this work was not considerable, seeing that the only important cut he contributed was the large engraving of the " Sad Historian," p. 36.

Mr. Bulmer, in the advertisement, thus speaks of the embellishments :—" They are all engraved on blocks of wood by two of my earliest acquaintances, Messrs. Bewick, of Newcastle-upon-Tyne and London, after designs made from the most interesting passages of the poems they embellish. They have been executed with great  care, and I may venture to say, without being supposed to be influenced by ancient friendship, that they form the most extraordinary effort of the art of engraving on wood that ever was

---

[1] Printed from the original holograph in the collection of the publisher.

produced in any age or any country. Indeed, it seems almost impossible that such delicate effects could be obtained from blocks of wood."

This beautiful volume possesses unusual interest for the Bewick collector. In it are combined the talents of the two brothers, in union with undisputed examples of the genius of Robert Johnson and his cousin John. These early pupils of Bewick could not engrave on wood, and the efforts of the former on copper do not rise above mediocrity. Their forte lay in another direction. As skilful artists in water-colour painting, they possessed a truly original genius. The designs of Robert Johnson in particular are distinguished by much elegance, simplicity, and truth. The early death which befel both must ever be mourned as a serious loss to the Fine Arts in this country.

My unique copy of Goldsmith's Poems is rendered valuable and very interesting on account of its containing Bulmer's own written directions to the engraver, neatly mounted on blank leaves, and endorsed by Miss Jane Bewick.

Opposite the cut of " The Traveller " is the following :—

"Mr. Westall,[1] you will see, has drawn an outline to this painting, which will assist you much. Be very particular in finishing this block, and above all things preserve the characteristic sentiment of the face, which so happily accords with the language of the poet. Without this, the whole force of the drawing will be lost. The shrub, too, must be exactly copied. Omit the ' R. W.' at the corner."

(" Westall designed 'The Traveller.' ")

"The small drawing marked No. 1 is, in my idea, a most beautiful conception, and given altogether in a manner that is really astonishing."

" From Wm. Bulmer
to
Thomas Bewick ! ! !

" This criticism must refer to the above head-piece.
"J. B."

---

[1] Richard Westall was born about the year 1765. Like Bewick, he was apprenticed to an engraver of heraldry on silver and other materials, and died in 1836. John Thurston and he were, much about the same period, largely patronised by publishers in designing book illustrations.

R. Johnson, del.   T. Bewick, sculp.

THE HERMIT, ANGEL, AND GUIDE.

Published, March 1887, by Robert Robinson, 21 Pilgrim Street,
Newcastle-upon-Tyne.

To face page 97.

The exquisite cut of Roman edifices in ruins is the one intended.

Before that of " The Departure" we read—

"Give as much character to the faces as you possibly can, and suppose you make the foreground rather coarser than you generally do, in order to form the stronger contrast with the fine finishing of the block. Let this picture have one-eighth of an inch more in depth."

" This criticism was written
by Wm. Bulmer,
addressed to Thomas Bewick.
"JANE BEWICK."

And again, as regards the beautiful cut of " The Hermit, Angel, and Guide," instructions are given remarkable for the knowledge of effect and attention to details bestowed by Mr. Bulmer in the production of the work, every care being taken to render those marvels of art worthy of the artists by whom they were designed and executed :—

"Give the Hermit more of age and feebleness, and keep the Landscape part and bridge gloomy, rugged, and dangerous. The drowning man to remain as it is. If the depth of the picture was increased abt. an $\frac{1}{8}$th of an inch at top, I think it would amend it. Let the drapery of the Angel seem floating and free, and the face delicate and sweetly interesting."

" Directions by Wm. Bulmer
to
Thomas Bewick."

This criticism, so full of interest, is rendered more intelligible by having two impressions of the cut facing each other, one being in the first state, before the suggested alterations were carried out by the engraver. It is a proof on yellow India paper, and, I have reason to believe, the only one in existence. In it the glory above the head of the angel is wanting, the flowing robe of the celestial messenger is much darker than in the altered cut as we have it in the book, and the foliage a

N

shade more sombre.   Art critics will differ as to the propriety or otherwise of the changes made in Bewick's first treatment of the cut, especially as to the glory and darkening of the foliage.

The face and garment of the angel appear more in accordance with one's idea of a citizen from the realms of light and beauty.

However admirable the illustrations in this work are, they are distanced both in design and execution by the companion volume issued by Bulmer in the following year, 1796, from the Shakespeare Press.   This was a truly splendid edition of Somervile's Chase.

The drawings were made on the wood by John Bewick previous to his leaving London for the last time, in the vain hope of recruiting his strength by again breathing his native air.

Alas! too soon was the agreeable social companion and talented artist destined to rest his weary frame beside his father and mother in Ovingham Churchyard.

THE unfortunate death of John Bewick seemed likely to occasion some delay in the fulfilment of the engagement entered into with the publisher.   Mr. Bulmer, who was a keen man of business, addressed himself therefore at once to his brother, and urged him by a "bold effort" to engrave the cuts within the time originally agreed upon.

This was accordingly done: no second appeal was needed. Before proceeding with the work, I have little doubt that the engraver, with his accustomed ability and good taste, corrected and considerably improved the whole of the drawings already made on the wood, in loving memory of his brother. Mr. Bewick would not allow the last offspring of his genius to go forth to the world with any faults it lay in his power to remove. The precept, "Let brotherly love continue," was one he was not likely to forget.

In 1797 the first volume of Bewick's great work, the "History of British Birds," was given to the world, and imme-diately became popular. It com-prised the Land Birds only. The commencement or first step in this enterprise was a visit to Wycliffe-on-the-Tees, the seat of Marma-duke Tunstall, Esq., whose magni-ficent Museum of Natural History afforded him an opportunity of making drawings of such birds as he was not likely to see alive.

Two months were spent at this place, after which Mr. Bewick returned home laden with a folio of drawings, the fruit of much study and close application.

These he immediately began to engrave, but soon dis-covered that the preserved specimens which he had copied so faithfully had been very inartistically executed—so much so that the labour expended over them had been almost thrown away. As the undertaking became known, much interest was excited, and gentlemen from all parts forwarded to him such rare birds as they had shot, and in some instances even living birds.

The beautiful cut of the Corncrake or Land Rail, now classed by the scientists among Water Birds, was drawn from a

living specimen presented by Major Harry Gibson, son of a
former town-clerk of Newcastle.   This bird was given to
Richard Wingate to preserve, and many years afterwards was
sold, when his extraordinary collections in Natural History were
brought to the hammer.   To my regret I missed buying it, but
determined if ever I had a second chance it should be mine.
After the lapse of twenty-one years, I was employed to catalogue
the library, Roman coins, pictures, and rare china at Greencroft Park, near Lanchester, County Durham, the property of

The Conceited Magpie—From *Tales for Youth*, 1794.

John Clavering, Esq., deceased.   On entering the hall, the first
object that met my eye was this well-remembered figure of
the Corncrake, in its curious oval case, which I was glad to
purchase along with some of the best of the coins, books, &c.

This interesting specimen I embraced the first opportunity
of submitting to my friends the Misses Bewick, who were so
much pleased with the sight of the bird that Miss Jane requested me to leave it with them for a few weeks.   The fine
cut of the Swan Goose appears in the second edition of the
"Water Birds" (1805), p. 281.   Like the Corncrake, it was

domesticated in Bewick's house at the Forth. A tub of water was sunk for its use in the garden, but after being kept for some time it was found necessary to part with it. The letterpress, or descriptive history of the Birds (Land), contained in the first volume of the work, was written by Mr. Beilby, subject to the corrections of his partner, and most ably did he accomplish his share of the work, though it must be deemed inconsiderable when compared with the part which Bewick performed, and to which he alone was equal amongst all living artists, not in

The Wilful Boy and the Hornets—From *Tales for Youth*, 1794.

England only, but throughout the nations of the Continent, those venerable centres of the arts and civilisation. It is scarcely to be supposed that, without some previous knowledge of the subject, Mr. Beilby could have so admirably acquitted himself in the literary portion of the work. His descriptions are free from the charge of being too diffuse, or the opposite fault of a meagre and spiritless style. The following copy of a very curious handbill, dated 1790, goes to prove that he possessed some knowledge of and taste for Natural History, thoug' followed only as a recreation.

BEILBY'S CURIOUS COLLECTION OF PRESERVED BIRDS AND SHELL-WORK,
The Sight of which will strike the Beholder with Wonder and Astonishment;
every Bird is fixed in so lively an Attitude, and in so great Preservation, that
Life cannot be more striking. This beautiful Collection will be put up by
Subscription at 1s. each Subscriber; to be 360 Subscribers, and prizes as follow,
at Mrs. Henzel's, in Mosley St., on Monday the 17th May inst., at 6 o'clock in
the evening.

PRIZES.	£	s.	d.
1. A Beautiful Pheasant and other Birds . . .	3	3	0
2. A Case of Birds and Squirrel	1	1	0
3. A Basket of Flowers from Nature	2	2	0
4. One ditto	0	16	0
5. A Nest of Birds and Old Ones	0	15	0
6. A Large Case of Various Birds	1	1	0
7. The Squirrel, preserved	0	10	0
8. Two Cases of Flowers	0	15	0
9. The Green Plover, preserved	0	10	0
10. The Fell Faire	0	8	0

Twenty Cases of Birds at 5s. each prize. Fifteen Prizes of the King and
Queen at 2s. 6d. each.

May 7th, 1790.

The device of a lottery for the ready disposal of pictures,
fans, and other articles of taste was quite common in those
days, and did not in the least detract from the position and
standing of the owners.

In a letter addressed to the artist by Thomas Pennant, the
well-known naturalist and antiquary, dated 28th June 1798,
thanking him for the present of a copy of the second edition of
the first volume of the "Birds," 1798, he begs his acceptance of
some token of the sense he entertained of the favour. "I sent
last week," he adds, "a copy of my 'History of London,' the
best edition, to Mr. White, bookseller, Fleet Street, to be
delivered to your order. May it prove some amusement to

you." It is inscribed, " To the ingenious Mr. Bewick, with the author's compliments. June 14, 1798."[1] Bewick gave the work to his wife, who had it bound in morocco. Above the title is written, " The bequest of Isabella Bewick to her daughter Elizabeth." The book is now in my collection.

In reply to Mr. Bewick, who had expressed a wish to have a portrait of Moses Griffith, Pennant writes a few weeks afterwards: "Sir, I will endeavour to get Moses to draw his portrait, and if I succeed, will send it in a frank," &c. This portrait, when sent, proved to be an admirable likeness of Bewick's father, and in the opinion of himself and his wife the resemblance was so perfect that had he sat for it nothing better could have been produced. It formed part of the valuable assemblage of drawings, pictures, miniatures, and choice woodcuts presented by the executors of the late Miss Bewick to the Newcastle Museum of Natural History.

Pennant presented portraits of himself and the Rev. John Lloyd, rector of Caerwis, his constant friend, companion, and assistant in his tour in Wales, to Mr. Bewick. The former is after a picture by Gainsborough, painted in 1776, and engraved by W. Ridley; the latter, an oval, from a drawing by Moses Griffith, engraved by P. Mazel. Both are in the original black and gold frames, and are now in my possession.

---

[1] Memoirs of Marmaduke Tunstall, Esq., and George Allan, Esq., with Notices of the Works of Thomas Bewick. By G. T. Fox, F.L.S. 8vo. 1827.

EWICK'S famous workshop in St. Nicholas' Church-yard, where so large a part of the life of the great wood-engraver passed in cheerful and unremitting industry, has been often drawn and engraved; with it we are all familiar. This, however, was not the original scene whence his first efforts date their beginning. Joseph Barber, the bookseller, had his shop and circulating library at Amen Corner, St. Nicholas' Churchyard. Next to it was an old red-brick house having two queer-fashioned wooden spouts projecting from above the upper windows far into the yard, like no other but itself. It was here Ralph Beilby carried on the business of a copperplate printer and engraver when Bewick first entered his service. This house, though hitherto unnoticed, witnessed the buddings of his genius and the commencement of his subsequent success. The late Miss Jane Bewick more than twenty years ago gave me this information. She said, " I never pass by the old place without doffing my bonnet." The con-struction of Dean Street diverted a large amount of business from the Side, which had hitherto been the main connecting link not only between the upper and lower parts of the town, but also between Newcastle and Gateshead, and the country south of the Tyne. The new street was a great improvement, and the public were not slow to avail themselves of it, thereby avoiding the narrow and steep ascent of the Side.

In consequence, Messrs. Beilby and Bewick determined to remove from their old quarters to other premises at the south-east end of the yard. This house was leasehold, and bought by the firm of Serjeant Bayles,[1] the " eloquent sword-bearer."

---

[1] Dr. Nathaniel Bayles, the patriotic champion of the rights of the burgesses in respect to the herbage of the Town Moor and Castle leases.—*Vide* " Bewick's Memoirs," p. 68.

They were thus brought nearer to the more fashionable and popular thoroughfare, without losing the advantage of a retired and quiet situation so essential to artists and literary men.

This took place in 1795. Mr. Bewick's neighbour for many years previous to the change, had been Joseph Barber, music and copperplate printer. In 1741 this gentleman, whilst located on the Sandhill, published "the first copperplate engraving done in Newcastle." The subject was "A Curious Draught of the famous manag'd Horse call'd the Marbled Persian. Price One Shilling."

In 1743 this was followed by a very large and curious copperplate of the equestrian statue of King James II. which stood on the Sandhill, and was thrown into the Tyne by a Protestant mob at the Revolution. It was advertised as "just arrived from London," and to be had, price 5s., of Joseph Barber, in Humble's Buildings, Newcastle. Round the margin of the print, which is extremely rare,[1] were the coats of arms of the subscribers, 200 in number. These were afterwards cut off and sold to them at 2s. 6d. each, together with 100 impressions to be used as book-plates. We afterwards find Mr. Barber in business as a bookseller at the sign of the Duke of Cumberland, at the Golden Ball, at the head of the Flesh Market, his business card having a well-engraved portrait of the hero of Culloden at the top. He afterwards removed to Amen Corner. At an early period Mr. Bewick engraved for him a shop-card of elegant design, and subsequently another cut to be used as a book-plate. This is of great artistic beauty, not exceeded as a work of art by anything he afterwards produced of the same kind. It is very scarce ; indeed the only impression I have ever seen is a fine proof inserted in my "Bewickiana."

---

[1] An impression without the armorial bearings is in the collection of Jos. Crawhall, Esq., of this town.

O

The Catalogue of Barber's Circulating Library, probably the first of its kind established in Newcastle, is a literary curiosity. I hope to be excused for giving its quaint title *in extenso.*

A

NEW CLASSICAL

CATALOGUE

O F

B A R B E R's

ORIGINAL

Circulating Library,

C O N T A I N I N G

Above Two Thoufand V O L U M E S,

in all Branches of Polite Literature.

✠✠✠✠✠✠✠✠✠✠✠✠✠✠✠✠✠✠✠✠✠✠✠✠✠✠✠✠✠✠

To be Lent out to Read, at Two SHILLINGS and SIXPENCE *per* Quarter in the Town, and THREE SHILLINGS in the Country.

✠✠✠✠✠✠✠✠✠✠✠✠✠✠✠✠✠✠✠✠✠✠✠✠✠✠✠✠✠✠

Where Ufeful, Entertaining, and Polite,
Collected, join the Curious to invite :
As Sermons, Comments, Pray'rs, religious Mifteries,
Lives, Geography, Memoirs, Tracts, and Hiftories ;
Voyages and Travels, where'er Sea or Shore is,
Romances, Novels, Tales, and Comic-Stories ;
With Num'rous of the MUSES rapt'rous Lays,
From good ELIZA's down to GEORGE's Days.
Which will be lent to read, by Week or Quarter,
At JOSEPH BARBER's Shop, in AMEN-CORNER.

☞ CATALOGUES may be had, Price *Three-pence,* at the LIBRARY ; to Subfcribers (*gratis*)

Mr. Barber died 4th July 1781, aged 74 years, and is buried under a table-monument at the north-east corner of St. Nicholas' Churchyard. The good man little dreamt that more than a century after his  decease a new tomb would be built to perpetuate his memory by one of the most distinguished scholars of the age, Joseph Barber Lightfoot, D.D., Lord Bishop of Durham. Joseph, his eldest son, settled in Birmingham, and from the marriage of his daughter Anne Matilda with Mr. J. J. Lightfoot comes Joseph Barber's great-grandson, the eminent prelate just named.

Barber was succeeded in business at Amen Corner by his son, Martin Barber, who died in London in 1799. As a memento of this old Newcastle bookseller, I have pleasure in using at the tea-table a handsome black cocoanut sugar-basin, richly ornamented with silver, with his initials, M. B., on a silver shield, engraved, no doubt, by either Beilby or Bewick.

The following letter, now published for the first time, from Mr. Bewick to George Allan, Esq., of the Grange, refers to the approaching dissolution of partnership with Mr. Beilby, after existing for twenty years. The matter had been debated in the family ever since the publication of the "Quadrupeds." Mr. Bewick did not derive from his incessant labour and the unsparing exercise of his great talents, that amount of pecuniary advantage from the sale of his works that he might reasonably have expected. And this arose from his having to share the profits equally with his partner and publisher.

"NEWCASTLE, 5th Decr. 1797.

"SIR,—It gives me great pain to think that you shou'd have been made the least uneasy or anxious respecting the invaluable Books which you have so obligingly lent me. They, as well as your Draft, was safely received; and although, perhaps, nothing ought to excuse me for not answering your obliging letter sooner, yet I cannot forbear telling you that they arrived at a time when I was in the middle of more business or rather confusion than I cou'd possibly get through—for you must know that *Mr. Beilby and I will be no longer connected in Business together than until the last day of this month.* The accounts for years back I am struggling to get set right—the sale of the 'Book of Birds,' the heavy payments to make up for the paper, &c.—and, in the midst of all this, by way of complicating the overload, I am obliged to be the acting Overseer of the Poor. Perhaps I have troubled you too much with this recital of my own affairs, instead of filling my letter with grateful acknowledgments for your kind attention and friendship towards me. I expect to be employ'd by the Durham Agricultural Gents. in taking drawings of their best and worst Sheep, Horses, Bulls, Cows, &c., some time in the latter end of next Spring; if so, I shall accept of your kind invitation and make the Grange my home. There were a great many additions to the two last Editions of the 'Quadrupeds,' and if you have the least desire to have one of them, you need only drop me a hint and I shall think myself happy if you will accept of it from me. We have just eight of the third Edition, common paper, left on hand.

"I am, Sir,

Your obliged and humbl. Servt.,

"THOMAS BEWICK.

"GEO. ALLAN, Esq., Darlington."

In his Memoir, p. 183, Bewick records a visit to Darlington, "to make drawings of cattle and sheep for a Durham Report." When these were made they proved to be *too like* the animals to please his employers. "He objected to put lumps of fat here and there, where he could not see it," to please "fat cattle-makers; and the journey ended in nothing;" so he observes, "I got my labour for my trouble."

In the year 1800, Mr. Bailey of Chillingham, and George

Culley, Esq., of Fowberry Tower, published a valuable Report concerning the State of Agriculture in Northumberland. Both gentlemen were friends of Bewick, and kindly mentioned in the Memoir, which accounts for their joint work being illustrated with several vignettes that had previously appeared in the "Quadrupeds." This was an unusual favour.

THE following correspondence between Mr. Bewick and Mr. T. Vernon, picture merchant, of Liverpool, was occasioned by the latter forwarding two folio volumes (blank) for his friend to fill with such stray cuts or proofs as might and would no doubt lie about the shop, and be accounted of little or no value. The three books mentioned in the first letter refer to copies of the "Land Birds," and vignettes, printed two on a page, without letterpress, in 1800. That Bewick thought much of this issue appears from the fact that he carefully reserved a few copies for *particular friends.* Mr. Vernon seems to have suggested an illustrated edition of Burns's immortal poem of "Tam o' Shanter," the incidents of which are well fitted to bring out the talents of the artist. This may be considered to have been at least partially accomplished in the Alnwick Edition of Burns's Poems, published by Catnach & Davison in 1808.

From a second most interesting letter, addressed to the same gentleman at the close of the year, we learn the estimate the writer had formed of the character and tastes of his clever pupil, Henry Hole. His master evidently considered that much reading and studious habits were calculated to disqualify him for that active rude intercourse with the world he was then about to enter. He had dwelt too much in the regions of imagination, and Bewick sought to interest his friend in promoting the interests of one in whose happiness he felt deep concern. Who their common intimate Mr. Harvey was (spelt Hardy afterwards) I have not been able to discover—probably the keeper of some tavern. Fortune dealt kindly by Mr. Hole.

He was not destined to end his days in monotonous and weary toil. On the death of an uncle he succeeded to a considerable estate at Ebberley Hall, Devonshire. The bashful and retiring spirit shown by Robert Bewick when a youth of sixteen was not shaken off when manhood was attained. Diffidence in his own powers was the prevailing feature in his passage through life.

Mr. Thomas Bewick *to* Mr. T. Vernon.

"Newcastle, *6th January* 1801.

"Sir,—I sit down to ansr. your Letter of the 21st ultmo., but when I may meet with an opportunity of getting your 'Books of Birds' sent by a safe conveyance I know not. If I send it by the Waggon, in all probability it will never more be heard of, and there is pretty nearly the same chance of it being lost by the Mail, besides their unreasonable charges for the carriage of small parcels. However, I shall be upon the look-out for a private hand, who may be willing to do me the favor of taking charge of it; and if my patience shou'd be wearied out, it is but to venture upon the other modes of conveyance at last. You'l see I have sent 3 Books. If my friend Mr. Gregson has a mind to have one of them, let him have it; but if not, perhaps you may have an opportunity of selling them. I have only a few of these Books on hand for my particular Friends, for as soon as Mr. Mawman saw a specimen he ordered the whole Edition. The retail price is half a guinea. I hardly know what to say to you about doing 'Tam o' Chanter' on wood. I cannot undertake to do it untill I have got quite done with the Second Vol. of 'Birds.' Everything that causes a delay in the publication I consider as taking a liberty with an indulgent public, who have a right to expect it as soon as I can; and yet it is not in my power to keep closely upon the 'Birds' while I keep a shop in the manner I do; and indeed, to tell you the truth, I am almost wrought to death—the ⌒ is kept continually bent, and I find myself not very well. I had lately an application to engrave a Bank note plate; and while I was doing it, a scheme came into my head to attempt something to prevent the forgery of it, and in this I think I have compleatly succeeded, by a manner of engraving perfectly new, and which I am of opinion, from the nature of the work, cannot be in any way exactly imitated. I suspect that this may cause a *run* upon me for orders in this way, which will still keep me from the 'Birds.' I gave you all the loose impressions of the 'Birds' I had, and I suposed there wd. be none a wanting; however, if I can find those you mention among any strayed proofs, I will send them. I would be much obliged to you to desire Mr. *Happy* Scott of your place to pay for his Book £1, 1s. to Mr. Gregson. Mr. Gregson can readily remit me anything in this way to N'Castle.

> "I am, Sir,
>> With my best wishes,
>>> Yours, &c.,
>>>> "THOMAS BEWICK.

"To-morrow by the Mail I will send your Parcel; it is needless waiting any longer.

"*Jany.* 23, 1801.

"*P.S.*—The Birds you mention are no doubt *water*, for the Second Volume. I have a great number of both them and new tailpieces proved, which I am unwilling to be made public untill the Book is out. I will then send or save *a compleat set of them for you.*   Miss Gostling has got all the little sketches of Tail-pieces, &c., from my little Boy, for I cannot be at the trouble of taking care of such things myself.   I think I have burnt 100ds. of them, and untill he took a fancy to save them none were saved by me."

By the "little sketches" mentioned above, impressions of woodcuts are meant.

"NEWCASTLE, *4th Decr.* 1801.

"Dr. Sir,—I cannot remember whether I ansrd. your kind letter of the 1st of March or not, for at that time, and for a long while after, I was so badly of the dizzyness in my head, accompanied with faintness and inability to look after anything properly, that it is most likely I had laid your letter, as well as many others, to a side.   I have now the pleasure, however, of telling you that I am at this time, I may say, *immensely better,* and I think—indeed, I doubt not, that this change has been brought about by relaxation from business and sea bathing. I trust it will continue, as I am determined to do otherwise than I have done. Your elegant ptfolios arrived by the Carrier long since, and I fear you have been disappointed at my not returning them long before this time; but I don't know how I could have done better for you, for I never took any care of Impressions from my Cuts, and those wch. found their way to the Forth were very often given to the Children to play with, and by that means lost or destroy'd; however, my little Boy is now very careful of them, and you may be assured that I will pull out his stores (such as they are) for you; and as soon as the 'Water Birds' are put to press I will take care that you shall have the whole of the Impressions from them.   I know not what I can say more on this business; for, were it not entirely to oblige you, I cou'd not bring myself to anything like a resolve to take the least care in collecting or preserving any Impressions from the Cuts wh. I execute.   I cannot look at them any longer than while they are quite new.   The 'Birds' will be *set about* in earnest as soon as I can be certain whether Parliament will or will not take off the late heavy and *prohibitory* Tax wch. they laid upon it last Session; but, at any rate, I think I have done right in delaying the publication, for certainly paper will now be cheaper.

"The Bearer of this—my late pupil, Mr. Henry Hole—intends to begin business in Liverpool, and probably it may be in your power to shew him some civilities in the shape of advice, &c.   He knows but little of mankind and the world into which he is just launched.   You will find that he has read a good deal, is of a poetic and romantic turn of mind, is unsettled, and does not know

Northumberland Bank

N°

N°

Promise to pay the Bearer on Demand ONE POUND, Value rec.

NEWCASTLE the day of 18

For John Reed, Reed & C°

One Pound

Engd. Wm Winton

Bewick

where to cast *Anchor* and *moor in Safety*. I cannot help figuring in my mind that he is like a Ship without a Pilot, and for his safety and welfare I am extremely anxious; and indeed (although I shall not shew it to him) I shall be inwardly much grieved at bidding him farewell, for I think I shall never see him again. I hope, however, from his sobriety and attention, that he will, when more settled, make a figure in the line of his profession, and be a credit to the place where he was reared.

"I sometimes have a Pint of Beer at your friend Mr. Harvey's, and our chat is often turned upon you. He is always enquiring when I heard from you— how you are, &c. Both he and Mrs. Harvey are very well, and desired me to give their Compts., best wishes, &c., to you and Mrs. Vernon.

"I am, Dr. Sir,

Yours, &c.,

"THOMAS BEWICK."

"NEWCASTLE, 18 *May* 1803.

'DR. SIR,—Your Letter catched me in the midst of anxiety and bustle, preparing to go to press with the second volume of 'Water Birds,' the paper for which is now *all at Sea—I fear at a bad time ;* but, however, I must hope it will arrive in safety. When I get to press I shall be enabled to save you an Impression from each cut for your splendid, or rather your massy volumes. My little Boy has gathered a few of one kind or another for you. Such as they are you are welcome to them, for they are only such as have been left, and the rest were picked out by comers and goers who are as fond of such things as yourself. For my part I cannot be at the pains to trouble myself about them any longer than a first peep at the proofs, and were it not that my Boy is more careful of them, I should not have one left. I missed or rather mistook the Carrier day, which is *Monday* to *Edinburgh ;* and as you have hinted that your stay at that place is uncertain, I *must hear* from you again before that day, informing me whether it will be safe for me to send them to you by next *Monday's* Edinburgh Carrier or not. I often spend an Eveg. at our friend Mr. Hardy's. Both he and Mrs. Hardy are very well, and desired me to return their best respects to you and Mrs. Vernon, to whom also with mine,

"I am,

Your most obet. Servt.,

"THOMAS BEWICK."

P

Mr. Vernon *to* Master Robert E. Bewick.

"My Young Friend,

"Accept of this Cup, not in return for the obligations I feel myself under to you, but as a cement to that Friendship which I hope will subsist between us when you are of riper years ; and I trust your own good sense will point out to you the benefits you will find, in your progress through Life, by following the example your Father has shewn you. Wishing you health,

"I remain,

Very truly yours,

"*Decr.* 12, 1804."

"T. VERNON.

"Dr. Sir,—When your Messenger arrived with your handsome present, I was at a loss at the moment what to say to you, and am not less so still. When Robt. came in, read your letter, and saw your present, he blushed over the ears, and felt so embarrassed that he cou'd not wait upon you to return his thanks—your kindness has made him ashamed to see you, and he has not been accustomed to make compliments.

"I was writing to Mr. Gregson of Liverpool when your present arrived, and I told him what you had done, &c.

"Shall I see you at Hardy's to-night?

"I am,

Dr. Sir,

Yours, &c.,

"*Wednesday,* 12 *Decr.* 1804." [1]

"THOMAS BEWICK.

[1] I am indebted to the liberality and kindness of J. W. Pease, Esq., Pendower, who owns the identical volumes thus enriched by Bewick, for permission to publish this correspondence. The impressions of the cuts are brilliant.

Presented to Mr Robert
Robinson by J & E Bewick
Sep.r 11 1876
West Street Gateshead on—

Miss Esther Elliot
Forth
Newcastle

To be left at J. Bewick's work Shop
St Nicholas Church Yard

(to be delivered immediately)

Tynmouth, Tuesday night.
13 October 1801

Dear Aunty

I have just now received a Letter from Luke, informing me that the Newcastle Bank wants a number of Bills printed immediately; therefore, as soon as you recieve this Letter you must go along to the Shop with the Key of the Desk, which you will find in my Pocket Book, in my right Cap Drawer,— it is the largest Key of the bunch ——and when you have opened the Shop Desk with it, you must desire George to get the Bill Plate wanted, which he will find in the bool hole over which there is a paper, pasted, with NOTES upon it —— Luke does not know the Plate, it is on that acct. that you must get George to seek it out from amongst the other plates of the same kind, which are in the same place along with it ———

—— When you are out, if convenient, you may call at Mr. Bells, we are very desirous to know how he is — also you may tell John that Robert received his Letter at wch. he was both pleased & disappointed — he longs much to have his company among the Rocks at Tynmouth, & we think it a pity he shou'd let the opportunity & the fine season pass away, without reaping the full bene-:fit he woud recieve from it — Little Rob: is /while I am writing this/ playing John's new Tunes of "peace & plenty" &c to old Willy Dean, in the Kitchen —— Jane desires her compts to Mary & hopes she is very well since her return to N Castle — Jane has met with a misfortune to day, her bathing ? was stolen from off old Willy's Garden dike, & the Thief has has escaped —— Give our Compts to our Neighbours at the Forth

J Bewick

HEN on a visit to the Misses Bewick one afternoon in September 1876, the ladies, in the course of conversation, kindly presented me with an autograph letter of their father. I have read it over many times with pleasure, and have no doubt my readers will be glad to have such a capital example of the writer's pleasant homely style in perfect fac-simile.

It is addressed to Miss Esther Elliot, a sister of his wife, who resided with the family at the Forth from not long after Bewick's

From the *Adventures of a Fly*, 1790.

marriage, and removed with them to Gateshead in 1814, where she continued to act as housekeeper until her death. It is written in reply to a letter from his apprentice Luke Clennell. Bewick's copper-plate printer at that time was George Barber, a near relative of Joseph Barber the bookseller. Mr. Joseph Bell, who is named in it, was a portrait-painter of some ability. His house and shop were in the High Bridge, next to the premises now occupied by Mr. Henry Watson, the eminent brassfounder. His house was decorated with great taste, the ceiling of the sitting-room being painted light blue and studded with golden stars. On the walls were large landscapes in compartments, within rich borders of flowers. John Bell, his son, and his daughter Mary, were intimate friends of the Bewicks. "Little Rob," the artist's only son, then in his fourteenth year, was already a skilful performer on the North-umberland pipes.

"Willy Dean's Cottage," where Bewick lodged, stood on the banks overlooking the short sands, at Tynemouth.

The second volume of the "British Birds," containing the "Water Birds," was not published until 1804. The letterpress was the work of Bewick himself, who in the advertisement acknowledges his obligations to the Rev. H. Cotes, vicar of Bedlington, County Northumberland, for his literary corrections. Mr. Beilby, who had hitherto mainly supplied the descriptions to the "Quadrupeds," and the first volume of the "Birds," retired immediately after the publication of the latter. Mr. Bewick, as we are informed (Memoir, p. 164), "was obliged, from necessity, not choice, to commence author. As each bird was finished on the wood, he set about describing it from the specimen before him, after consulting such authorities as were within his reach, adding from the stores of his own knowledge such particulars as appeared of value, and likely to interest his readers."

The following is an extract from a page of Ralph Beilby's ledger, and records the final settlement between himself and Mr. Bewick, with the amount received for his share in the copyrights :—

1802	THOS. BEWICK.	*Dr.*
April 15th.	To my third share of the "History of Quadrupeds," sold this day	£100
1804		
Novr. 1st.	To my half share of the first vol. of the "History of British Birds"	£300

The payment of these heavy sums, drawn from a property entirely of his own creation, was not only a severe strain upon the resources of the artist, but would naturally bring to his remembrance the words of his late brother, "that things might have been managed more to his advantage." A dissolution of partnership in 1790 was a step he strongly recommended. Mr. Bewick remarks in the Memoir, pp. 162–3, that—

"On some disputes happening respecting the printing of the 'Quadrupeds,' Mr. Beilby, who now sought repose, sold me his share of that publication. Some time before the second volume of the 'Birds' was put to press, he also sold me his share of the first volume. I had no sooner agreed to give the price demanded than many recollections of the past crowded upon my mind, and, looking at the unfavourable side, I could not help thinking of the extra labour and time I had spent in the completion of these works, wherein he had borne comparatively a small part; but, having promised to pay the sum, I made no further observations to any one."

The "Seasons," by Thomson, was a great favourite with Mr. Bewick. He engraved a series of woodcuts after designs by Thurston, for a fine edition, published by Jas. Wallis, Paternoster Row, in 1805. In the following year Jas. Catnach, of Alnwick, brought out an edition of the "Hermit of Wark-

The Hive—*Thomas Bewick*, 1806.

worth," for which Bewick executed the cuts from drawings by Mr. Craig. The third and best edition of the "Hive of Ancient and Modern Literature" appeared also in 1806, from the press of Mr. Solomon Hodgson. It contains fourteen large and beautiful woodcuts by Thomas Bewick. Three of the original drawings—viz., those that illustrate the story of "Fidelia," "Le Fevre," and the "Wounded Soldier"—are in my collection. These were obtained from Miss Isabella Bewick. The remaining cuts (with sixteen vignettes showing the Sports of Youth) are entirely the work of Clennell. His initials are on several of the more important. These are fine examples of genuine wood-engraving, and I am happy in being able to adorn this work with such an interesting series. The merits of the master and his brilliant pupil may thus be viewed side by side. The extracts in prose and verse have been selected with great care from the best English writers, and do credit to the judgment of the publisher.

The Siege of Calais—From *The Hive, L. C.,* 1806.

About this time Bewick was much occupied in devising means to prevent the forgery of bank notes. After considerable time had been consumed, and a very lengthy correspondence with bank officials, he found, like many other ingenious men, that his suggestions had only served to build up the fortune of others. Sir William Congreve, who was in a position to "cull and select from" the designs contributed by various talented artists, and appropriate ideas thus made known to him, some-what disguised by modifications of his own, reaped in the end

all the honour and advantage.   In the spring of 1881, Miss
Isabella Bewick presented me with a letter (endorsed, "For
Mr. Robinson") written by Mr. William Bulmer to her father.
The reader will observe that in it he asks his old friend "if he
had thought of any little poem that he would wish to illustrate"
—presumably in the style of Goldsmith's Poems and Somer-

vile's Chase, which had both proved
such a great success.   Miss Bewick
said that Allan Ramsay's Poems and
those of Burns had been suggested by
Bulmer.   It is matter of regret that
the idea was not taken up.   Bewick,
however, did not feel inclined to re-
spond to the invitation.   Bulmer drove a hard bargain with
respect to the cuts recently supplied him by the two brothers,
and this want of liberality did not dispose the great wood-
engraver to engage again in similar work for a like remuneration.   The sum of sixty pounds was all that Mr. Bewick
received for the splendid cuts which illustrate Somervile's
Chase.

Mr. WILLIAM BULMER *to* THOMAS BEWICK.

"*July* 21, 1802.

"DEAR BEWICK,

"By this day's Mail Coach I have forwarded to you a deal box
containing 6 copies of Somervile's Chase, agreeable to your Order ; and as the
Newcastle people seem fond of our joint efforts, I have likewise inclosed 4 copies
of the 2nd edit. of Goldsmith's Poems, which it is very probable some of the
Booksellers may wish to have, as I have not above a dozen Copies of this edition
on hand.   The Trade price is 17/-, the retail 1 Guinea.   I have sent them by
the Mail, as our friend George Gray means to go to Newcastle partly by the
Coach and occasionally to walk a little, which prevents me the opportunity of
sending them by him.   The expense of this parcel, as well as the former one,

you will make me debtor for. . . . Have you yet thought of any little poem or poems that you would wish to engrave some blocks for?

"I am, Dr. Bewick, yrs. very truly,

"W. BULMER.

Mr. T. BEWICK

1802	*To* W. BULMER.	*Dr.*
July 21	To 6 Somervile's Chase in boards at 11/8 . . .	£3 10 0
	To 4 Goldsmith's 4to Poems at 17/- boards . .	3 8 0
		£6 18 0

July 26	Charnley, 2 Goldsmith's	£1 14 0
	Sands, 1 Somervile .	0 11 8
	Akenhead, 2 Somervile's	1 3 4

"MR. THOMAS BEWICK,
   ENGRAVER,
      NEWCASTLE-UPON-TYNE."

GEORGE GRAY, the fruit-painter and enthusiastic student of Nature, was a frequent visitor at the Forth. A half-length portrait of John Bewick, painted by him in crayon, is now in the Museum of the Natural History Society, Newcastle. He is represented as wearing a dark-brown wig, bright-green coat, buff vest, and frilled shirt. When this was taken he would probably not be more than thirty. His finely formed forehead and dark luminous eyes vividly remind one of Nasmyth's well-known portrait of Burns. Gray, who lived in a small white-washed house at the foot of the Pudding Chare, opposite to the Crown and Thistle yard, was of an exceedingly humorous and merry disposition.

As drawing-master at one of the most respectable schools for young ladies in the town, his entry in a morning was the signal for a general hum of pleasurable excitement among the pupils.

Q

Eccentric, but of a truly honourable and independent spirit, he would never incur the slightest obligation.

On the occasion of his calling at Mr. Bewick's house, he never could be prevailed on to take tea, but remained standing,

garnishing his discourse with observations remarkable for shrewdness and pungent wit. Mr. Gray was an able mineralogist as well as an artist. His ardour in the study of botany led him to visit the wilds of South America, and wander for years amongst the savage inhabitants. Mr. Bewick had a pair of good-sized stockings woven by Gray from the stalks of nettles after being macerated in water. Miss Bewick showed me one of them, the colour, fabric, and quality being excellent. He had his little stocking manufactory to carry out the process in Jesmond Dene.

To the trade in particular the following letter will recommend itself, as showing the liberal terms on which booksellers were supplied. The writer announces the publication of the fifth edition of the " Quadrupeds," published 13th May 1807. The " Birds " referred to is the second edition, 1805. The demy copies named would be the second impression of the " Land Birds," printed in 1798 with the date of 1797, and the first edition of the " Water Birds," 1804. There are demy copies of the " Land Birds " substantially the edition of 1797, but having on the last leaf and title the words " printed by Edw. Walker," with the date " 1804."

Mr. Bewick gave the trade long credit for large orders. I have in my possession an acceptance for £100, payable fifteen months after date.

"NEWCASTLE, *May 29*, 1807.

"SIR,—A new Edition of the ' History of Quadrupeds' being now ready for delivery, and as I have determined to throw the sale open to the whole of the London Trade upon equal terms, I take the liberty of soliciting your orders for whatever numbers you may be inclined to take. The following are the terms of Sale :—In Boards—Imperial, £1, 2s., sells £1, 11s. 6d.; Royal, 15s., sells £1, 1s; Demy, 9s., sells at 13s. In sheets—Imperial, £1, 1s.; Royal, 14s. 4d.; Demy, 8s. 6d.

"'British Birds'—of them I have Imperials and Royals on hand; the Demy were sold some time ago. In Boards—Imperial, per Volume, 17s.; Royal, per Volume, 13s. Six, nine, and twelve months' Credit will be given for large Orders, and your acceptances taken at those Dates. The Books are to be Shipped at your risk and expense.

"I am, Sir, your most obedt.

"MR. J. PAYNE,   "THOMAS BEWICK.
    BOOKSELLER,
        MEWS GATE, LONDON."

HE want of a bridge between Prudhoe and Ovingham had been long felt by the inhabitants on both sides of the river, particularly by the farmers. Many fatal accidents had occurred in fording the stream from time to time.

Mr. Bewick inserted a letter in the *Newcastle Courant* (17th May 1816), under the *nom-de-plume* of "The Hermit of

The History of Joseph—From *The Hive*, 1806.

Horsley Wood," urging the building of such a structure as a fit monument to the Duke of Northumberland, to whose public spirit the county was so largely indebted, in preference to a column, on the ground of utility. "Here," he observes, "many a man and many a team have by the sudden floods of the Tyne been swept away." Sixty-seven years afterwards this desirable work was begun, and the foundation-stone of a bridge laid, amid general rejoicing among the villagers. This was within a few days of the funeral of the last daughter of Thomas Bewick, who died at the age of ninety-four.

In the early part of 1883 the Ovingham Bridge Company

(Limited) was formed, with John Hilton Ridley, Esq., of Well-
burn, Ovingham, as chairman.   On June 21st the foundation-
stone of the north pier was laid by Mrs. Ridley.   His Grace
the Duke of Northumberland, as owner of the land at both
ends, gave every support to the company.   The bridge was
publicly opened on the 20th of December following.   Mr.
Hubert Laws was the engineer, who completed the work in the
short space of six months.   After the bridge was opened the

The Story of a Disabled Soldier—From *The Hive*, 1806.

company partook of luncheon at the Ovingham Inn.   The
health of the Duke of Northumberland was proposed by the
Rev. John Frederic Bigge, Vicar of Stamfordham.   A ball was
held in the same room in the evening, largely attended by the
neighbouring gentry.

STORY too good to be omitted is given of the poet Campbell in W. B. Scott's "Memoir of David Scott, R.S.A.":—

"Some of the earliest pupils of Robert Scott (David's father), stimulated by the success of Bewick's 'Birds' and 'Quadrupeds,' employed their inexperienced hands on a series of animals. Mr. Scott applied to Thomas Campbell, then a student at Edinburgh, to write the descriptions of birds, beasts, and fishes, which Campbell undertook to do. But Campbell worked but slowly, and the engraver, whose patience was worn out, visited the poet's lodgings one evening without finding him at home, and collected the books he had sent for the task, in order to place them in other hands. One of these, Bewick's 'Birds,' was found in a sadly dilapidated state—several leaves had been torn in half from the end. The landlady was called in and questioned, her children being suspected; but these she exonerated by exclaiming, 'Oh, that's the book Mr. Camel lichts his canelle wi' when he comes hame at nicht!'"

From this time up to 1818 nothing deserving of special mention came from the hand of Mr. Bewick. To particularise every cut he executed during the interval forms no part of the plan I have marked out for myself. This has been already done most amply by the late Rev. Thomas Hugo in the "Bewick Collector." In 1812 he had a severe illness, and believed himself to be on the very confines of another world. All the past history of his life presented itself to his mind with a freshness and reality which could not be exceeded had the events been the actual occurrences of the previous day, so vivid was their memory. His mother once said to him, shortly after he had taken up his abode at the Forth, that he would not remain there long. He replied that he would never leave it till he was carried out. And this really took place; for after the property was sold, and he was obliged to seek another residence, he had, through weakness, to be carried out. His hands were swollen and painful in consequence of the gout. In this state he was removed to lodgings at Carr's Hill, near Gateshead. Having recovered health and strength, a project long entertained was set about in good earnest. This was no other than the publication of an illustrated edition of the "Fables of Æsop," uniform in size with the "Quadrupeds" and "Birds." Greater difficulties had to be encountered, we are informed, in the production of this work than he had experienced with either of those just mentioned. The most able of his pupils at this time were William Harvey and William Temple, who engraved nearly the whole of the cuts, assisted by Mr. R. E. Bewick. The publication had been looked forward to with much interest, and was at length given to the world on 1st October 1818.

Unlike his previous works, it failed in obtaining that praise and commendation which greeted his earlier efforts.

The manner in which the cuts were engraved was different from his ordinary and well-known style. It lacked that boldness of stroke to which the public had been accustomed, and which had hitherto distinguished the work of his hands. The general opinion, shared by Mr. Bewick himself, was that the printing of the cuts did not come up to the high standard formerly obtained. A very curious receipt was given to subscribers, adorned with a sprig of sea-weed printed in red from a copper-plate, over a woodcut. This was done at Bewick's own office : the object was to detect copies obtained by stealth, and not from himself. The effect was both novel and pleasing : connoisseurs never fail to acknowledge the taste and ingenuity of the device. Bewick's signature is sometimes *written*, a genuine autograph, but generally printed : the quaint conceit of his *thumb mark* is amusing. In 1823 a second edition was called for. In it the printer was thought to have been more successful, but the unfavourable impression produced at first continued.

The late Miss Jane Bewick many times declared to me that, in her opinion, the cuts had not had justice done them.

There have been but two editions of the Fables, and sixty-three years have now elapsed since its last appearance. In the meantime there has been a complete revolution in public opinion regarding the merits and undoubted excellence of the work. What was once disparaged is now held by general consent to be truly admirable, and worthy of Mr. Bewick's great name. The originality of the designs is remarkable, and where the cuts in Croxall's Æsop have manifestly suggested the idea, the

From the *History of a Fly* (Newcastle Edition).

treatment of the subject has been so wonderfully improved by Bewick that it becomes a new composition altogether. Sixteen guineas is not now thought to be too much for an uncut copy in imperial octavo. Miss Bewick once offered me the whole of the woodcuts for Æsop's Fables, including the copyright, for £500.[1] In 1876 a most absurd offer was made for the Fable cuts by an eminent London publisher, which was rejected by Miss Bewick with just indignation. "Rather," she said, "than my father's cuts should be sold for such a sum, I would take them down to the bridge, and drop them one by one into the river."

---

[1] Miss Bewick valued the entire collection at £3000.

JOHN TROTTER BROCKETT F.S.A.

HE ensuing correspondence between Mr. Bewick and John Trotter Brockett,[1] the well-known north-country antiquary and collector of rare books and coins, is now published for the first time, from the original letters in my possession. The smartness and spirit shown on both sides is characteristic of the writers. Indignation, keen and intense, was felt by each towards the other, from an acute sense of insult and injury. They had long been friendly, and it is to be regretted that any estrangement should have taken place. When the *editio princeps* of the "Fables of Æsop" was about to be put to press, Mr. Brockett conceived that a set of impressions from the cuts, on India paper, would be a valuable acquisition to his large and choice collection of literary rarities. What passed when the matter was first mooted in conversation be-

---

[1] John Trotter Brockett, F.S.A., one of the Council of the Society of Antiquaries, Newcastle, and a Secretary of the Literary and Philosophical Society. This accomplished lawyer, bibliophile, and numismatist was a native of Witton Gilbert, near Durham. On the removal of his father to Newcastle, his education was confided to the care of the Rev. William Turner, and at the proper age he selected the law as a profession. The duties connected with this honourable calling henceforth became the business of his life. He was mainly instrumental in establishing the Newcastle Typographical Society, several of whose most valued publications had the benefit of his careful editorship.

The sale of Mr. Brockett's choice cabinet of coins and valuable library, &c., took place at Sotheby's in 1823, and occupied twenty-four days, the proceeds amounting to upwards of £6000. The prices obtained were at that time thought excessive. It would mightily gladden the heart of a Newcastle bookseller at the present day were he able to purchase Bewick gems in such bindings and condition for such small sums.

He compiled the Memoir of Thomas and John Bewick prefixed to Charnley's excellent reprint of the "Select Fables," published in 1820. But it is upon his "Glossary of North-Country Words" that he will be best known to posterity. He was one of that literary coterie accustomed to assemble in the back shop of worthy Mr. Charnley, the prince of north-country booksellers, along with the Rev. John Hodgson, the eloquent and learned historian of Northumberland; Vicar Smith; the Rev. W. Turner; John Adamson, the distinguished Portuguese scholar and translator of Camoens; William Nicholson, the artist; Thomas and James Hodgson, the former learned in Roman antiquities, whilst the latter edited the *Newcastle Chronicle* newspaper with much spirit and ability; Thomas Doubleday, brilliant alike in prose and rhyme; with others less known to fame. Mr. Brockett died at his residence in Albion Place, Newcastle, 12th October 1842, aged fifty-four.

R

tween him and Mr. Bewick I know not.   The India paper was
duly bought and forwarded by Mr. Brockett, but, alas! only
to be returned in the same condition.   A disappointment so
unexpected went to the very heart of the antiquary, and his
wrath found vent in letters to Bewick full of bitterness and
anger.   Mr. Brockett had no claim to be so favoured over
many friends of long standing.   With him, to be baulked by a
rival collector of a Roman denarius with a rare reverse, of a
unique tractate from the Allan Press, or even of one of Prynne's
miscellaneous works needful to complete his set, would at once
constitute an offence not to be condoned.   Again, he collected
not so much with the intention to keep, as to sell when opportunity offered.   On the other hand, the great wood-engraver
through life never could understand or reciprocate the ardour
of a genuine collector, or enter into the feelings of the curious
in such matters.   He was thoroughly utilitarian in all the pursuits of life.   Impressions on white satin or vellum of several
of his finest cuts, particularly of the " Birds," are to be found
in the collections of connoisseurs, but these were struck off by
the pressmen *sub rosa*, without the knowledge or consent of
Mr. Bewick.

Mr. Bewick *to* Mr. John Trotter Brockett.

"*Decr. 9th,* 1818.

" Mr. Brockett.

"Dear Sir,—I beg to advise you of having returned the India paper, and
to inform you that, before I received it, I had cleaned and gone through a great
number of the Fable Cuts ; consequently I cannot at present take off a set of
Impressions such as you want.   It will afford me much pleasure to meet your
wishes when the work goes again to press.

"I am, Sir,
Your most obedt.
"THOMAS BEWICK.

" *To* Mr. Brockett."

Mr. BROCKETT *to* Mr. BEWICK.

"SANDHILL, 11*th Decr.* 1818.

"SIR,—I have this morning recd. your extraordinary Letter, dated two days ago. Taking all the circumstances into consideration, I consider your conduct towards me as to the Cuts for the Fables to have been uncandid and un-handsome in the extreme. With that conviction on my mind, I can place no reliance on the future Promises of one who has not only broken those already made, but has throughout the whole Affair betrayed such a littleness of mind as really makes the Transaction without a Parallel.

"Sir,
Your obedt. Servt.,
"JOHN TROTTER BROCKETT.

"Mr. THOS. BEWICK."

The Reply.

"ST. NICHS. CHURCHYD.,
"12*th Decr.* 1818.

"Mr. BROCKETT.

"SIR,—By your arrogant and offensively impudent Letter, you have pre-vented me from answering it any otherwise than by merely saying, it has put an end to all future correspondence or connection between us.   Farewell.

"I am, &c.,
"THOMAS BEWICK."

Mr. BROCKETT'S *Rejoinder.*

"SANDHILL, 12*th Decr.* 1818.

"SIR,—My Letter was intended to produce the Effect your very polite note of this morning has anticipated; for I assure you your shuffling and insincere Behaviour (to say no more of it) could never allow me for one moment to hold further communication with one who has forfeited the best Protection which can bind man to man.   I still suspect there is some dirty fellow in the back Ground.   If it is the Person I suppose, I should like him to know that I consider *his* Conduct as despicable as his Character has proved itself to be worthless.   I remain for the last time,

"Yrs.,
"JOHN TROTTER BROCKETT.

"Mr. THOS. BEWICK."

EWICK had a memory richly stored with local anecdote. No man possessed a better knowledge than he of Northumbrian phraseology, or could have rendered more valuable help in perfecting Mr. Brockett's instructive and entertaining "Glossary of North-Country Words."

An *illustrated* glossary of words in use by the peasantry and common people one hundred years ago from such a hand

Ingratitude Punished—From *Tales for Youth*, 1794.

would now be highly prized by all students engaged in the study of words. What such a *brochure* would have been, a tolerable idea may be formed by quoting instances where Mr. Brockett has sought to impress his verbal definitions on the mind of the reader by a reference to the graphic pencil of Bewick. Thus, in the first edition of the Glossary, we have—

"*Neddy, Netty,* a certain place that will not bear a written explanation, but which is *depicted to the very life* in a tail-piece in the first edition of Bewick's 'Land Birds' (1797), p. 285. In the second edition a bar is placed against the offending part of this *broad* display of native humour."

"*Nose-on-the-grindstone,* a simile for the fate of an improvident person. See an illustration in Bewick's Æsop, p. 128."

"*Oysters*—'E-shee-ke-le-kaul-er-oysters,' the famous cry of the elder oyster-wenches in Newcastle, but now rarely carried to this musical extent. Bewick has figured two of these dames in a tail-piece to his 'Land Birds,' ed. 1821, p. 20."

"*Pant*, a public fountain. See a representation of a north-country pant in Bewick's Æsop, p. 334."

"*Hikey*, a swing. It is much better represented than I can pretend to in Bewick's tail-piece of two monkeys engaged in the sport. See 'Quadrupeds,' p. 484, ed. 1820."

"*Shuggy-shew*, a swing. A long rope fastened at each end, and thrown over a beam, on which young persons seat themselves, and are swung backwards and

ALCESTES and PRÆTUS—From *Tales for Youth*, 1794.

forwards. See Bewick's Æsop, p. 4, where his Satanic Majesty is amusing himself in this manner."

"*Howdy*, a midwife; *helter-skelter*, in great haste. *Vide* Bewick's 'Land Birds,' p. 157, ed. 1797."

In this vignette the good woman is represented as being carried along at a somewhat reckless pace by a messenger on horseback, half dressed, the case being urgent. Part of the cut is covered by a large leaf, to denote that the scene about to take place requires to be concealed. What the good lady may bring forth is still one of the secrets of nature. John Jackson, who was a native of Ovingham, and for a short

time a pupil of Bewick's, projected an " Illustrated Glossary of
North-Country Words" some time before his death.   A number
of cuts were engraved for the purpose, and a considerable
number of words (not in Brockett) gathered together.   Had
he lived to carry out his idea the result of such a performance
could not fail of agreeably extending our knowledge of what
is fast becoming obsolete.   It is to be hoped that his brother,
Mr. Mason Jackson, will find leisure amid his arduous duties
to complete the work.

   The second portrait taken of Mr. Bewick was a miniature

by Murphy, amusingly alluded to by him in a letter dated
18th April 1803, addressed to Mr. Christopher Gregson,
London, a son of his old master, and quoted by Jackson in
his " Treatise on Wood Engraving."   In it Bewick humorously
alludes to his *beauty* when a boy, and to the state of his
coat-sleeve, in consequence of his using it instead of a pocket-
handkerchief.   Bewick, it is to be observed, was very hard-
featured, and much marked with the small-pox.   After mentioning Mr. Murphy as "a man of worth, and a first-rate artist in
the miniature line," he thus proceeds : "I do not imagine, at
your time of life, my dear friend, that you will be solicitous

about forming new acquaintances ; but it may not, perhaps, be putting you much out of the way to show any little civilities to Mr. Murphy during his stay in London. He has, on his own account, taken my portrait, and I dare say will be desirous to show you it the first opportunity ; when you see it, you will, no doubt, conclude that T. B. is turning *bonnyer* and *bonnyer* in his old days. But, indeed, you cannot *help knowing this*, and also that there were *great indications* of its turning out so *long since*. But if you have forgot our

The Cuckoo and the Swallow—From *Tales for Youth*, 1794.

earliest youth, perhaps your brother Philip may help you to remember what a *great beauty* I was at that time, when the grey coat-sleeve was *glazed* from the cuff towards the elbow."

This portrait was afterwards neatly engraved by J. Summerfield, and published in 1815. Little is known of the engraver, who seems to have led a wild and irregular life, and to have joined a militia regiment stationed at Newcastle in the early part of the present century. As an artist and an engraver, he would soon become known to Mr. Bewick, and if any one could have reclaimed him from a life of folly and unhappiness, the prudent and wise counsel of his friend would have done so. William Carey, the author of "Memoirs of the Progress of the Fine Arts in England during the Georgian Era," 4to, 1826, and other works, had, it appears, entertained the idea of writing a sketch of his life, and applied to Mr. Bewick for any material he could supply. This was the occasion of a letter sad enough to read, and now printed for the first time (from the original), by the courtesy of J. W. Pease, Esq., Pendower, Newcastle. Summerfield appears to have been a pupil of F. Bartolozzi, R.A. The engraving of "Rubens and his Wife," alluded to therein, was published in February 1801, and ought to rank amongst the best of the English school. It was my good fortune to secure this print at the sale of the Bewick Collection, February 1884, and it now hangs in my Bewick room with other relics of the artist. It is done from a painting by Rubens and Snyders.

"NEWCASTLE, 4*th April* 1818.

"DEAR SIR,—It is long since I had given up the thought of ever hearing more of my friend Mr. Carey, having from time to time made many enquiries for that end, but to no purpose. Time was beginning to wear out the recollection of what had so agreeably passed between us and our friend, the late Mr. Joseph Bell, until your letter brought back to my recollection many of the circumstances you name; but my young folks, who were pleased with reading your letter, repeated over to me, pit-pat, everything that had happened between us while you were here. They are all well, and were pleased to find you the same. I cannot pretend to give you anything like a full memoir of poor Summerfield; this wou'd take a long time to do such an article any justice. I can only answer some of your Queries shortly, and perhaps not so accurately as I wish. He appeared, on the whole, to me to be a *man* on whom Nature had been very liberal of her bounties, and that he threw her favors in her face. I had a very great regard for him, and was much with him the latter part of the time he was in Newcastle. I know not how long he might be altogether in Newcastle, but I suppose from the time the militia Regt. to which he belonged to were first here, and until some time after the quarrells which took place among the officers *broke them up*. After this happened he lodged at various places, and lived all the time in expectation of his opulent friends sending him supplies, but which they either did not do at all or totally withdrew their bounties. I do not know how this was, but I know he became involved in debt and difficulties, insomuch that, to avoid the [Sketch of three devils], he took private lodgings somewhere about Benwell, where he remained *incog.* during the week, but invariably (I think) visited me at my house at the Forth on the Sundays, when, after spending the day, to avoid being watched to his home, he crossed the Tyne by the Bridge, walked up its south banks, crossed it again, and walked (perhaps in the dark) up the bank to his lodgings. During this time he appeared to be fast losing his health, and before he bid me farewell his handsome and manly looks were much faded away. Before parting, I most earnestly implored him to leave off his dissipated course of life, and to begin in earnest with his engraving; and this, with his last words to me, he promised me he wou'd do; but, but ! this had not, I fear, been done. I had much reason to know that he was of a good-natured and pleasing disposition. I have also seen him, on being insulted, act the part of the roused Lion. He made me a present of the print of ' Rubens and his Wife.' I never saw him at work with the plate of the ' Dead Christ,' &c., you name, and do not now remember whether or not he engraved it at Newcastle. I was much grieved at parting with him. This happened in 1809, and I think it was in the autumn of that year. Thus, my dear Sir, I have, tired and wearied out, almost asleep, set about giving you a hasty scrawl, which, so far as it goes, may perhaps aid you a little in giving your Memoir of poor Summerfield, in which I wish you may be rewarded for your trouble. It will make his name linger a little while longer here than it would otherwise have done; but that is all, for he is gone where all will go— to the land of forgetfullness.

" I am, Dr. Sir,

With Best wishes,

" THOMAS BEWICK.

" Mr. Wm. Carey,
    35 Mary-le-bonne Street,
        Piccadilly, London."

Mr. Carey does not appear to have ever carried out his intention of giving to the world the life of his unfortunate friend. Miss Isabella Bewick, in one of our last conversations, told me that she believed he had never done so, or they would have been sure to have had a copy.

Mr. Bewick could enter into the feelings of an honest trades-man contending with difficulties in the outset of his career. In 1819 a stationer on the Quayside, Newcastle, stood indebted to Messrs. Tipper and Fry to a considerable amount. An acceptance had been given, which was dishonoured, and Bewick was asked to wait upon him and request immediate payment.

The Wounded Soldier—From *The Hive*, 1806.

This was done, and the cash faithfully promised in three or four days. Mr. Bewick, in a letter to those gentlemen, thus represents the case:—

"Mr. G—— is at present not well, but he closely attends his shop, and I dare say is using his utmost endeavours to do well. I do not think he is doing anything in a large way, and I fear he begun upon a small capital, so that he must have to struggle on some time with difficulty, but he is attentive, sober, and active."

Time being allowed, the defaulting debtor was enabled to dis-charge the account, and continued in business for many years afterwards.

MERSON CHARNLEY, a highly respected book-seller in Newcastle, purchased in 1818, of Messrs. Wilson and Spence of York, printers and publishers, twelve hundred woodcuts, many of which were formerly the property of John White, who established the *Newcastle Courant* newspaper in 1711. This collection contained wood-blocks of the seventeenth century, together with the earliest and best productions of Thomas and John Bewick, including the cuts for "Tommy Trip," "Gay's Fables," and the interesting series which embellish the little volume of "Select Fables" published by Saint in 1784.

These Mr. Charnley rightly considered might be used again to illustrate a superior edition of the same work, and thereby show the progress Bewick had made, and the gradual development of his genius when contrasted with his later productions. Mr. Bewick judged otherwise: he did not wish his first efforts, made to adorn school-books, to be now brought before the public in a more respectable form. The subject is well reasoned from his point of view in the following letters and statement, which impart much curious and interesting information.

The original correspondence between Mr. Bewick and his local publisher is now printed *verbatim* for the first time. It forms not the least important part of my private collection.

Mr. T. BEWICK *to* Mr. CHARNLEY.

"NEWCASTLE, 11 *May* 1819.

" Mr. CHARNLEY.

"DEAR SIR,—In consequence of your advertisement in the *Courant* and *Chronicle* of 'Select Fables,' &c., I have thought it proper to communicate to you the inclosed, which it is my intention to insert in the Newcastle, York, Manchester, and London Papers. It is exceedingly painful to me to obtrude myself upon the public, and most particularly so in a matter where you, whom I have always considered my Friend, and for whom I have ever had the greatest respect, will not now stand upon the vantage ground you have hitherto done. You must allow that if the Book is published in the form of my other works it will make a sorry figure, not only from the badness of the Engravings but from the want of Tail pieces. *If those are supplied by others,* with what truth can it be said that the embellishments are the works of myself and my late Brother, as advertised? But you will see by the inclosed that in that particular you have already committed yourself. As my name is now considered by the public of some little estimation in the woodcutting Business, it will be readily admitted, upon seeing the work now advertised, that if I had been concerned in no other, my reputation might as well have hung by the Cut of a halfpenny Ballad : consequently your success must depend upon my after acquired name. I believe I anticipate the sentiments of every enlightened mind when I declare that your undertaking can alone be supported by the cunning and trick practised by needy adventurers, or those regardless of character. Therefore, my dear Sir, reflect maturely before you go further. I believe you little to blame; I believe you have entered upon the undertaking without reflection. No man has a higher opinion of your honour than myself. I can assure you I have no animosity; I breathe nothing but goodwill toward you : if any other feeling, you must be sensible I would not have handed you the inclosed for your consideration. I have no motive otherwise than honestly to protect Property of which I am the guardian, and to prevent the illiberal and unhandsome use of my name, which must evidently tend to bring it into contempt, and thereby materially affect the after sale of my Works. Before I do anything I shall wait your answer. I have always acted with candour towards you, and wish the return.

" I am,

Dear Sir,

Yours sincerely,

"Mr. Emerson Charnley,   " THOMAS BEWICK.
    To the care of
      Messrs. Baldwin, Craddock & Joy,
        Booksellers,
(*Post Paid.*)   London."

"To the Printer, &c.

" Newcastle, *May* 11, 1819.

"Sir,—Observing an advertisement in your paper of 'Select Fables,' with cuts designed and engraved upon wood by Thomas and John Bewick previous to the year 1784, to be published by Mr. Charnley—as I lately published an Edition of the 'Fables of Æsop' and others in form corresponding to the work now advertised by Mr. Charnley, and as that Edition has been most favourably received by the public,[1] and Mr. C. was the principal purchaser, it may be believed that I am a party concerned in the present publication. I think it therefore necessary to declare that I have no interest in the undertaking ; nor were the cuts confined to the workmanship of my late Brother and myself. I recollect the work, with many particulars respecting it, and when I inform the public that 10s. was the price paid for each cut, and that price considered exorbitant by the publisher, they will readily agree with me that no great excellence could be expected in the execution. At the same time it is but justice to the late Mr. Saint, for whom the cuts were engraven, to state that it was intended by him only as a common School Book, and in that form it was introduced to the world ; and if Mr. Charnley had republished it in its original shape, and for its original purpose, I should not have troubled you with this letter. The book had no reputation, and has remained in an unproductive state for many years; but as this is the Age of Bookmaking, and every artifice used to decoy the public, and as my name is considered of some little value where there are woodcut embellishments, many unwarrantable liberties have been taken with it which I have never noticed, nor would I in the present instance, had it not been used unworthily in opposition to a work which has cost me the labour of years. When the 'History of Quadrupeds' was first undertaken it was only intended to supersede the 'Three Hundred Animals.' In the execution of that work I am sensible that nothing would please long, but just representations of general nature ; I was, therefore, more anxious about the accuracy in the drawings than the mechanical nicety of the cutting, as the printer, inexperienced at that time in woodcut printing, did not make good work from a finely executed Engraving. I therefore date the 'Quadrupeds' to be my commencement of Wood Engraving worthy of attention. Before that period I was engaged in the general work of a Country Engraver's Shop ; one hour employed on copper, another on wood, another on silver, another on brass, and another on steel—indeed, ready and willing to undertake any description of work. Under these circumstances Mr. Charnley may as well collect every sixpenny job which has been done in my premises during the last forty-five years, many of which possess more merit, and certainly produced more gain, than these famed ten shilling Cuts, executed partly by my late Brother, when he was an apprentice, and partly by *David Martin*, whom I

---

[1] Being nearly out of print, and I am under conditions with Mr. C. not to put it to press again for two years.

respected as a Man, but who was obliged from inability to seek some other line of work. As I have hitherto found in Mr. Charnley the same honourable Sentiments and Integrity of mind which distinguished my sincere and worthy friend, his late revered Father, it is extremely painful to me that he should descend from the proud eminence on which he stood, and lend himself to a disreputable concern—I say, lend himself, as I am persuaded the matter has not originated with him, nor has he reflected upon the impropriety of the undertaking. It may be said that the work is intended for the curious, merely that a comparison may be made between it and the improvement of my after works; it is certainly announced 'that the Impression is to be "limited."' What is limited? The new cant of the most experienced Book drudge of the Day! A Bait to hook the poor Bibliomanist! In this obtruding myself upon the Public to guard both my reputation and property, I am aware that many may consider me as interested and of a contracted disposition. Those who know me will readily acquit me of an excess of zeal in the pursuit of advantages personal to myself; to those who do not, I think proper to declare that I have ever considered it the Duty of a Parent to provide for his Family, and promote its Prosperity by every honourable means. Under such sentiments, I conceive my conduct would be highly censurable if I were indifferent to the defence of property of which I feel myself the natural Guardian.

"THOS. BEWICK."

Mr. Charnley to Mr. Bewick.

"London, Saturday Evening.

"Dear Sir,—I received your letters this day, but shall not at present attempt answering them at any length, but should wish you to suspend your opinion of my undertaking till I can have a personal interview, which, as I return to Newcastle in a week, will, I think, be to our mutual advantage. There is one part of your letter, however, I do not lose a moment in replying to, and that is the imputation of my wishing to injure your fame by the intended publication. I am too great an admirer of your genius even to take any step which may be construed into a wish to detract from your well-earned reputation; and my view of the work was to shew the world the promise of that talent afterwards so eminently displayed in your later publications, viz., the 'Quadrupeds,' 'Birds,' &c. Should the work, after it is printed, in the opinion of our mutual friends, be thought to detract from your reputation, I should be the first to propose its destruction. In the advertisement prefixed to the work every particular shall be faithfully given of the origin of the publication, &c. &c. All the cuts of the Fables shall be those Mr. Wilson sold me as yours and your Brother's cutting. The truth of Mr. Wilson's statement I cannot immediately ascertain, as Mr. Wilson is at present in Ireland; but if you prove to my satisfaction that you did not engrave any of the cuts of the Select and Gay's Fables, part of which latter are to be inserted in this work, I shall immediately make a bonfire of the cuts, and have no doubt Mr. Wilson will return me the money I paid him for them, as they were only valuable to me as being the production of your early labours; the only new cuts are a few tailpieces, of which I had not a sufficient number.

"I should be doing an injustice to you to allow Nesbit, Willis, or Nicholson's cuts to be confounded with yours. That I feel that I am not injuring your Fables, I am quite ready immediately to enter into a treaty to purchase the engravings of that work, and would thank you to inform me if you should like to dispose of them, and on what terms. This part of my letter respecting the purchase of your Æsop I should feel obliged by your answering me immediately; and as I shall not leave London before Sunday or Monday week, I can receive an answer from you in time. Thanking you for the candour of your communication,

"I am, Dear Sir, yours truly,

" E. CHARNLEY."

Mr. BEWICK's *Reply.*

"NEWCASTLE, 21 *May* 1819.

"DR. SIR,—It was with painful feelings that I set about writing to you on the subject of the old Fables, and I now can assure you that it was with pleasure I read your reply. I should suppose it scarcely possible that you and I can quarrel on this business; perhaps our mutual friends will easily set the matter to rest. One of the leading considerations with me is that it may be understood by the public that I have no interest in the work, nor any desire to feed the whimsies of the Bibliomanists. In the expectation of this reaching you before you leave London, I have lost no time in attending to what you have said, and to answer your letter as soon as I was able. To your question respecting my selling you the Fables, I have to answer that I will gladly do so as soon as I can inform myself of the real value of that work; and if, upon your consulting your London Friends, you can say what you will give, I shall not be long in saying whether I will accept your offer or not.

"I am, Dr. Sir, yours truly,

"THOMAS BEWICK.

"Mr. EMERSON CHARNLEY,
    At Messrs. BALDWIN, CRADDOCK & JOY's,
        BOOKSELLERS, PATER NOSTER ROW, LONDON."

Mr. Charnley's handsome and elegantly printed volume of
"Select Fables," with cuts designed and engraved by Thomas
and John Bewick, and others, previous to the year 1784, made
its appearance in 1820, in imperial, royal, and demy octavo, to
range with the "Birds," "Quadrupeds," and "Fables of Æsop."
The objections Mr. Bewick so strongly expressed against this
work at the beginning had given way on calmer reflection, and
the old friendship between this respected tradesman and his
distinguished correspondent remained firm as in days gone by.

The Perfidious Duck and the Stork—From *Tales for Youth*, 1794.

It is matter of regret that, even previous to the publication of the "Quadrupeds," down to a late period of his life,
Bewick had unfortunately been forced into several disputes,
many of which he could well afford to have let alone.   Nothing
further took place with respect to the purchase of the cuts and
copyright of "Æsop's Fables."   These, together with the cuts
for the "Birds," "Quadrupeds," and "Memoir," remained in
the family to the last.

As a proof that all irritation had ceased, Mr. Bewick
allowed Charnley the use of the wood-blocks of the Peacock,

Great Bittern, Lion, three beautiful tailpieces, and two cuts from "Æsop's Fables," to adorn a set of titles for his works in the various sizes. The printing of these titles was charmingly executed at the *Chronicle* Office by S. Hodgson. The date, however (1822), might have been omitted.

The next letter is addressed to a London author and publisher in answer to one Mr. Bewick had just received. The balance unpaid has reference to the cuts done for "Thornton's Family Herbal," published in 1810. The defaulter is well reminded that "the sum left standing is not less due for having stood so long unpaid." Let us hope that this appeal to the debtor's sense of what was just and right did not prove unsuccessful.

" Newcastle, 19 *June* 1820.

"Dr. Sir,—I received your letter requesting to know if I would undertake to execute some Cuts for you for School Books. This we will do with great pleasure ; but not knowing what time they may take doing, until we see your designs, we cannot promise you to do the first parcel you name in the time you limit us to ; we will, however, do them without delay. It is painful for me to name to you again the sum you left standing unpaid for the Botanical cuts, £4, 19s. 1d., since June 1809. It is not less due for having stood so long unpaid, and I hope you will remit me the amount. I am, at this time, struggling hard to make the 'History of British Birds' complete. I intend to make a Supplement of such Birds as I can get, for the purpose of furnishing my friends with them who have got the former Editions without the Figures. A New Edition of the 'Quadrupeds,' printed much better than any that has been done before, is now ready for Sale. I am at press again with the 'Birds,' which I also hope will surpass any of those which were done before.

"I am, Dr. Sir

(for Son and Self),

Your most obedt.

"THOMAS BEWICK."

T

OR profound erudition, painful and laborious inquiry into the records of distant ages, the name of the Reverend John Hodgson will ever rank among the most distinguished and learned antiquaries of this country. His invaluable " History of Northumberland " was the result of intense study and application. He delighted in exploring the mines of antiquity, and was thus engaged in collecting materials for his great work for the long period of twenty-two years, sustained by a rare spirit of devotion.

The Envious Dog and the Ermine—From *Tales for Youth*, 1794.

Mr. Bewick engraved views of Chipchase Castle, Warkworth Bridge, and Copeland Castle, to illustrate Hodgson's account of those places, and had friendly literary intercourse with the author. Mr. Hodgson was born in the year 1779, and died on the 12th of June 1845, loved and honoured by all who knew him. His piety resembled, in its gentleness, purity, and love of truth, that of George Herbert and Izaak Walton and White of Selborne.

In the course of business many schemes were resorted to

Engraved by E. Scriven, from a Miniature by Miss H. F. S. Mackreth.

THE REV.ᴰ JOHN HODGSON. M.R.S.L.

Vicar of Hartburn Northumberland.

&c. &c.

by unprincipled strangers and others to get work done without
any intention of paying for it. One winter night, Miss Bewick
said, a woman came for some job just finished, which she wished
to take away on credit. Being unknown, this was refused.
Suddenly she snatched up the parcel and ran out of the shop.
Bewick followed, and caught hold of her gown as she was
running down the stone steps leading into Dean Street. In
doing so, a part of her dress unfortunately became detached
and was left in his hand.

The Peacock and the Blackbird—From *Tales for Youth*, 1794.

It was in the heyday of his early manhood, in August 1776,
that Bewick first saw Edinburgh, and now in the evening
of his days he again longed to revisit that beautiful city. On
the 11th of August 1823 he went through by coach, and
whilst there received much kind attention from Professors
Jameson and Wallace, Mr. Nasmyth, the eminent landscape-
painter, and the leading engravers of the day, including
William Nicholson, who some years before had migrated from
Newcastle. Before leaving, after a stay of twelve days, he
called upon Messrs. Ballantyne & Robertson, the well-known

lithographic printers. Whilst at their office, he was pressed
by those gentlemen to make a sketch on stone, which was
done on the following morning before breakfast. A few impressions were struck off on the same day, and the print is
now known to collectors as the "Cadger's Trot." This slight
sketch represents a man on horseback riding in the midst of
a drifting storm of rain and sleet. This is Bewick's only
attempt at lithography. Not more than thirty copies were
printed on white and tinted paper, when the design was rubbed

Instance of Filial Duty—From *The Hive*, 1806.

off the stone; they are consequently of considerable rarity.
Mr. Bewick left Edinburgh on the 23d of August 1823; "and
I think," he remarks, "I shall see Scotland no more." On
his return to Newcastle, he addressed himself to the task of
pushing through the press the eighth and last edition of the
"Quadrupeds," consisting of the same number of cuts as in
the three previous editions. This was published in 1824.

On the title of an edition of the "Quadrupeds," printed in
4to, without letterpress, in the same year, there is an interesting
vignette, representing a man riding on horseback in the midst

of a storm of wind and rain. The same cut occurs at p. 5,
vol. i., of the last edition of the "Birds," 1847. In the two instances of its use, however, it presents a considerable difference
—the rain appears *black* in the "Quadrupeds" and *white* in
the "Birds." That the rain might be dark, as in Nature, it
was requisite that a second block should be provided: this
was accordingly done. The lines pencilled on it were left
untouched by the graver, and the intervening spaces carefully
cut away, this process being the reverse of the practice usually

CELADON and AMELIA—From *The Hive*, 1806.

followed. When this second cut, consisting of fine diagonal
lines only, representing rain, was printed over or above the
first, on which the entire subject was engraved, the desired
effect was produced. Mr. E. Walker, in whose office the
printing was done, was staying at Croft at the time. The first
impressions or printing were taken off on a Saturday afternoon,
and as the *modus operandi* was intended to be kept a profound
secret, Mr. Bewick agreed with his pressman, Thomas Kay,
that the second printing should take place on the following day.
On Sunday morning they went together to Mr. Walker's house

in Pilgrim Street, and, after much persuasion, succeeded in obtaining the key of the office from the servant girl. It being Sunday, they entered through the rear of the premises in the Manors. Two blocks were cut for the second printing. The first of them did not answer the purpose intended; the second was a complete success. Three "points" were used by Kay to ensure accuracy, that the second printing might fall immediately over the first. When these "points" were noticed by the workmen on the following morning, they were much puzzled, and laughed at Kay for using "points" in printing such a simple job as a title. Bewick and his pressman were equally delighted with the success of the experiment, the former exclaiming, "Would that I had been but twenty years younger!"

On the work being finished, every scrap of paper on the floor used in proving the cut was destroyed by Bewick. The titles were all packed up, and taken by Kay to Bewick's shop. When Mr. Walker returned home, he soon learned the unauthorised use that had been made of his office in his absence, and great was his displeasure at such a liberty. He was still further irritated, both against Bewick and his own workman, for refusing to tell him the nature of the job, or even to show him one of the titles. He could not understand how one block could be printed above another. Kay said that Bewick called it "cross-hatching," and that was all he knew about it. This Sunday job, however, together with Kay's refusal to inform his employer how he manufactured a composition which he had invented for making printers' balls, at last cost him his situation. For this information, which the late Mr. Hugo highly valued, he was indebted to me. My informant was Kay himself.

EWICK'S views with regard to the best means to be adopted for the regulation of our salmon fisheries are worthy of attention. The original of the following letter is in the collection of J. W. Pease, Esq., Pendower :—

"NEWCASTLE, *April* 26, 1824.

"Mr. HOPPER.

"SIR,—I have met with few things in passing through life that have given me more pleasure than the information you have this morning imparted to me respecting Mr. Brandling's intention of laying before Parliament the various causes which, taken together, throw obstructions in the way of the Salmon tribe breeding in the Tyne in the same overflowing numbers as of old, and in putting together a few remarks in as short a way as time permits, to state my opinion as to the reasons for such an immense falling off. When a boy, from about the year 1760 to 1767, I was frequently sent by my parents to the fishermen at Eltringham Ford to purchase a salmon, and was always desired not to pay 2d. a pound, and I commonly paid only a 1d. and sometimes 1½d. Before, or perhaps about this time, I have been told that an article had always been inserted in every indenture of apprenticeship in Newcastle, that the apprentices were not to be forced to *eat salmon above twice a-week*, and the same bargain was made with common servants. I hope the time will shortly come when the same overflowing bounty of Providence will again enrich my beloved Tyne. Whatever obstructions are thrown in the way to prevent the salmon from ascending as far up the river and rivulets as they can reach, for the purpose of spawning, is the first and great cause of the breed being thinned ; therefore every weir and every dam ought to be removed. The fishermen's weirs are bad, but those of Bywell dam are the worst; they both have their rise in a greedy and selfish disposition, to prevent other fisheries from catching or partaking in a due share of the fish. You will be able, as well as I can, to point out to Mr. Brandling the evils arising from the use of nets of various kinds, which obstruct the fish from ascending the river, as well as those which arrest the fry in their way to the sea. Should the business of the wears and dams be settled, then River Conservators should be appointed to guard the spawning fish (usually called kipper fish) from being killed (which they are) in this sickly state. These Conservators ought also to be empowered totally to prevent *wicked destruction,* occasioned by putting lime into rivulets, as they kill millions of spawn, as well as every living creature in the water within its extended reach. Fishermen may grudge to see the angler fill his creel with a few scores of the fry, which would perhaps return to them as salmon in a short time; but when it is considered that a pair of salmon will breed more of this fry than all the fair anglers can catch from the head to the foot of the river in a season, I think it is cruel to debar such from enjoying the diversion. Fish are not like game which are fed by the farmer. Their food costs nobody anything, and ought only to be preserved so far as may be for the public good; therefore I have always felt disgusted at what is called preserved rivers. In these, because they run through the land of some freeholder, the fish is usually claimed as his own. The disposition which dictated claims of this kind is the same which would, if it could, restrict the use of the sun and rain. The angler is debarred the most delightful of all recreations, which ought to be the birthright particularly of the sedentary and studious. It is the healthiest and comparatively the most innocent of all diversions; it unbends the mind, and enables such as the pale artist to return to his avocation or studies with renovated energy, to labour for his own and the public good. I ought also to name to you the uncommon destruction of the fry, which frequently happens when they are hastening to the sea, by the stopping a mill race with thorns and then letting the water off some other way, by which it has been known that a cart load of fry have been taken at once. I named to you the kind of weirs which ought to be made out of the tide-mark, to increase the depth of every river in the middle, by which a more equal chance would be given to all fishermen to come in for their due share, and at much less trouble and expense than they have hitherto been put to, and would, besides, open a free passage for the fish to where they instinctively ascend to the proper spawning ground.

"I am, yours, &c.,

"THOS. BEWICK."

N June 1825 it was proposed by a few friends to have a marble bust of Mr. Bewick executed by an eminent sculptor, and placed in the new Library of the Newcastle Literary and Philosophical Society.

Mr. Armorer Donkin, Bewick's solicitor, took an active part in forwarding this object, and invited the co-operation of Mr. John Trotter Brockett, between whom and Mr. Bewick the sharp passage-at-arms took place, already noticed. That gentleman, forgetful of past differences, at once cordially responded, and I have much pleasure in recording the steps taken to accomplish the resolution come to. The original letters are in my collection.

Mr. A. DONKIN *to* Mr. BROCKETT.

"NEWCASTLE, *4th June* 1825.

"DEAR BROCKETT,

"It is proposed that a few friends of our distinguished Towns-man, T. Bewick, shall meet at Fletcher's, the Turk's Head Inn, on Monday Evening, the 6th inst., at 8 o'clock, for the purpose of organising a Subscription for a Bust of Bewick, to be placed in the Literary and Philosophical Society, or in some other Public Situation. I took the liberty of mentioning to the parties among whom the idea originated that I thought you would be a zealous pro-moter of the object in view, and I had no doubt would be happy to attend the meeting, at which, I presume, a committee will be formed to carry the design into effect. It has consequently fallen to my Lot to solicit your attendance. May I rely upon you?

"Yours sincerely,

"ARMORER DONKIN.

"J. T. BROCKETT, Esq."

Mr. BROCKETT'S *Reply.*

"SANDHILL, *4th June* 1825.

"DEAR DONKIN,

"You may rely on my attending the Meeting to which you invite me, and if any exertions of mine can tend to promote the Object you have in view, I shall feel extremely happy. No man can appreciate more forcibly

U

than I do the uncommon Genius and extraordinary Talents of the Individual of whom you are desirous of having so deserved and so imperishable a Memorial.

"Believe me, Dear Donkin,
  Very sincerely yours,
    "JOHN TROTTER BROCKETT."

                                              "*July* 30, 1825.

"The Committee for managing the Subscription for Mr. Bewick's Bust are requested to meet at the Turk's Head on Monday Evening, at 8 o'clock.

              "WILLIAM TURNER, *Secretary.*

"J. T. BROCKETT, Esq.,
    ALBION STREET."

It was now determined to issue a circular, of which the following is a copy, having the names of about seventy gentlemen attached, who had become subscribers.

"BUST OF MR. BEWICK.

"A few Friends, admiring the Talents and esteeming the Character of Mr. THOMAS BEWICK, whose various *unique* Works reflect so much Honour on himself, and on the town of Newcastle-upon-Tyne, have conceived that it would be an appropriate Tribute to his Merit to have a Bust in Marble, executed by an eminent Sculptor, placed in the New Building for the Literary and Philosophical Society. For this Purpose a Committee has been formed, and E. H. Baily, Esq., R.A., has been engaged, and is expected shortly to visit Newcastle, to prepare a Model for the Purpose.

"In Order to give Mr. Bewick's numerous Friends an Opportunity of gratifying their Feelings, the Subscription of each Individual is limited to ONE GUINEA."

The following is from an elegant article by the late Thomas Doubleday, Esq., in the *British Quarterly Review* :—

"To expect the artist to go to London to sit to any sculptor there was a somewhat hopeless expectation, and was therefore not entertained; but Mr. Baily was brought down in order to make the model from which the bust was to be executed. So far all went smoothly; but when it came to be debated in what 'costume' he should be taken, a sore controversy arose. The sculptor, as is usual, insisted upon covering the engraver's shoulders with some kind of drapery which, for want of a better word, we shall call *Romanesque.* Whether it was precisely a 'toga' or not we cannot say; but it was, no doubt, something classical, in so far as it was not English! Against this, however, Bewick at once rebelled. He was resolved, if he must appear on earth after his death, to do so after the fashion of Hamlet's father,

'In his habit—as he lived,'

and from this resolution he would not budge. The 'toga' was accordingly given up, and the artist was taken in his coat and waistcoat, not forgetting his neckcloth and ruffled shirt; nor can we say that the likeness was thereby injured, whatever may be the case with the classicality."

The plaster cast was taken by Mr. Baily in the drawing-room at West Street, Bewick reclining on a couch with small pieces of quill in his nostrils, as usual, to enable him to breathe. Miss Bewick remarked, in giving this information, that she did not at all like to see the operation.

The distinguished sculptor employed succeeded in rendering an admirable likeness of the artist, to the great satisfaction of the committee, as well as that of Mr. Bewick and his family. These gentlemen were not left without a valuable souvenir of the work, as will appear from the following letter :—

THOS. CRAWHALL, Esq., *to* Mr. BROCKETT.

"NEWCASTLE, 12*th April* 1826.

"DEAR SIR,—Mr. Baily having forwarded to my care a Cast from the Bust of Mr. Bewick for each Gentleman of that Committee without annexing Names to them, and some being slightly injured, I therefore request the favour of your attendance at my house on Friday Evening next, at 8 o'clock, to determine by ballot their distribution.

"I remain, Dear Sir,
Yours truly,
"THOS. CRAWHALL.

"J. T. BROCKETT, Esq."

The solid casts alluded to were very fine, and have now become scarce. I am happy in possessing one of the best, as perfect as the day it left Mr. Baily's hands.

The Rev. William Turner, who kindly acted as secretary to the committee, was a dissenting minister, well known in Newcastle for his large benevolence and scientific attainments. These were ever directed to the promotion of the knowledge of God in Nature to both old and young. His amiable disposition, coupled with public usefulness wherever good might be done, caused him to be highly valued, irrespective of creed or politics.

As early as 1784 he succeeded in establishing two Sunday schools, and was one of the first projectors of the Literary and Philosophical Society, to which, in 1802, he was appointed Lecturer on Natural and Experimental Philosophy.

There is a Memoir of Bewick by him, prefixed to the sixth volume of Jardine's "Naturalist's Library." Though a resident in Newcastle from about 1782, and an intimate friend of our artist, it is surprising how little he had to communicate of interest on the subject. Mr. Turner left Newcastle for Manchester in 1847, at the advanced age of 81, where he died, April 24, 1856, aged 97.

The Rev.ᵈ William Turner

Secretary to the Lit: & Phil: Society of Newcastle.

&c. &c. &c.

Engraved by William Collard from an Original Picture by A. Morton.

N 1826 the sixth edition of the "Birds," the last
published in the lifetime of the artist, was given
to the world. This, bearing the impress of the
author's own and last hand, is much and deservedly esteemed.   In the Preface, dated Newcastle, July 1826, the writer reviews the past, and looks forward
to the future, in a strain so well worthy of regard, that a few
extracts will not be deemed out of place.   Mr. Bewick observes—

"My writings were intended chiefly for youth; and the more readily to
allure their pliable, though discursive, attention to the Great Truths of Creation,
I illustrated them by figures delineated with all the fidelity and animation I
was able to impart to mere woodcuts without colour; and as instruction is of
little avail without constant cheerfulness and occasional amusement, I inter-
spersed the more serious studies with *Tale*-pieces of gaiety and humour; yet
even in these seldom without an endeavour to illustrate some truth or point
some moral. . . . Many have imagined, and some few have publicly asserted,
that having, with scanty literary education, been brought up an engraver, the
whole of my department has been confined to the figures and embellishments,
and that I have had very little, or indeed no share in the composition of the
history or observations. But my education was not so scanty as many imagine;
I was sent early to a good school, and regularly kept there, and from the freshest
vernal years of my infancy was enraptured with nature." . . .

He thus concludes—

"The conscious integrity of my intention imparts a reasonable expectancy
of a continuation of the happiness I have hitherto enjoyed in this life, and
a cheerful hope of the eternal existence hereafter; and with these feelings I
offer, kindly and respectfully, to liberal and enlightened minds, the last edition
of this work which I may, probably, at my advanced age, live to republish;
though, if it please Heaven to allow me the blessings of health and sight, I
shall continue to throw off my inoffensive fancies, wherein I perceive no
deficiency of imagination, and apply my graphic labours, whereof I seldom
feel wearied; it being my firm resolution not to claim the privileges of senility,
or suffer inert idleness to encroach on reasonable repose."

As I have found this most interesting Preface wanting in
many copies of this edition, I have much pleasure in bringing

these last aspirations of the venerable artist before the notice of my readers.

There seems to have been some hesitation about its insertion, for whilst Mr. Bewick and his daughters were at Buxton in 1826 he addressed a note on the 6th of June in that year to Mr. Edward Walker, his printer, in which he says: "I trust you will be so good, as soon as you can, to send me a proof of the Preface to this *edition* as on the other side, without any alterations, as I am determined to have it so."

In a letter to W. C. Trevelyan, Esq., dated 4th November 1826, he alludes to his "late very severe illness" and "aversion to stir from home." He complains of being baffled in cutting a numerous set of vignettes by reason of the weakness of his eyes. These were no doubt the tailpieces for the intended "History of Fishes." Age and infirmity were fast stealing round the old man, already enfeebled with pain and sickness, so that, whilst engaged on the cut of the Alpine Vulture,[1] we hear him lament, "I cannot get so fast forward as *I used to do*."

---

[1] *Vide* Bewick Correspondence, communicated to the *Transactions of the Natural History Society of Northumberland*, &c. (vol. vii.), by Sir Walter Trevelyan, Bart.

N the 12th of January 1876 the writer purchased of his late honoured friends, the Misses Bewick, their father's last and largest woodcut, "Waiting for Death." The accompanying illustration is printed from the original wood-block. No reproduction can possibly do justice to or adequately represent the merits of this extraordinary work. It was an attempt to produce by means of two or more woodcuts, printed over each other, the

admirable effects obtained by William Woollett in his excellent copperplates. There is a marked resemblance between the foliage of both those artists—the same breadth and freedom of style is common to each. Unhappily for the Arts, the engraving was left unfinished by the rather sudden death of Mr. Bewick. Had he lived to finish what had been so successfully begun, there can be no doubt that this inimitable work would have added much to his great fame, as it has certainly shown the kindness of his heart in thus endeavouring by pen and pencil to instil a more humane and compassionate feeling towards the horse. The history of the animal is well

told in the author's own words, written so far back as 1785.[1]
The cut measures 12 inches by 9 inches, and is formed of four
blocks closely joined together, and mounted on two transverse
mahogany panels, to prevent warping. A second block, exactly
the same size, had been prepared : on it an impression of the
cut was transferred, but not a line engraved.   There was also a
third block.   This was provided should further tints and more
colour be deemed necessary to perfect the effect.   It has been
said that the head of the horse is too large, but I have been
assured by an eminent anatomist that this results from the fact
that the head of the animal is less emaciated in proportion to
the body, by reason of its bony structure, and not a consequence
of bad drawing.   The cut was proved at Walker's office, in the
presence of Mr. Bewick, on the Saturday before he died.

Four proofs were taken, and distributed among the members
of his family.   In 1832 a small impression of "Waiting for
Death" was printed for Mr. R. E. Bewick by Messrs. Vizetelly
and Branston, accompanied by a sheet containing the descriptive letterpress.

---

[1] The original sketch, in pencil, is dated 30th November 1785.

IXTY-TWO years had now rolled away since, as a young lad fresh from the country, somewhat rude in manner and unpolished in speech, but of an intrepid heart, and full of life and hope, Bewick travelled towards Newcastle along with his father and the village parson.

The final return journey was near at hand. The sprightly object of their care and solicitude was now an old and broken-down man. His parents, a brother and a sister whom he tenderly loved, with the aged parish priest, had long since departed to their eternal rest, and he looks forward to the time when his ashes shall mingle with theirs in the lone churchyard at Ovingham.

It is singular that Bewick's first-known sketch, and the last time he took pencil in hand, was to portray the same object—an old horse " Waiting for Death."

I can state on the authority of Miss Bewick that the White-throated Nightingale was the last bird drawn and engraved by her father, and that the last vignette he ever cut on wood is that placed at the conclusion of the Memoir—viz., the Funeral Procession from Cherryburn. In the hedge may be observed a bright shining cross, to indicate the Christian's hope in life and death. This is placed in advance of the mournful spectacle.

The governing passion continued with him to the end, for whilst slumbering during his brief illness, he would in imagination revisit the green fields so well known to his boyhood, and those burnsides where, with schoolfellows gay and light-hearted as himself, he was wont to stroll through the long summer day. On being asked, when awake, about what he had been thinking,

X

he replied, with a faint smile, that he had been devising subjects for some new tailpieces.

That wonderful power so long exercised for the delight and instruction of mankind was then fast ebbing away. Happily free from all mental or physical suffering, his spirit passed into the hands of his Creator.

Thomas Bewick departed this life on the morning of Saturday, 8th November 1828, aged 75, and was interred on Thursday, 13th November, at Ovingham.

"He mused on Nature with a poet's eye."

Mr. Robert Bewick wrote to his father's old friend, William Bulmer, informing him of his death, and Mr. Bulmer acknowledges the sad intelligence by a letter, dated 17th November 1828, in which he feelingly condoles with him for the loss the family had sustained. " He little thought, when he parted with the friend of his youth only a few months back, that it was for the last time.   They were companions in boyhood, and past memories crowded on his mind.   He had known his father upwards of fifty years, and they had passed many happy and pleasant days together. . . . Mr. Bewick had spent a laborious life;" and he conjures Robert to follow in the footsteps of his father, in truthfulness, patient industry, and rectitude; above all, not to let the art of wood-engraving perish, which had slept from the time of Albert Durer until recovered by his father.

WAITING FOR DEATH.

In the morning of his days he was handsome—sleek as a raven, sprightly and spirited, and was then much caressed and happy.   When he grew to perfection, in his performances—even on the turf, and afterwards in the chase and in the field—he was equalled by few of his kind.   At one time of his life he saved that of his master, whom he bore in safety across the rapid flood; but having, in climbing the opposite rocky shore, received a blemish, it was thought *prudent* to dispose of him, after which he fell into the hands of different masters; but from none of them did he ever eat the bread of idleness, and as he grew in years his cup of misery was still augmented with bitterness.

It was once his hard lot to fall into the hands of *Skinflint*, a horse-keeper— an authorised wholesale and retail dealer in cruelty—who employed him alternately, but closely, as a hack, both in the chaise and for the saddle; for when the traces and trappings used in the former had peeled the skin from off his breast, shoulders, and sides, he was then, as his back was whole, thought fit for the latter; indeed, his exertions in this *service of unfeeling avarice* and *folly* were great beyond belief.   He was always, late and early, made ready for action—he was never allowed to rest.   Even on the Sabbath day, because he could trot well, had a good bottom, and was the best hack in town, and it being a day of pleasure and pastime, he was much sought after by beings *in appearance* something like gentlemen, in whose hands his sufferings were greater than his nature could bear.

Has not the compassionate eye beheld him whipped, spurred, and galloped beyond his strength in order to accomplish double the length of the journey that he was engaged to perform, till, by the inward grief expressed in his countenance, he seemed to plead for mercy, one would have thought, most powerfully?   But alas! in vain.   In the whole load which he bore, as was often the case, not an ounce of humanity could be found ; and, his rider being determined to have pennyworths for his money, the ribs of this silent slave, where not a hair had for long been suffered to grow, were still ripped up. He was pushed forward through a stony rivulet, then on hard road against the hill, and having lost a shoe, split his hoof, and being quite spent with hunger and fatigue, he fell, broke his nose and his knees, and was unable to proceed ; and becoming greased, spavined, ringboned, blind of an eye, and the skin by repeated friction being worn off all the large prominences of his body, he was judged to be only fit for the dogs. However, one shilling and sixpence beyond the dog-horse price saved his life, and he became the property of a poor dealer and horse doctor.

It is amazing to think upon the vicissitudes of his life. He had often been burnished up, his teeth defaced by art, peppered under his tail, had been the property of a general, a gentleman, a farmer, a miller, a butcher, a higgler, and a maker of brooms. A hard winter coming on, a want of money and a want of meat obliged his poor owner to turn him out to shift for himself. His former fame and great value are now to him not worth a handful of oats. But his days and nights of misery are now drawing to an end ; so that, after having faithfully dedicated the whole of his powers and his time to the service of unfeeling man, he is at last turned out, unsheltered and unprotected, to starve of hunger and of cold.

THOMAS BEWICK.

THE author has been favoured with the following lines from the pen of the Rev. William Kingsley, Rector of South Kilvington, Thirsk, an experienced art critic and admirer of Bewick.

"This woodcut, 'Waiting for Death,' is the last work of Bewick, and was intended to be printed, not as it is now presented, but with additional lines printed over what is here given. The object he had in view was to give greater fulness of tint and a better rendering of effects depending upon crossed lines than could be given by the ordinary method of wood-engraving.

"A few words to explain the process of wood-engraving will make this clear. If a wood-block is inked, and paper laid upon it and pressed down, the result is of course a black impression of the block ; but if lines are cut upon the block, and the printing process repeated, these lines will appear white on a black ground. Hence it is necessary, in wood-engraving, to cut away all the surface of the block excepting where the black lines are to appear in the impression. This is the very reverse of what is done in engraving a copper or steel plate, for the lines cut in such plates hold the ink and print dark. Now it will be seen that the lines which are very easy to draw with a pen are very difficult to cut in a wood-block, as all the whites have to be picked out; but in a copperplate such lines are easy, as they are at once cut with the tool. It will also be seen that it is not possible to cut such lines on a wood-block and secure the freedom of the original drawing, and in all cases of refined expression crossed dark lines cannot be used in a woodcut.

"To obtain dark tints, either with a pen or copperplate, crossed lines are most effective, and what is called 'crossed hatching' is constantly used; but such work is quite wrong in woodcutting, though it is constantly seen in modern woodcuts and in very old ones. Bewick in his Autobiography refers to this in the large woodcuts by Albert Durer, and expresses a doubt of their being printed from a single block. In all probability Durer made the drawings on the blocks, and left them to be cut by the very clever school of engravers then existing at Nuremberg. In these cuts a large amount of cross-hatching occurs in all parts, and most commonly on walls in shade and such places, where any method of obtaining the right degree of shade would have done just as well. These cuts by Albert Durer are the grandest examples of the art the world has yet seen, but the grandeur depends on the power of the draughtsman, and not on that of the engraver: indeed it may be doubted whether there is one single cut in which there are not serious failures of engraving, arising from the difficulty of keeping the freedom of line in the original drawing. These Durer cuts are large and the lines thick, but the delicacy of a line does not consist in its thinness, but in the truth of its edge; and in power of drawing these cuts are unrivalled.

"Then came a time when prettiness and fine cutting were more admired than powerful drawing, and the art of wood-cutting sank into a clever imitation of copperplate engraving, and thence most rapidly into the vilest rudeness and coarseness.

"It was from this state that Bewick raised it; and if any one will compare any of the woodcuts of the last century with Bewick's 'Birds,' he will see at once the enormous step Bewick had taken in the art, and also see that to him is due the wonderful amount of good wood-cutting to be found in almost any cheap illustrated work of the present day. It would take too much space to show that his work is still far superior to all that followed it, but as bearing upon this plate of 'Waiting for Death' it is necessary to point out in what respect Bewick's work excels. It mainly consists in this—he was both artist and engraver, and so had learned how to make the most use of the special facilities wood-engraving afforded in rendering the picture in his mind. He in fact *drew* at once with his graver. He maintained that all tints could be got without crossing his lines, and his Birds are a proof of the correctness of his assertion. It may be questioned whether the difficulty of drawing without crossing lines is not so great as to be beyond the power of ordinary men; at any rate it was so difficult that he tried to avoid the difficulty by using more than one block, printing first from one and then on the impression from another block. The vignette on the title-page to the 'Quadrupeds,' 4to, 1824, is an example. The subject is a man riding over a moor in a storm: the rain is printed from a second block, and crosses all sorts of lines without losing any freedom. There were, of course, difficulties in the process, but they are not so great as may be supposed. Great care is needed in 'keeping the register' in printing, but that is perhaps the greatest difficulty. However, the success of the small cut was sufficient to prove to Bewick that he could produce a large cut such as the world had not seen, and this 'Waiting for Death' was from the first block—the rain, &c., having to be printed on the impression from other blocks, which he had not begun. His death, however, just after the first impression had been taken, deprived the world of the realisation of his design. Much as we may regret the unfinished state of the engraving, it ought to be a satisfaction to all who look at it to remember that the artist died in harness; and, unlike the poor horse, 'his eye was not dim, nor his natural force abated.'"

WHILST at work Mr. Bewick invariably wore a brown silk cap. When a child he unfortunately got scalded, and in consequence of this accident became bald on the crown of his head ever after. In the days of his early manhood, agreeable to the fashion of the time, he wore a wig, and of course used hair powder; when this commodity was not to be had, flour formed a ready substitute. Bewick seldom smiled; but once was he known to dance, and that was at his own house with a young lady, the daughter of a very intimate friend—Miss Jane Ann C—w—ll. Though acquainted with many, especially local songs, on one occasion

only was he ever heard to sing, and that was Allan Ramsay's
beautiful ballad of the

WAUKING O' THE FAULD.

" My Peggy is a young thing,
　　Just enter'd in her teens,
Fair as the day, and sweet as May,
Fair as the day, and always gay.
　　My Peggy is a young thing,
　　And I'm nae very auld,
　　Yet weel I like to meet her at
　　The wauking o' the fauld.

" My Peggy speaks sae sweetly,
　　Whene'er we meet alane,
I wish nae mair to lay my care,
I wish nae mair o' a' that's rare.
　　My Peggy speaks sae sweetly,
　　To a' the lave I'm cauld ;
　　But she gars a' my spirits glow
　　At wauking o' the fauld.

" My Peggy smiles sae kindly,
　　Whene'er I whisper love,
That I look down on a' the town,
That I look down upon a crown.
　　My Peggy smiles sae kindly,
　　It makes me blythe and bauld,
　　And naething gi'es me sic delyte
　　As wauking o' the fauld.

" My Peggy sings sae saftly,
　　When on my pipe I play,
By a' the rest, it is confest,
By a' the rest that she sings best.
　　My Peggy sings sae saftly,
　　And in her sangs are tauld,
　　Wi' innocence, the wale o' sense,
　　At wauking o' the fauld."

In both dance and song he acquitted himself remarkably
well, having a good ear for music ; but he could not play on any

instrument, and in this he differed much from his younger brother
John. Ramsay's charming pastoral, " The Gentle Shepherd,"
was a great favourite with Mrs. Bewick, who could repeat
almost the whole poem from memory. It was once performed
by a Scotch regiment quartered in Newcastle, at the " Turk's
Head Long Room" in the Bigg Market, a place of entertain-
ment well known to the inhabitants sixty years ago, and gave
great satisfaction.

Bewick and his family were seldom seen at the theatre, or

indeed at any other place of amusement. During the Race
Week, on Thursday, when the Gold Cup was run for, he used
to take his children to the Moor for an afternoon's recreation,
taking care, however, to avoid the pressure of the crowd. In
the interval between each race little Robert and his sisters
amused themselves by making caps and whips of the rashers
or rushes which grew around. On these occasions *paterfamilias*
always provided an ample supply of nuts to eat as they sat on
the green sward.

At that time the Town Moor was in a comparatively wild

state. The population being small, the attendance at this great annual festival, though more select, fell short of that mighty multitude brought together from all parts of the country by rail in late years. Then the aristocracy and patrons of the Turf usually came into town on the Friday or Saturday before the races, which began on the following Monday, and continued five days. Pilgrim Street, the principal thoroughfare, was during their continuance gay and lively with the many carriages and rich equipages of the nobility and gentry, as they streamed

Returning Good for Evil—From *The Looking Glass for the Mind,* 1792.

northward through its grey and aged gate to enjoy the sports beyond—the Queen's Head, the principal inn, being thronged with company.

Newcastle Races, familiarly known as household words, are now a thing of the past. That brilliant assemblage of beauty and fashion which in the days of our grandfathers graced the grand stand, the dress-circle at the theatre, or the ball at the Assembly Rooms, will never be seen again on a like occasion.

v

STEPHEN KEMBLE,[1] whilst manager of the Theatre Royal, at the beginning of the present century, by reason of his obesity did not like to venture out at night in the dimly-lighted streets during the winter months, when not required at the theatre. He resided in a large house nearly opposite the White Cross, on the east side of Newgate Street. Here in winter time Mr.

Bewick and he spent many a pleasant evening. The elegant and finished conversation of the accomplished actor would contrast with the shrewd remarks and strong provincialism of the talented artist. Mr. Kemble often spoke of the honour and

---

[1] Portrait of Stephen George Kemble in the character of Sir John Falstaff. Engraved for the Admission Ticket to the Boxes of the Newcastle Theatre on the occasion of Mr. Kemble's Benefit. Mr. Kemble, who was the only "Falstaff" *without stuffing*, died June 6, 1822. When this ticket was engraved he was the manager of the Theatre Royal, Newcastle, Glasgow, and Edinburgh.

high principle which actuated so many of the performers, their self-denial rather than run in debt, and of the kindness and generosity they displayed to fellow actors when in trouble or distress.

The great wood-engraver was simple in all his habits, and inexpensive in his indulgences. Frugality approaching to parsimony prevailed in his household arrangements. Had it been otherwise, Mr. Bewick would have had but little to leave behind for his family. Miss Jane assured me that it was not until after the publication of Æsop's Fables, 1818–23, that they could feel assured of even a moderate competence. This uncertainty would at times weigh heavily on the mind of the father of four children, three being daughters. At page 116 of the Memoir Mr. Bewick speaks of his "little happy cot at the Forth," where his eldest sister died in 1785. It was here he first commenced housekeeping, some years before his  marriage, in 1786, having bought part of the furniture belonging to the previous tenant, Dr. Hutton, the eminent mathematician, for whose "Treatise on Mensuration" he had cut the diagrams in 1770. Both were self-taught men, and had achieved celebrity at a time when Free Libraries and Mechanics' Institutes were equally unknown. It was a fine low old-fashioned house, pleasantly situate in what was called Circus Lane, having a garden extending backward almost to the old Town Wall, and embracing a view of the semicircular bastions of West Spital Tower and Gunnerton Tower. It was well stocked with fruit trees and flowers, especially roses, in the culture of which Bewick and his accomplished family took great pleasure, though he, through a long life, never allowed recreation to interfere

with business. West Spital Tower had been transformed into
a genteel residence, where Bewick's partner, Ralph Beilby, and
his family dwelt, amid a delightful orchard, not far from where
the Central Railway Station now stands.   A most pleasing
vignette at page 109 of the first edition of the "Water Birds,"
1804, represents one of those old towers as seen from Bewick's
windows, which in summer time were thickly wreathed with the

fragrant jasmine.   A venturesome youth, with a companion—
probably scholars from the neighbouring Grammar School—is
depicted in the act of climbing its venerable wall in search of
birds' nests, thereby disturbing a colony of jackdaws in their
secluded retreat.   The Norman keep of the Old Castle is seen
in the distance.

In this garden, on a Sunday afternoon, he used to enjoy
himself in quiet meditation, and the grateful feelings of his

heart found expression in the lines of his favourite poet, Thomson :—

> " Soft roll your incense, herbs, and fruits, and flowers !
> In mingled clouds to Him, whose sun exalts,
> Whose breath perfumes you, and whose pencil paints."

Had I not known Mr. Bewick's partiality for the author of "The Seasons," I should certainly have thought Goldsmith would have held the first place in his estimation, the sentiments of the "Deserted Village" being congenial with his own cherished convictions.

CAROLINE : A Lesson to Cure Vanity—From *The Looking Glass for the Mind*, 1792.

This humble abode, secluded as it was, became in time the joy of his heart. In it his children were born, and here he first felt the endearments of domestic life. It consisted of only five rooms, and the rental was but £8 per annum. The family had a pew in St. John's Church hard by, and nothing gave Mrs. Bewick more pleasure than to see her son and daughters, neatly dressed, attending their Parish Church, where they had been baptized.

The congregation comprised the *élite* of Westgate Street and Charlotte Square, then both very aristocratic, together with the Forth, Elswick, and Benwell.

The Misses Bewick have often described to me the dress of the ladies, and the large handsome fans they used in church in summer time. When service was over the quality repaired to the Forth, to inhale the fresh country air under the shade of two rows of lime trees.

HE summer walking attire of the fair sex appears to have rivalled in our good town the splendour of Ranelagh, Kensington Gardens, or St. James's Park. These were mostly of white, light blue, or other coloured muslins, worn very low in the neck. The gipsy chip, straw, or Leghorn bonnets were of various

From *Harrison's Picture Book.*

hues; some pink, nankeen, pea-green, or lilac, tied under the chin, and ornamented with flowers in front.

The Rosina hat was a general favourite, trimmed with a wreath of flowers; whilst low shoes, red, pink, or yellow, with silk stockings, completed the costume.

The high and costly plumes of ostrich and bird of paradise feathers I do not attempt to describe.

A lady named Hunter, who lived in Charlotte Square, and a Mrs. Lloyd, whose husband was in the Newcastle Fire Office, were by general consent accounted to dress in the best taste. Mr. Lloyd was at one time most friendly with Bewick, but after the publication of the "Land Birds" became indignant at the character of some of the tailpieces, and threatened a prosecution.

Conspicuous amongst the many whose habit it was to enjoy a walk in the Forth in the cool of the day was Lieutenant

Rosina ; or, Froward Girl Reformed—From *The Looking Glass for the Mind*, 1792.

Hamilton, of the King's Land Forces.[1]   This gentleman had received a wound in the side (not in the groin, like my Uncle Toby), and as the bullet could not be extracted, the result was a stiff neck and a peculiar gait when walking.   This compelled him to turn round whenever accosted by a friend—and he had

---

[1] Joseph Hamilton, Esq., resided in Newcastle for about twenty years. He lodged at a house on the right-hand side on entering Lisle Street, where on Saturday morning, 29th September 1798, he dropped down dead whilst dressing. This gallant officer was in the sixty-sixth year of his age, and was buried at St. Andrew's Church, Newcastle.

many, by reason of his politeness and gentlemanly manners. He wore a cocked hat and bag-wig, light-coloured breeches and blue stockings, with large silver buckles on his high-lows. The distinguishing feature of his dress was a large red and white checked plaid or cloak, which he was accustomed to wear both in winter and summer. His extraordinary motions and rolling about when spoken to inflated this garment every now and then, and obtained for him, amongst the vulgar, the nickname of "Peter Waggy."

The Story of Le Fevre—From *The Hive*, 1806.

THE Bewick family rose at six o'clock in the morning—sometimes earlier. The young ladies would, as was natural, fain have reposed a while longer; but their father's voice, "Come down and get dressed," being more than once repeated, they would say to each other, "We may as well get up, for there will be no peace till we do so." In summer time, when the weather was fine, they strolled up Summerhill, and then turned along Elswick Lane.

> " Forth issuing on a summer's morn, to breathe
>   Among the pleasant villages, and farms
>   Adjoined, from each thing met conceives delight ;
>   The smell of grain, or tedded grass, or kine,
>   Or dairy, each rural sight, each rural sound."

It was on one of these early morning walks that Bewick, accompanied by his little daughters, made a sketch for the beautiful cut of the Pintado (" British Birds," vol. i. p. 293, ed. 1797).

The bird belonged to John Hodgson, Esq., the hospitable owner of Elswick Hall. The gate of the yard being fast, he had to climb over the wall to gain admittance, and he has represented this incident in the background to the cut. Though very minute, the resemblance of the figure on the wall to himself is perfect. The Rev. Thomas Hugo was indebted to me for this anecdote, which he inserted in the " Bewick Collector." This I had, with other interesting information explanatory of the vignettes, from the Misses Bewick. The limit of their ramble reached, they would now, invigorated and strengthened, direct their way homeward by a pleasant footpath through some delightful meadows that led to the river's side, near to a place rightly named Paradise, listening meantime to a carol from on high by our earliest songster.

> " Married to morning by a sweeter hymn
>   Than priest e'er chaunted from his cloister dim
>   At midnight, or veiled virgin's holier word
>   At sunrise or the paler evening heard."

Mrs. Bewick frequently went to meet her husband and children, and all returned together. The repast that awaited them

was somewhat homely. The family never tasted tea for breakfast; good wholesome hasty pudding was the common dish, each
using a wooden spoon marked with his or her initials. In 1768,
whilst Bewick was an apprentice, Souchong sold for "twelve
shillings, and the finest Hyson at twenty shillings per pound, at
Watson's, the Teaman, in the Bigg Market, where also might

be had The Ladies' Sticking-Plaster, Daffy's Elixir, Godfrey's
Cordial, &c." Bewick's dinner hour was two o'clock.

Sixty years ago, when a lad, I was often sent to the grocer's,
and remember paying eight shillings per pound for tea, and
sevenpence for moist sugar. The *Courant* newspaper (weekly)
then cost sevenpence.

ISS JANE BEWICK once told me that when it became known that her father proposed to adorn his " History of Quadrupeds" with vignettes or tailpieces, there were not wanting those who at once condemned their use, on the somewhat singular ground that they would be objected to and considered *vulgar* by persons of taste and education. In this, as in other points, the artist boldly adhered to his own ideas and resolves, without regard to the advice tendered by his would-be critics. The originality and unity of purpose existing in his own mind he rigidly adhered to, and is most observable in the "History of British Birds." The history, explanation, and significance of the charming tailpieces and backgrounds to so many of the cuts in this, the artist's greatest work, was often adverted to when on visits to my venerable friends. On the holidays at Easter, and in the Race Week, I was for years a regular visitor, and always invited to tea. The ladies expected my coming, and would say to the maids, " Mr. Robinson is sure to be here this afternoon." On leaving Bewick House I immediately began to turn over in my mind the topics which had formed the subject of our pleasant gossip. On reaching home, I wrote down all that was worthy of remembrance. The connection and relationship between the figure described in the text and the accompanying vignette is well worthy of attention, as well as the apposite nature of the designs in regard to the position they hold in the book. One brain conceived, one pencil designed, and only one graver could execute those matchless creations of genius and poetic fancy. For the sake of illustration, it is only necessary to take the admirable cut on the title-page of the first volume of the " Birds." The arms and crest of the

town appear on a boundary stone in the centre; over against
a thicket of brushwood a fine blackbird is seen perched on a
spray, *apropos* of coaly Tyne.   The Rev. James Murray, in his
"Travels of Imagination," takes notice of the song of a blackbird saluting him on reaching the south side of the Tyne, after
being drawn across the river in a ferry-boat, when on his way
to London.   A fleet of keels in full sail are going against the
tide, laden with coals, commonly called "the black fleet."   On
the near side are two others empty; the crews are pouying
their keels by three stowers; the long wooden erection called
a staith is seen close to the shore on the opposite side of the
river; the Windmill Hills appear in the distance.   A colliery in
full work is a prominent object to the right.   Two waggons are
on the incline—one filled with coal running down to the staith;
the other at the same time being drawn up, after discharging
her cargo at the staith.   Two keels are using their sweeps, a
very long oar which is guided by one man at the stern, whilst
the rest are pouying.   The third is drawn along shore by a rope.
What a wonderful amount of incident and detail is contained in
this small picture!

HE lovely cut of the Bird's Nest and Eggs heading the Preface fittingly introduces the reader to a history of the feathered tribes and their young. The drawings of William Hunt, with all the aid of colour, do not call up a more intense feeling for the beautiful than this little gem in black and white.

A pedlar wearing a cocked hat and spatterdashes, with a well-filled box strapped on his shoulders, is appropriately placed before the Table of Contents. He has come from Newcastle, and has five weary miles yet to travel before the next village is reached, where he can display his wares before the farmers' buxom wives and sprightly daughters.

Mr. Bewick's choice of Nature was most felicitous and original. His art resembles poesy, for in it

> "Are numberless graces which no methods teach,
> And which a master hand alone can reach."—*Pope.*

And if, as Ben Jonson remarks, "even one verse alone sometimes makes a perfect poem," how truly is this verified again and again in Bewick's charming vignettes. Each little picture is a poem.

How fertile is the imagination of the artist! He may indeed have witnessed what his pen and pencil here represents and describes so well. "A magpie is seen busily engaged in collecting materials for her nest from the back of a cow, whilst her mate is observed flying towards the nest persecuted by a hawk, which in turn is harassed by two crows and a third magpie" ("British Birds," vol. i. p. 74, 1797).

Then there is, at page 78 of the same volume, the admired cut of the Snow-Man, a boyish reminiscence. The youth mounted on a three-legged stool, Miss Jane Bewick informed me, was her father. The stout well-dressed boy, Willy Johnson, lived in the adjacent hamlet, and in after years became a farmer at Prudhoe; his other playmate, the less-favoured urchin, Joe Liddell, was a son of Anthony Liddell, mentioned in Bewick's Memoir, p. 221. The background is a view of Cherryburn: the "little window at his bed-head" is seen below the gable.

Another charming bit of rustic life (p. 147) is that of tracing a hare in the snow. The figure in the distance behind the hedge is Mr. Bewick; the man in the foreground with the gun, the lock of which he so carefully protects with the tail of his coat, is Joe Liddell, just mentioned, but now grown to manhood.

N depicting the varied seasons of the year Bewick is always at home, and never more so than in his winter scenes. There is a cut at page 162 which, along with many others, attests the truth of this remark. Here the severity of the season is still felt, though the cut stack—a favourite object with the artist— indicates its approaching close. Long icicles hang from the

gable of the roof, which is thickly covered with snow: heat from the chimney has kept others from forming near it. Two lads are seen watching their success in snaring birds, their footsteps marked in the snow. Outwardly all is bleak, but still there is an air of comfort about the little dwelling, arising from the feeling that warm and honest hearts are sheltered within.

MARSDEN ROCK, NEAR SOUTH SHIELDS.

There is a very pretty cut at page 202, in which the decrepitude of age and the joyous spirit of youth are well contrasted —the ruins of St. Edmund's Chapel, Gateshead, in the background.

Above the Table of Contents to the second volume of the "Birds," 1804, is a cut full of humour. An old poulterer, with pannier and basket full of birds, has broken his stick with beating his restive horse, that he may be in time for the market. "He has lost his hat," Bewick observes, "but not his patience" (Bewick's Book of MS. Annotations on Vignettes).

Views of Marsden Rocks and Bywell Castle are given at pages xx. and 23. The romantic scenery of the former place is renewed at pages 144, 156, and 161. Another local view, supposed to represent the Ruined Church of Alnmouth, now washed away by the sea, is given at page 245.

At page 348 of the same volume there is a little cut of a woman pumping water on the leg of an impotent man : his crutch and stick are lying beside him. Mr. Harry H——, a gentleman well known to Mr. Bewick, had a weak limb, and frequent recourse was had to this method of imparting strength and effecting a cure. A lover of mischief represented that this cut was intended to caricature his lameness, notwithstanding that Mr. Bewick protested that such a thought had never entered his mind. The untruth was believed, and a coolness ensued for many years in consequence.

The old sea-worn coble, with the ruined castle on the cliff, forms a telling and appropriate finis.

In villages and about farms it is no uncommon sight to see a number of geese follow one another in regular order ; the foremost turns round and cries "Ga, ga." In the fragment of a letter Bewick thus describes in short, natural, and expressive terms the flocks of geese he had seen "on their route to the Metropolis—a *hissing, cackling, gabbling,* but peaceful army, *waddling* along (like other armies) to certain destruction."

HERE is much meaning in many of the *tale-pieces,* not apparent at first sight, but requiring to be unfolded even to those who have given their days and nights to the study of Bewick; and better expositors there could not be than his own daughters. For instance, the admirable cut of "The Ovingham Dyers,"[1] so replete with humour, contains characteristic portraits of Thomas Dobson, dyer and bleacher, and his man, Geordie Carr. Dobson owned some property, and was esteemed a *laird,* as I have been told by Miss Isabella Bewick of Cherryburn. One of Carr's daughters, Mabel, married Robert Stephenson, the father of George Stephenson, the world-renowned engineer and originator of railroads. Worth in the humblest paths of life is akin to greatness. The following anecdote is illustrated in the background of the cut:—A certain laird, I remember the late Miss Jane Bewick telling me, made a vow that he would never again enter a public-house. He kept his promise to the letter; he would not dismount, but whilst sitting on his horse at the door, he would freely partake of a goodly tankard or two of the best ale the house could supply. Thomas Dobson's second son married Bewick's sister, Ann. My kind old friends in West Street always spoke highly of Geordie Carr as an honest and

---

[1] "British Birds," vol. i. p. 17, 1805.

upright man who had brought up a large family. His children were all a credit to him.[1]

Edward Willis, who served his time with Mr. Bewick as an engraver, was a grandson of George Carr. For him the Bewick family entertained the utmost respect. Mrs. Dobson had two children—a son, Thomas, and a daughter named Jane. Both, with their father, died young. To his sister, Ann, Mr. Bewick was much attached. After the death of her husband, who was a cooper, and lived in the Close, she removed from Newcastle to Ovingham, and commenced keeping a small school.

At page 135, vol. i., "British Birds" (1826), we have an example of a sport far from uncommon even now amongst idle lads in country places—that of tying a tinpot to the tail of a dog, and then setting it adrift. The terrified animal is here seen wildly dashing along amidst the hooting and stone-throwing of its bare-legged persecutors, whilst a great hulking fellow, with folded arms, enjoys the cruel pastime. Bewick, with his daughters, when young, watched for a long time to see how the leather leggings were fitted on this man, who was a tanner living in the West Gate, whose place they often passed in their morning walks.

Then we have, at page 223, the capital vignette of "The Burglar Disturbed." It is a summer morning about sunrise, for the chimneys are not yet smoking; an open gate shows too well how the thief has obtained an entry; when attacked by the dog, his booty, in the form of a large portmanteau, has been thrown upon the ground. His mode of fence consists in holding a stick (across) before him by the ends; by this means he expects to baffle a rather awkward assailant.

---

[1] George Carr lived in a cottage opposite the "Brick House," Ovingham, where Mr. Bewick's father-in-law, Robert Elliot, had farmed. Every other house in Ovingham was built of stone.

T the beginning of the present century a spacious mansion stood near the foot of Westgate Street, where the Library of the Literary and Philosophical Society now stands, having twenty-five windows in front, and is engraved on the margin of Corbridge's rare plan of the town (1726), and marked "Mr. Thomas Ord's House."

It was afterwards occupied by William Gibson, Esq., who was town-clerk for nearly thirty years. There was a large garden behind, and in front the ground was tastefully laid out,

and displayed an abundance of snowdrops and other spring flowers in their season. At the time I write of this house had become a boarding-school for young ladies, under Miss Smith, a person of the highest respectability. Here the Misses Bewick finished their education. Elementary instruction had already been imparted at a seminary close to their home at the Forth, kept by Miss Stevenson.

The landlady to whom this property belonged had a large conservatory in her garden, to which Bewick and his family had free access, he being her agent, and collected the rents. Miss

Isabella used to go there to learn her lessons, and was often startled by hearing the large apples fall from the trees. The late Mr. Barnes of Whitburn, who, whilst a lad, resided with his uncle, Alderman Forster, close by, attended the same school. The room was reached by a wooden staircase at the outside, having formerly been a hayloft. Now and then he played the truant, and would visit Bewick's workshop to pass away the time. For some fault he was one day "kept in" by himself. He longed for an apple or two from a tree which stood near the window but beyond his reach. At last he thought of the school tongs, and contrived by their means, after one or two failures, to secure some of the tempting fruit. Bewick observed this juvenile prank, and made a sketch of the amusing incident, as he was accustomed to do when any occurrence struck his fancy.

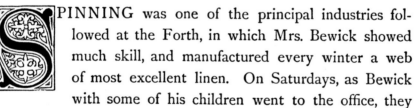

PINNING was one of the principal industries followed at the Forth, in which Mrs. Bewick showed much skill, and manufactured every winter a web of most excellent linen. On Saturdays, as Bewick with some of his children went to the office, they used to pass a woman wearing a gipsy hat, sitting on a basket at the foot of St. John's Lane, selling bands for spinning-wheels. Her cry was, "Now then, lasses, don't forget your wheel-bands." This most useful old-world employ has now gone out of fashion. Not long ago a lady from London, on a visit to the Misses Bewick, saw a spinning-wheel in the room, and innocently asked if it was a musical instrument!

Eighty years ago early rising was more general in New-castle than at present. Those of the inhabitants who wished to spend a day at Tynemouth were much inconvenienced, for there was but one coach, which left in the morning and returned the same day. The passage down the river was pleasant, but very long and tedious. It took three hours in going by the "Comfortables," a kind of covered passage-boat used on the Tyne before the introduction of steamboats. Robert Bewick and his sisters were wont to prefer the road, and walk the distance, leaving home at six o'clock in the. morning. After enjoying many hours of healthful pleasure they would return

The History of the Empress Catharine—From *The Hive*, 1806.

in the same way, sometimes meeting Stephen Kemble on the road, who tried by such exercise to keep down his constitutional tendency to increase in bulk.

It is related that whilst Liston, the comedian, was performing in Mr. Kemble's company, a dispute arose between the manager and the performers respecting the arrangements made by the former for playing on alternate nights at Newcastle, Shields, Sunderland, &c., by which the latter were much harassed. A rebellion being likely to ensue, Mrs. Kemble

NORTH SHIELDS—THE LOW LIGHTS.

was reported to have said that the company might leave as soon as they choose, "for there were actors to be got on every hedge." Shortly after, Liston and some others, walking along the road from Newcastle to Shields, perceived a post-chaise at some distance behind them, which they knew was conveying Mrs. Kemble to the place of their destination. Immediately Mr. Liston clambered among the bushes to the top of the hedge, and when the chaise came up, Mrs. Kemble, astonished at seeing him in such a situation, cried out, "Mr. Liston, what

From the *History of a Fly* (Hodgson's Edition).

are you doing there?" "Looking for actors, ma'am," replied he; "but I can't find a single sprout." It is needless to add that he was instantly invited to enter the chaise. On another occasion, as he was walking between Newcastle and Sunderland, he was overtaken by one of the coaches which ran on that road (then and long after proverbial for the slowness of their motion), when the driver asked him if he was for a ride. "No, thank you," said he; "I am in a hurry!"

HILST the Rev. James Lushington was Vicar of Newcastle, and for a lengthened period non-resident, his curate, the Rev. John Ellison, resided at the Vicarage in Westgate Street. This house was "large and ancient, suitable to hospitable times." Here the worthy gentleman used at Christmas and at Midsummer to give parties to the young ladies and gentlemen round about, including the daughters of Thomas Bewick and their brother, where, amongst others, they used to meet

From the *History of a Fly* (Hodgson's Edition).

with the two daughters of Lord Collingwood, who, with Lady Collingwood and her relatives, the Blacketts, lived in Charlotte Square. On such interesting occasions there was much to delight the eye, and an abundance of fruit, cake, and all that was good, to satisfy the desires of his young guests. Innocent mirth and good humour was pictured in every pretty face.

A glowing fire, with many lights, reflected upon the polished oaken floor and quaint old furniture, frequently in striking contrast, when the hour for parting came, with the view presented outside of this venerable mansion, its many antique gables and mullioned windows being covered with snow, in token that Old Christmas had come again, in fitting mantle clad. In extreme old age the ladies remembered with pleasure the reminiscences of their youth, and delighted to recall the recollections of bygone days. The fine old oak staircase, the rich clusters of large red-currant berries that grew in the Vicarage garden, the

laburnum and lilac trees which spread so gracefully over the garden wall into the street, were never forgotten.

The time came when Mr. Bewick would in all probability have to leave his much-prized "cot in the Forth." In consequence of the death of the owner, the property had to be sold. The old tenant was loth to leave; he had a strong desire to buy his house at a reasonable price. At the auction he had to encounter the opposition of a Mr. Featherstone, a wealthy grocer in

Collingwood Street, who outbid Mr. Bewick, and became the purchaser at £360.

The large garden was sold as a separate lot.   Mrs. Laidler's land at the Barras Bridge was bought by Messrs. Burnup, builders, for £2000.   Long previous to this Bewick had made many endeavours to buy a little land in the neighbourhood of Eltringham, but was always forestalled by the landowners whose estates adjoined.   The many little pleasures the family had enjoyed at the Forth never passed out of remembrance, and the kindness of the Waldies and other neighbours in times of sickness was not forgot.

The apple tree, with its golden pippins, which stood before the door, and under the shade of which they often took tea and had their evening meal, the field in which his children used to play, all served to endear an otherwise humble dwelling to those who had known it so long.

R. BEWICK was now approaching his sixtieth year, and in ill-health. Many old haunts were now being gradually forsaken; the long and toilsome ascent to his new abode in Gateshead began to tell even on so stout a pedestrian.[1] The practice of temperance and assiduous application to hard work had not so enriched the artist that he could afford to venture upon a more desirable residence in Newcastle. Whilst at the Forth he frequently began work at six o'clock in the morning, and continued until nine at night. He used to say that "he could get better on with what he had to do after the lads had left." At his solitary bench he would hear the curfew bell "swinging slow with sullen roar" from the tower of St. Nicholas. And when he had *lapped up* for the night, he had to pass on his road home by a strange and uncouth group congregated near the south door of the church. This was the watch, who met there before departing on their nightly rounds, clad in topcoats with many capes, and wearing coloured neck-shawls. Each man was provided with a powerful rattle, which hung from a leathern belt buckled round the waist, a lanthorn, and a short staff with a hook at the end. The clock of St. Nicholas regulated most of Mr. Bewick's movements. He never had a watch; this was

---

[1] The following advertisement in the Newcastle papers first drew Mr. Bewick's attention to this property. Mrs. Bewick could see this house whilst building from their garden at the Forth.

A FREEHOLD DWELLING-HOUSE AND GARDEN, &c.,

To be Sold by Private Contract,

And may be entered upon at May first. All that substantial stone-built Dwelling-House, situated in an airy and pleasant road on the west side of Gateshead, called the Back Lane. The front commands a beautiful view of the country to the West, extending beyond Axwell Park, which affords an agreeable object. On the North and East are seen Newcastle, and a fine prospect eastward.

For further particulars apply to Mr. Hancock, Bridge End, Newcastle.

2 B

a luxury he did not care to invest in. His brother John was not so self-denying. The family at Cherryburn possess, along with other relics, his inexpensive silver timepiece.

WHEN a young man, Mr. Bewick, by always using his right eye with the glass, very much weakened the other. He applied to a Dr. Clark for advice, who recommended him to make a practice of plunging his head into cold water every morning. This he did at the pant in Darn Crook, in Newgate Street, until both eyes recovered strength.

Bewick one afternoon, whilst writing in his office, observed through a window his two apprentices, Harvey and Temple, writing on slips of paper, which they twisted up, and quietly passed to each other. Mr. Bewick got off his seat, went through to them, and managed to pick up a few of these missives, which he read. They proved to be full of impudence about "Tommy." He called them both into the office, where, after making them feel ashamed of their behaviour, they were told with much earnestness "that if ever he caught them again passing such remarks about 'Tommy,' he would knock their heads together so long as he had strength in his arms;" and there can be no doubt he would have kept his word.

Mr. Bewick whilst at work at night never used a lamp, as is usual amongst engravers; by the light of two candles with double wicks he could see to execute the most delicate and minute objects. In everything he was most regular and methodical, whether in regard to the business and routine of the shop or household affairs. Except on rare occasions he was seldom out of his own house much after ten o'clock, when it was customary with him to have bread and cheese, with a glass of good ale, for supper, or a little rum and hot water before going to bed. Among the early relics of Mr. Bewick preserved by the family is his silver punch ladle with ebony handle, inscribed "Thomas Bewick, Engraver, Newcastle, 1786."

An ill-mannered journalist, whose office was in St. Nicholas' Churchyard, once incurred the wrath of Bewick by a remark

From the *Life of a Fly* (Hodgson's Edition).

made in the course of conversation. This the irate engraver promptly resented by administering a sound slap on the cheek of the offender which made his ear tingle, saying "that he would not seek redress from a magistrate whilst he could vindicate his honour himself." Age had not tamed his old spirit in resenting an insult.

Bewick's supper beer, whilst he lived at the Forth, was brought in a bottle that held five gills (which served the whole family) from the Black Bull's Head, which stood at the foot of Westgate Street, nearly opposite Denton Chare. This old house—one could almost touch the gable—was famed for good beer. It has just been pulled down.

Mr. Robert Wilson, merchant tailor, now in his eighty-ninth year (1877), who, whilst I was an apprentice, lived in Richmond Court, Pilgrim Street, told me that he well remembered going down in an evening when the business of the day was over to the Blue Bell Inn at the head of the Side, then kept by William Cant, an admirable performer on the Northumberland small pipes. Here Mr. Bewick was accustomed to repair and regale

himself with a pot of good porter. His dog Cheviot invariably accompanied him, and lay down at his feet on entering the room. Bewick was the acknowledged chief and president of a harmless gathering of substantial Newcastle tradesmen, who met here to discuss the politics of the day. After having quietly occupied his chair for about an hour, Cheviot would get up, and, standing with his tail against the door, begin to whine and look hard at his master. To this well-known signal that time was up, the old gentleman would say, "Well, Cheviot, we must be off and home. I understand you, old boy." Then taking up his walking-stick he left along with his canine friend, who never allowed his master to remain too long without broadly hinting that it was time to be gone.

The same informant related a curious story about Cheviot. On the occasion of some repairs being done to Bewick's house in West Street, several masons and joiners were employed to complete the job. To one workman in particular the dog took a sudden and most decided dislike, for which no reason could be assigned. He growled and barked in such a threatening manner that the man became afraid to enter the house or come near the dog. Some time after this the Misses Bewick were staying with their relatives at Cherryburn, when a woman came to the farm one day with a basket containing laces, nightcaps, and other articles. She offered a cloth pelisse for sale, which was immediately recognised by Miss Bewick as having belonged to her, and been stolen some time before. It turned out that this woman was the wife of the workman who had incurred so unaccountably the anger of Cheviot.

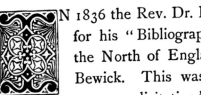N 1836 the Rev. Dr. Dibdin, whilst collecting material for his "Bibliographical and Antiquarian Tour in the North of England," paid a visit to the Misses Bewick. This was brought about, at "Dibdin's urgent solicitation," by the Rev. John Collinson, Rector of Gateshead. Miss Isabella Bewick's subscription copy of the "Tour" is now before me, with her autograph on the title, as well as on the book-plate in each volume. This was generously offered me by that lady—a present I was glad to accept. Miss Bewick has underlined several passages, added marginal notes, and inserted a few annotations on notepaper.

The first has reference to Dibdin's blunder in stating (p. 330, vol. i.) that her father was born in Gateshead. At page 333 he favours his readers with an account of his interview with those ladies and their brother at the family residence in West Street. Miss Bewick in strong terms expresses her sense of the injustice done to the memory of her father by the insinuations contained in the Doctor's remarks as to his religious belief. I am of opinion that "the tearful eye and the tremulous tongue" existed only in the Doctor's imagination. It was surely an un-

grateful return after the kindness and attention he had received. Miss Bewick continues—" This is a piece of unmitigated impertinence which never was named, nor had I ever occasion to shed a tear during the interview." Dibdin quotes a " Brief Memoir" (this was a single 4to page, published by a local bookseller after Mr. Bewick's death), in which it is said that Bewick was "jealous of his fame, and had not much affection for rival artists." Miss Bewick, in the margin, truly asks, " Of whom need Bewick be jealous ?" Certainly not of any one of the many talented pupils he reared, either as designers or

engravers on wood. Miss Bewick afterwards comments on a
note at page 336 of the " Tour " in reference to the progress
her father had made at the time of his death towards the
intended " History of Fishes."

The Doctor relates that " Miss Bewick was so obliging as to
furnish me with the following list of the woodcuts of what this
work upon ' Fishes' contained, namely, fourteen entire fishes
upon wood; seventy vignettes, chiefly of fishing scenes; about
forty drawings of fish, with a few descriptions and memoranda;
thirty-five sketches of vignettes, with a few slighter." This
statement calls forth the following observations :—" Miss Bewick
ventures here to express a wish that she had let the *list* suffice;
but on the worthy Doctor begging for the loan of a cut (viz., a
cat lifting its foot to a creel hung against a wall, allured by the
smell of the fish) to place in his ' Northern Tour,' she was so
simple as to confide this cut to his keeping, that ' he might give
it a place in this book;' he declaring that it would be such a
benefit 'that we might bless the day that brought him to call
here.' He begged hard also to have the loan of the portrait
(Good's portrait), for which he was prepared to give (I think)
£20, to get copied for his ' Northern Tour.' We never more saw
our beautiful cut, nor an impression from it in the ' Northern
Tour,' or anywhere else. But in a letter from him at last,
which began, ' I never in the course of a long life was so
pained, &c. &c.,' he ended by telling us that the cut was
burnt at a fire in a printing office (he did not inform us where
or when), where it was left by him, I suppose, to print. The
Rev. Mr. Collinson was much chagrined when I told him what
had occurred, as he had introduced the reverend gentleman to us.
I heard him preach at Gateshead Church from the last verses
of chap. xii. of St. Matthew, ' Who is My mother, and My

sister, and My brethren?' This cut may ooze out some time
or other." The drawing for this cut was included in the valuable present made by the executors of the late Miss Isabella
Bewick to the Museum of the Natural History Society of
Newcastle.

BOOK
III

MY first acquaintance with the Misses Bewick began about thirty years ago. Since then I have spent many, very many, pleasant hours in the society of these ladies, Miss Jane and her sister being ever most liberal in displaying their artistic treasures. Folios of engravings and rare children's books, not to be found in "Bell" or "Hugo," were brought out for inspection on the occasion of my visits.

About the earliest subject we spoke of and discussed was the publication of the manuscript left by their father. I respectfully urged Miss Bewick to publish the work herself, if it was to be done at all, now whilst she enjoyed health and strength, and not to leave the Memoir to be mangled probably by others after her decease. The topic was renewed time after time throughout a lengthened period. I considered its performance to be a duty she owed to the memory of her father and herself, as well as to the public, and that it should not be delayed any longer. This Miss

Bewick readily admitted, but urged the great trouble and anxiety it would entail at her advanced age. After much consideration the task was at length undertaken, and proceeded apace. Thus the world is indebted to my representations and persuasion that the Memoir was at length put in hand, and brought out under the best of all possible editorship.

My calls on the ladies were mostly in the afternoon or in the evening. My stay was usually about three hours or more. Miss Bewick often favoured me by reading extracts from the proof-sheets, as they were received from the printer, to my great delight. These were carefully examined, she noting on each sheet the date when received, and how long it had been in hand, often expressing displeasure at the delay which now and then took place.

On my pointing out that the poet Thomson's name had been spelt with a "p" at page 257, she observed that "that was so. In the *revise* it had been carefully corrected, but that the self-sufficiency of printers was so great, there was no putting them right."

The chapters treating of religion and politics I strongly objected to, especially the former, and begged that they might be omitted. But Miss Bewick would not listen to this. She replied with much spirit, "That would not be my father. I wish to show him to the world not as an artist only, but as a philosopher."

The impression on my mind all along as to the tenor of the Memoir in regard to remarks on some of his contemporaries had been something very different from what the book proved itself to be, and in this misconception I was not alone. Years before its publication was determined upon, I remember the late Mr. Robert White, the historian of the Battle of Otterburn, asking my opinion as to whether it would ever come to light, or was likely to share the fate of Lord Byron's Memoirs. And when it was at last given to the world, Mr. John Fenwick, a well-known local collector, and who had at one time been Bewick's solicitor, remarked in the course of conversation, "Sir, if the Memoir had been published as written, it would have immediately given rise to half-a-dozen actions at law." The observation was truly professional. Such anticipations never had any foundation in fact. The woodcuts are certainly

The Wanderer Destroyed—From *Tales for Youth,* 1794.

disappointing; they must be considered as the last efforts of a great man, and preserve much of his old power and individuality. The great merits of the work are now recognised, and the author's literary fame rests on a surer basis than before. The all-accomplished art critic, John Ruskin, recommends the book to his students at Oxford as one of the first they ought to study. The freshness and truth with which he describes Nature in the varied year will always be read with pleasure. Miss Jane Bewick was a lady of rare intelligence and capacity, and fitted to edit the Memoir written at her request. She knew the world well, and could gauge the character and mind of those with whom she came in contact with nice discrimination, inheriting much of the shrewd and close observation of men and things for which her father was so noticeable. In many little peculiarities she instinctively followed him. It is said that Berghem used to be always singing whilst at work; Bewick had an inveterate habit of whistling. Miss Jane, when busily employed in arranging and selecting woodcuts or drawings, an occupation in which she never appeared to tire, indulged in something faintly approaching that modulation of the lips. Miss Bewick was lady-like in manner, and in her best days stately, resembling her father in personal appearance. A well-informed mind, united to a most retentive memory, rendered her conversation most enjoyable. One winter evening, whilst speaking of Shakespeare, she recited, with animation, the speech of Queen Katharine at the Trial (Henry VIII. Act ii. Scene 4).

During the last four years of her life her memory failed very much, and Miss Isabella was often called upon to assist her sister with respect to names and dates.

This venerable lady departed this life on the 7th April 1881, in the ninety-fourth year of her age, to the deep regret of many old and attached friends, and the great grief of her sister, the last surviving child of Thomas Bewick. They were never separated, but lived in sisterly love and affection, "being ever from their cradles bred together."

April 29 my dear sister Birthday

Dear Lady Turner

How little would it enter my dear Father and Mothers mind that when from little ailing Girl would be left in this world and at such an age and with so many cares with so many upon her weak shoulders and yet how thankfull I am to a kind providence that he has seemed fit to do long prolong my life as to enable me to smooth my dear Sisters passage to her Grave, her last moments were quite like falling

into sweet sleep with her eyes fixed on my face and hold of my hand her face placid and angelic and I am happy to, without the least pain, and this look continued till the sight of her last was for ever in this world. She was interred at Ovingham where when it pleases the disposer of event to remove from earth my poor feeble body will be laid beside her and the love of her and the love of ones I have outlived. my sight is getting my so faor excuse ommission and believe me with the greatest respect Isa Bewick

Fac-simile of a letter written by Miss ISABELLA BEWICK in her 92d year, printed for "THOMAS BEWICK: his Life and Times," by R. Robinson, by the kind permission of LADY NORTHBOURNE, to whom it was addressed.

Lithographed by Banks & Co., Grange Printing Works, Edinburgh.

OME notice of Mr. Bewick's residence at 19 West Street, Gateshead, and its contents, may not be without interest. On the walls of the dining-room or parlour were a few engravings in old black and gold frames, including one of "Rubens and his Wife," a gift from poor Summerfield the engraver; a portrait of Captain Coram after Hogarth, "The Spanish Pointer," "The Rural Cot," "The Apple Gatherers," "Celadon and Amelia," and a landscape after Poussin, all engraved by William Woollett; a portrait of Robert Elliot Bewick when a boy (an oil-painting), by Joseph Bell; a plaster cast from Baily's marble bust; and an old mahogany bookcase, with green curtains in front, containing the artist's little library. Before one of the windows of this room the old gentleman used to sit in his declining years, busied in engraving the cuts for his intended "History of British Fishes." One evening, when about to leave, Miss Isabella directed my attention to her father's neat work-table, with one drawer, from which he regularly took a single fig every day at twelve o'clock.[1] The sitting-room, immediately above, will never be forgotten by me, for there I was favoured, through long years, with the hospitable kindness and instructive conversation of those venerable ladies, whose retentive and well-stored memories, rich in old local information and gossip, which they were ever pleased to impart, was a treat in which I delighted.

The apartment had three windows. Formerly pleasant fields and gardens lay in front: these have now given place to a dismal-looking Mechanics' Institute and buildings of an inferior

---

[1] This valued relic, filled with choice wood-blocks, the masterpieces of Bewick and his brother, is now in my Bewick room.

description.   On the white marble mantelpiece there was a mirror, to the left of which, near to the couch on which the ladies usually sat, hung Good's fine portrait of Bewick, representing the old gentleman in a sitting posture, with one leg folded over the other, dressed in a black coat and vest, kerseymere breeches, and blue worsted stockings, home-made—an admirable example of the artist's skill in giving a pleasing radiance to the side face.   His intellectual and finely-formed forehead is well brought out; the eyes are full of animation

From the *History of a Fly* (Hodgson's Edition).

and intelligence, whilst a ruddy and genial glow suffuses the whole countenance.

Under this picture was a beautiful miniature of the artist on ivory by Plymer.   To the right was a portrait of Northcote by Ramsay, and below it Murphy's miniature, also on ivory.   This has been engraved by Summerfield.   In a recess between the fireplace and the window was a large mahogany case, resting on a card-table, containing a portion of the precious woodcuts of Birds, Quadrupeds, and Fables of Æsop.   The great bulk of the cuts were contained in a press in the kitchen, on the basement at the back of the house, whence they could easily be removed through a window into the garden in case of fire. In the opposite compartment stood a handsome pianoforte, and above it an antique china bowl, richly painted with flowers and gilt. In the middle of the room, on a noble centre table, there was another of larger size, filled with rose-leaves. "The fragrance is all the more grateful," Miss Bewick once remarked, "from having come from Cherryburn." Between the windows were choice impressions of the Chillingham Bull, the Whitley Ox,

From *The Oracles,* 1792.

and the rare lithograph called the "Cadger's Trot." The opposite wall displayed a curious half-length portrait of John Bewick (crayon), by George Gray. He is represented in a blue dress coat, buff vest, and wearing a wig. This was found by Miss Bewick a few years ago at the bottom of a drawer, unframed, unknown till then. Under it was suspended his pretty silver-mounted cane with ebony gibb. Near this hung a proof of the Chillingham Bull on parchment, in the first state, with the ornamental border. It is but just to myself to point out that this impression, now in the Museum of the Natural

History Society, Newcastle, with other impressions I have seen
in the same early state, do not exceed in excellence that given
in this work.   In company with the above were beautiful proofs
of Pidcock's Lion and Elephant, the original drawing in colours
for Spearman's Kyloe Ox, frames containing highly finished
drawings of Birds, and vignettes of the same high quality as
those recently presented to the nation by the Misses Bewick,
and now in the British Museum.   On the wall to the right of
the door was a fine large portrait in crayons of the late Miss
Jane Bewick, drawn by J. Gilbert in 1852, together with proof
impressions of some of the best cuts done by John Bewick to
illustrate Trusler's "Progress of Man in Society," "Robinson
Crusoe," &c.   At the bottom of this apartment, Ramsay's
portrait of Mr. Bewick, so well known by Burnett's engraving,
hung above a small sideboard.   This portrait was a present
from the artist to Mrs. Bewick.   On each side were closets
well filled with family relics, silver plate, folios of drawings,
and scrap-books abounding with rare woodcuts.   A large and
splendid Wedgwood vase, with other articles of taste, occupied
side-tables, and finished the decoration of the room.   Gas never
found an entrance at 19 West Street.   As soon as it turned
dark, two elegant silver candlesticks were brought in by a
maid, and placed on a table near the fire, and the wax candles
lighted.

O N my first entering the room Miss Bewick would say, "I am glad you have come, for I am weary and tired out with this work," viz., the sorting and arranging of woodcuts and piles of old letters of her father and Uncle John. These were at once put aside for the night. After having tea, I had the privilege for two or three hours of feasting my eyes in looking through a collection of Bewick treasures, neatly mounted in folio volumes, which the ladies kindly placed before me. The cuts, as far as possible, had

The Story of Obidah—From *The Hive,* 1806.

been arranged in chronological order. For two of these books, one of which I bound myself, I offered more than once, on behalf of a wealthy customer, the sum of one thousand pounds —(this was before it was determined to present them to the nation)—but my offer was declined. They have since then been taken to pieces, their contents framed, and exhibited to the public in the King's Library at the British Museum. For a time I respectfully pressed on the Misses Bewick the claims of Newcastle for the precious gift, but the National Museum appeared to the donors to be the only fitting receptacle, London being the grand centre to which not only all Englishmen resort most frequently, but also students from America, France, Germany, and other countries.

In ordinary use at the tea-table was a carved cocoa-nut cup or sugar-basin, mounted in silver, and inscribed on the rim, " Thomas Bewick, Newcastle, 1779." It was the first article bought before he began housekeeping. This relic the Misses Bewick said, on Christmas Eve 1876, they intended to leave me, but could not bear to part with it while they lived. Meantime, as a pledge that it should be mine afterwards, Miss Isabella gave me the pretty turned stand on which it originally stood before Mrs. Bewick had it mounted with silver. At the same time I was presented with an interesting little copper jug which belonged to their father: on it is engraved, " Thomas Bewick, 1780."

After Miss Bewick's death I duly received the following note from the solicitors :—

> "UNION CHAMBERS, NEWCASTLE,
> *3d September* 1883.

"DEAR SIR,—We have been requested by Messrs. Joseph Crawhall and John Wheeldon Barnes, the Executors of the Will of Isabella Bewick, deceased, to inform you that under this Will you are entitled to the legacy mentioned on the other side (silver-mounted cocoa-nut cup).

> "Yours faithfully,
> "HODGE & WESTMACOTT."

The cup, which is exquisitely carved, was received a few days afterwards.

Miss Bewick kindly favoured me, on one of my visits, with a sight of her father's box of tools, many of them well worn, including his eye-glass, gravers used for making outlines, with part of the handles cut off, tint-tools for cutting parallel lines, gouges for scooping out the wood towards the middle of the block, and chisels for paring away the edges of vignettes. The box contained two or three pieces of chalk, just as when last used by Mr. Bewick; there was also a rest. These relics are now in the possession of Joseph Crawhall, Esq. The tools

The Story of Melissa—From *The Hive*, 1806.

needful for wood-engravers are but few, but these are of various sizes.

On a call I made Miss Bewick in August 1881, four months after her sister's death, I found the old lady knitting. She was, of course, in mourning, and wore a small gold brooch, having the date of her mother's death, and a lock of her hair. She had on a pair of gold spectacles, her eyesight now beginning to fail. I noted these little particulars, so as to refresh my memory in after years, when all the dream of life should be well-nigh over, and not without some hope that my readers might not altogether disapprove my recording them here.

T is unpleasant to remark that, in a special number of the *Graphic* (4th June 1881), published to commemorate the Centenary of George Stephenson, there is a woodcut portrait of Thomas Bewick, professedly taken from Ramsay's full-length portrait of the artist. In it the engraver has striven, most unworthily, to render Bewick's appearance as contemptible as possible. This at the time gave great pain to Miss Bewick, that lady being then in her ninety-second

The Story of Maria—From *The Hive*, 1806.

year. The accuracy of the scribe who represents the great North-countryman as having been born at *Ovingham*, and caricatured by *one of his sons* on a pane of glass in the workshop window, is on a par for truthfulness with the woodcut itself. It is needless to say that Mr. R. E. Bewick's filial respect for his father would never allow him to be guilty of such an act. I was glad to learn afterwards that a playful urchin had sent his ball through it, and smashed the precious relic, the work of some idle tenant long after Robert Bewick had been forced from the premises. The property was leasehold.

Drawn by E. Train. 1830.

Etched by T.E. Nicholson

Robert Roxby

My last interview with Miss Isabella was on an evening about a month before her lamented death. The conversation turned on Robert Roxby, the bard of North-country anglers. This gentleman, with the late Mr. Thomas Doubleday, were both Tyneside fishers of renown, and enthusiastic in sounding the praises of their favourite streams. She mentioned the cut by her father on the title of Roxby's poem of the "Reedwater Minstrel."[1]

Miss Bewick did not seem disposed, as usual, to converse freely, yet to my surprise she recited with much feeling, although in her ninety-fourth year, George Pickering's beautiful fragment, entitled

DONOCHT HEAD.

Keen blaws the wind o'er Donocht Head,
   The snaw drives snelly through the dale ;
The gaberlunzie tirls my sneck,
   And, shivering, tells his waefu' tale:
" Cauld is the night, O let me in,
   And dinna let your minstrel fa',
And dinna let his winding-sheet
   Be naething but a wreath o' snaw.

---

[1] Robert Roxby died in Newcastle, July 30, 1846, in his seventy-ninth year. The deceased was born at Needless Hall, Reedsdale, Northumberland, and having lost his father at an early age, he was confided to the care of Mr. Gabriel Goulburn, an extensive farmer in the neighbourhood. With that person he led a rambling kind of life until his twenty-fifth year, when Mr. Goulburn became insolvent, and the small fortune of Mr. Roxby being lost in the wreck, he was cast penniless upon the world. About 1798 he became a clerk in the bank of Sir W. Loraine & Co., in Newcastle, and on the failure of that establishment he entered the bank of Sir M. W. Ridley & Co., where his cleverness as an accountant soon became remarkable. After composing various pieces of poetry of more or less merit, he published by subscription in 1808 an edition of 250 copies of " The Lay of the Reedwater Minstrel," a ballad poem which he had gradually expanded into three books from a mere metrical epistle of a few stanzas addressed to Matthew Forster, Esq., Broomyholme, near Chester-le-Street. In 1822, in conjunction with Mr. Doubleday, then a young man, he published what proved to be the commencement of a series of lyrical productions, which obtained a large circulation, and which since his death have been collected under the title of " The Coquetdale Fishing Songs." In these ballads he took great pride, which their popularity sufficiently excused. That their originator should predict that songs which have been sung on the banks of the Ganges and on the banks of the Hudson would not speedily be forgotten is quite pardonable.

Mr. Roxby was of middle height, had much colour, and a patch over one eye. He usually wore a dark-green dress coat, with light drab gaiters. On first entering the bank in the morning, he used to inquire of a young gentleman, a clerk in the establishment, who lived in Jesmond Dene, " Were the mennims loupin' in the burn this morning?"

" Full ninety winters hae I seen,
  And piped where gor-cocks whirring flew ;
And mony a day ye've danced, I ween,
  To lilts which frae my drone I blew."
My Eppie waked, and soon she cried,
  " Get up, gudeman, and let him in,
For weel ye ken the winter night
  Was short when he began his din."

My Eppie's voice, O wow ! it's sweet,
  E'en tho' she bans and scaulds a wee ;
But when it's tuned to sorrow's tale,
  O haith ! it's doubly dear to me.
" Come in, auld carl, I'se steer my fire,
  I'll mak' it bleeze a bonnie flame ;
Your bluid is thin, ye've tint the gate,
  Ye shouldna stray sae far frae hame."

" Nae hame hae I," the minstrel said ;
  " Sad party strife o'erturned my ha' ;
And, weeping, at the eve of life,
  I wander thro' a wreath o' snaw."

.   .   .   .   .

On leaving I promised to see her again very soon, but this was fated never more to be in this world. After a brief illness my venerable friend departed this life on the 8th June 1883, aged 93, and was laid under the sod in Ovingham Churchyard on the following Monday.

The morning of that day was lovely in the extreme. The solitary hearse, with the remains of the last child of Thomas Bewick, wound its way by Gateshead and the Redheugh Bridge to Newcastle, and so on by the west road, through Benwell, to Ovingham. The company invited, including the writer, went by rail to Prudhoe, crossing the river by the ferry-boat. Ovingham Church (dedicated to the Blessed Virgin Mary) is kept as all churches ought to be—the altar properly vested, and the door ever open to the parishioners and the casual stranger. In the Vicarage garden we were shown the original altar, with its crosses, incised stones beautifully adorned with the Christian emblem, pious memorials of the long-forgotten dead. The worthy vicar expressed a wish that those sacred relics might one day be built up in the church porch, and so preserved from further profanation.

The clergy, with a large and efficient surpliced choir, met

The Battle of Blenheim—From *The Hive*, 1806.

the corpse at the church gate, and went in procession towards that venerable house of God wherein the high-born noble and the humble peasant have knelt in worship through many centuries.

The ruins of feudal power and grandeur are here in immediate contrast with the still active and living ministrations of the imperishable Christian Church.

The sublime Service for the Dead was read by the Rev. William M. Wray and the Rev. John F. Bigge, the esteemed

2 E

vicar of Stamfordham.[1] After the funeral, a most delightful
walk by the river-side, amid high bushes rich with hawthorn
blossom, and the silver Tyne beneath, brought us all too soon
to Wylam, where we took train for Newcastle.   I was assured
by an old friend and much honoured priest of the Church of
England, who accompanied me a part of the way, that amongst
the most famed rivers of France, however picturesque and known
to song, there was not one to surpass the sylvan beauties of our
own noble river from Ryton westward—which I fully believe.

Before leaving Ovingham, whilst lingering over the tablets
in memory of the two brothers, and the vault which had just
received the remains of my good old friend, the words of
Garrick's inscription on Hogarth's monument in Chiswick
Church came to mind—

> " If Genius fire thee, Reader, stay ;
>   If Nature touch thee, drop a tear ;
> If neither move thee, turn away,
>   For *Bewick's* honour'd dust lies here."

---

[1] Both these worthy priests have since departed to their eternal rest.

R. BEWICK'S Family Bible (Ostervald's) is a fine large folio volume with plates, printed in 1782 by his early and dear friend Thomas Lawson, in Vine Entry, Flesh Market, Newcastle.

The following is a true copy of the Register, as written on the fly-leaf at the beginning. The entry of Miss Jane's death is made by her sister. One word, "Isabella," forms the last line, and in her own handwriting.

THOMAS BEWICK and ISABELLA BEWICK,
Newcastle,
Was married 20th April 1786.

Jane Bewick was Born 29th April 1787.
Robert Elliot Bewick was Born 26th April 1788.
Isabella Bewick was Born 14th January 1790.
Elizabeth Bewick was Born 7th March 1793.

———

Isabella Bewick died 1st February 1826, aged 74 or 5.
Thomas Bewick died 8th November 1828, aged 75.
R. E. Bewick died 27th July 1849, aged 61.
Eliz. Bewick died 7th April 1865, aged 72.
Jane Bewick died 7th April 1881, aged 94.
Isabella

A line may not be out of place explaining the origin of the relationship which subsisted between the late Mr. Robert Ward, printer and publisher, Newcastle, and the Bewick family. Mrs. Bewick's brother, Robert Elliot, who was a farmer, lived in the Red Brick House, Ovingham, from whence he afterwards went to Haydon Bridge, where he married. His daughter became the wife of Thomas Ward, farmer, Wylam, whose son, the late Mr. Robert Ward, residuary legatee of the late Miss Isabella Bewick, died at Newcastle-upon-Tyne, January 2, 1883, aged sixty.

Morning—From *The Chase*, by W. Somervile, 1796.

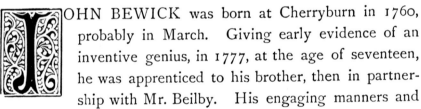

OHN BEWICK was born at Cherryburn in 1760, probably in March. Giving early evidence of an inventive genius, in 1777, at the age of seventeen, he was apprenticed to his brother, then in partnership with Mr. Beilby. His engaging manners and vivacity of disposition soon won for him many friends, who delighted in his ready wit and humorous conversation. But herein lay the source of after grief and sorrow. Serious disagreement and numerous altercations took place between him and his more prudent and circumspect relative. Thomas deeply deplored the erring course of life which wrong-headed and thoughtless companions were surely leading one to whom from infancy he was much attached. To wean him from their society, and habits so fatal to his future success in life, Mr. Bewick resolved to cancel his indentures after he had served about five years, and remove him from Newcastle to London—a change which

was attended with complete success. That freedom and latitude
he had allowed himself in the latter period of his servitude
were now found to be incompatible with his altered position.
Work in earnest was a necessity, and with the utmost diligence
he addressed himself to the task of obtaining an honourable
subsistence. Unfortunately his ill-requited labour induced a
rapid and hasty method of execution which did not tend to
increase his fame as a draughtsman or an engraver. In John
Bewick's circumstances at this time there was much to excuse
that want of proper care and attention which was only too
obvious to his best friend whom he had left at Newcastle.
The London booksellers supplied any amount of work, but the
remuneration was small. As his prospects brightened, the
more liberal terms he was enabled to command freed him at
length from a thraldom so irksome to an artist inspired with a
true love for his profession. To add celebrity to the name of
Bewick, already so distinguished in the art world, was an
ambition worthy of himself. That John Bewick contributed
cuts to "Gay's Fables," published by Saint in 1779, and the
"Select Fables," issued from the same press in 1784, has been
already stated.

In 1781 Newbery published a little volume entitled "Choice
Emblems," &c., adorned with woodcuts. These John Gray
Bell believes to have been done after his removal to London.
I am inclined to think they were executed before he left
Newcastle.

In 1786, after a short stay in the North, he finally settled
in the Metropolis, where he arrived on the 12th of August in
that year, and began business on the 15th of October 1787 at
No. 7 Clerkenwell Green. Here he worked by himself, without the help of an apprentice. He never had a pupil, or

published any work on his own account. The "Emblems
of Mortality," a reproduction of the "Imagines Mortis" of
Holbein, representing in upwards of fifty cuts Death seizing
persons in all ranks and conditions of life, was published by
Thomas Hodgson in 1789. This is a desideratum with all
Bewick collectors. The cuts were executed in London, and
are well engraved. The original drawings are in my collection. Several have been only slightly traced on the wood,
affording evidence how completely the feelings of the artist

The Envious Shepherd—From *Tales for Youth.*

had been enlisted in his work, and the confidence he felt in
his own powers. An inferior workman without innate genius
would have required every line to have been drawn on the
block before proceeding to engrave ; but this was not the case
with John Bewick. A copy of the third edition of the
"Imagines Mortis," 1545, the gift of the late John Adamson,
Esq., to Thomas Bewick, was once in my possession, but
afterwards parted with to the late Admiral Robert Mitford.

His continued industry and application in a sedentary occupation tended to injure his health, which at this time (1790)

began to break down. The very large number of woodcuts
executed for the Rev. Dr. Trusler testify that his brain was
not idle. "Proverbs Exemplified," "Proverbs in Verse," and
the "Progress of Man and Society" more particularly, show
a considerable advance in the artistic treatment, both in design
and composition, of such subjects. Proof impressions of most
of the cuts in the last-named work are in my possession. At
page 6 of the Preface to "Proverbs Exemplified" the author
mentions Mr. John Bewick as "an artist who knows how to

The Moth and the Water-Fly—From *Tales for Youth*.

illustrate the follies and vices of mankind better than most
men," and his having profited by his abilities in the adorn-
ment of the book. In the following touching letter to his
brother he already anticipates a fatal termination of his illness.
The symptoms named were calculated to dishearten and have
a depressing effect on a nature so sanguine, and unfit him from
following his profession with spirit and energy. The gratitude
of the sick artist to his brother for all past kindness is most
feelingly expressed, and cannot be read without emotion. He
alludes to the third edition of the "Quadrupeds," published

in the preceding year, and the general opinion entertained in London that the sale might have been conducted more to the author's advantage, but adds that he well knew "that the management of it was *not* in your hands." This is most significant. Bewick somehow is often thrown into the background. In the original prospectus to the "Quadrupeds," so wretchedly written, this is very apparent.

"Crouch End, *March* 31, 1793.

"Dear Brother,—You have often (and not without some reason) accused me for my long silence, which I always acknowledged as a fault, which fault I think you seem much inclined to imitate. I was told by Mr. Bulmer, I may say months ago, that you intended to write me soon, since which time I have with the greatest impatience waited till yours of the 15th inst., wherein I am extremely happy to hear of Mrs. Bewick's safe delivery, and that she and my little niece are both well, which I hope will continue thriving.[1] I am sorry that you should think that I am in the least dissatisfied with you respecting the *sale of your* 'History' in London, well knowing that the management of it was *not* in your hands. *What I said concerning the conducting of it from the beginning was the universal opinion of every well-wisher, and I still believe might have been managed much more to your advantage.* Far be it from me to upbraid you, or in the least harbour any such unjust thought. Your advice and utmost endeavours to serve me, I may say from my infancy, when Ill able to judge or serve myself, must to my last Day with gratitude be remembered, which I am afraid will be the only (tho' poor) recompense that may ever be in my power to make. My very poor state of health at present crowds with grief on my memory all these past obligations. My severe Illness last summer has not, nor, I am afraid, ever will, entirely leave me. I have for these few Days past spit a good deal of Blood, which has rather alarmed me, never before having been troubled with that Complaint, though we are always ready, and ever willing, to hope to get better. Yet reason tells me (from the many severe attacks which I have had of the same kind) that my Constitution must be much impaired. I am happy to hear of your improvements at the Forth, where I hope you and your Family will there long live to enjoy Health and Contentment. 'O Blessed and glorious Health, thou art above all Gold and Treasure ! He that has thee

---

[1] Elizabeth, youngest daughter of Thomas Bewick, born 7th March 1793, died at Gateshead, 7th April 1865, aged 72.

hath little more to wish for ; but he that is so wretched as to want thee, wants everything with thee.'

> ' When Health is lost be timely wise,
> With Health all taste of pleasure lies.'

" I sometimes have a wish to be with you in the North ; at other times think I am much better here with respect to my Health. Indeed, all agree that the warmer the Climate the better for my Complaint. Dr. Oliphant wou'd recommend a Voyage to some hot Country. I have moved from Mount Pleasant in October last, and now lodge and board with an old Widow Lady in the neighbourhood, who pays me every attention that a Nurse or Mother could possibly do. And as the weather gets warmer I hope, and please God, to get better. The two Mr. Bulmers, Mr. Gregson, and Mr. Pollard was to see me the other Sunday. Dined and spent the Day at Crouch End.

" I am, with Kind Love to Mrs. Bewick and all Relations and Friends,
Dear Brother,

" *Address—* " JNO. BEWICK.
Mr. BEWICK, FORTH, NEWCASTLE-UPON-TYNE."

In the " Looking Glass for the Mind," published by Newbery in 1794, will be found charming examples of his pleasing

The History of Jonathan—From *The Looking Glass for the Mind,* 1792.

style. The late Miss Jane Bewick greatly delighted in this little work, and not without reason, for the pure and childlike sweetness and innocence depicted in the looks and graceful form of young children, always a feature in John Bewick's juvenile portraiture, is in no work more observable.   The dress

The Rival Dogs—From *The Looking Glass for the Mind.*

Nancy and her Canary Bird—From *The Looking Glass for the Mind.*

and occupations of the little people, so simple and truthful, bring before the mind's eye pleasurable memories of the golden hours of youth and childhood.

In the same year Newbery brought out "Tales for Youth, in Thirty Poems," illustrated with thirty beautiful cuts by the same artist, "Many of them equal to the highest efforts of

The Silly Lamb and the Shepherd's Dog—From *Tales for Youth*, 1794.

The Cat and the Fish—From *Tales for Youth*, 1794.

his genius; that of a Prowling Cat, at page 55, has been pronounced the most natural likeness of that animal ever produced" (*Vide* "Bell's Catalogue," p. 27).

As impressions from the whole of the original wood-blocks, together with several in the "Looking Glass for the Mind,"

The Destruction of Envy—From *Tales for Youth.*

From *Harrison's Picture Book* 1792.

are given in this work, my readers will be enabled to judge for themselves. The "Blossoms of Morality" afford also cuts of equal merit.

The Ungrateful Fox—From *Tales for Youth.*

The Timorous Boy—From *Tales for Youth*, 1794.

The Contemplative Hero—From *Tales for Youth.*

In April 1794 a prospectus was issued by William Bulmer announcing the publication of a splendid edition of Goldsmith's Poems for the following January, comprising " The Traveller,"

The Turkey-Cock and Turtle-Dove—From *Tales for Youth.*

Avarice Punished—From *Tales for Youth*, 1794.

" The Deserted Village," and the " Hermit," by Parnell. The fine large cut of "The Sad Historian," drawn and engraved by John Bewick, was the only important woodcut he contributed

John Bewick, del. et sculp.

THE SAD HISTORIAN.

Published, March 1887, by Robert Robinson, 21 Pilgrim Street,
Newcastle-upon-Tyne.

to the work. His fame rests chiefly on the admirable drawings, made on the wood, to illustrate Somervile's poem of the
Chase. Bulmer remarks in the prospectus that Goldsmith
will be "enriched with Twelve Engravings on Wood, from
the most interesting Passages of the Poems, by T. Bewick of
Newcastle-upon-Tyne and J. Bewick of London, the whole
forming the most extraordinary effort of the Art of Engraving
on Wood that has ever been published." Gentlemen are invited
to inspect the engravings at the Shakespeare Printing Office in

Cleveland Row. They appear to have been already finished,
although the book was not published until 1795. This is the
only work in which the genius of Bewick's pupils, Robert and
John Johnson, may be seen combined with the skill of their
master and his younger associate. Two of the largest and
most important cuts were designed by the former. These,
together with the fine cut of " The Hermit at his Devotions,"
designed by John Johnson, were engraved by Thomas Bewick,
as was also the cut of " The Traveller," from a design by

2 G

Richard Westall. " The Sad Historian," an old woman gathering water-cresses, affords an excellent example of the peculiar
style of John Bewick, and his mode of treating foliage, which
was inferior to, and stands in contrast with, the unapproachable
fidelity in imitating Nature exhibited by his brother.   Another
main characteristic is that of contrasting positive black with
pure white.   Sickness and worry indispose the mind from
even attempting that which can only be attained when free

KING GEORGE III. Hunting in Windsor Park.—From *The Chase*, by W. Somervile.

from care and in the enjoyment of quiet and repose.   This,
unhappily, was not destined to be his portion in this life.

These illustrations, however beautiful, and their merits are
unquestionable, must yield in originality and elegance to those
contained in the companion volume, "Somervile's Chase,"
published by Bulmer in 1796.   These were all, with one
exception (a group of hounds from a picture by Halkart),
designed and drawn on the wood by John Bewick.   In consequence of his early and lamented death, it fell to the lot of
his brother Thomas to engrave the entire series, except the

last, which was done by Charlton Nesbit. Mr. Bewick did more than engrave those masterpieces of art. In affectionate regard for his brother's memory, I feel assured that, where needful, he improved the drawing in the original designs. The artistic beauty displayed in these charming productions, and the finely balanced composition of each, have obtained from competent judges and connoisseurs unqualified commendation. It is said that George III. could not be persuaded that such delicate effects were obtained by means of woodcuts, and that his bookseller, Mr. George Nichol, obtained for his Majesty a sight of the blocks to convince him of the fact.

In the vain hope that his native air would once more restore him to health and strength, John Bewick again sought the banks of the Tyne, but not, as in past years, to derive the much-wished-for benefit. Amid the haunts and scenes of his boyhood he was destined to breathe his last. He died at the residence of his sister, Ann Dobson (a widow), who lived at the Red Brick House, Ovingham. Mr. John Grey Bell errs in stating that his death took place at the residence of his brother William at Cherryburn.

Otter Hunting—From *The Chase*, by W. Somervile.

Mr. Bewick put up a marble tablet in Ovingham Church-yard, with the following inscription :—" In memory of John Bewick, Engraver, who died 5th December 1795, aged 35 years. His ingenuity as an Artist was exceeded only by his conduct as a man."

There was an amount of refinement in manner and speech about him that his more talented brother did not possess. John played well both on the flute and clarionet : Thomas was no musician.

When John visited Newcastle he invariably brought with him from London an assortment of entertaining books for children, with proof impressions of cuts he had executed, as presents to his little nephew and nieces. Miss Jane Bewick used to say that, when young, "she thought her uncle the funniest fellow she ever saw."

HAVE now before me a tiny tome, entitled " The Oracles," published by Newbery. On the fly-leaf is the following inscription: " The Gift of John Bewick to his nephew, R. E. Bewick, 1792." Below this Miss Bewick kindly added, " The Gift of Jane and Isabella Bewick to Mr. Robert Robinson, May 16, 1877."

Innocent mirth was a part of John Bewick's being. He was of a sallow complexion, and rather under middle size. In this he differed from his father and brothers, who were tall, portly, and ruddy. He was particular in his dress, as a young man ought to be who is desirous to please. Ordinarily he wore a green or blue coat with bright buttons, light-coloured vest and breeches, a beaver of the latest London fashion, a neat powdered wig, a shirt with three cambric frills, silk stockings, and silver buckles. A very pretty buckle that fastened his stock was remembered by Miss Bewick after ninety years had rolled by. Fine drawings of birds and animals, including a Prize Ox, a Turtle-Dove and Thrush, coloured and of the size in nature, the work of his pencil, are in the possession of the family at Eltringham.

The same love for a country life and rural quiet that so strongly possessed the mind of his brother through life, was not less intensely felt by John Bewick. Whilst yet a resident in the great city, he longed for a humble dwelling or hermitage on the richly wooded banks of the Tyne, between Prudhoe and Wylam.

> " And may at last my weary age
> Find out the peaceful hermitage,

> The hairy gown and mossy cell,
> Where I may sit and rightly spell
> Of every star that heaven doth show,
> And every herb that sips the dew."—*Milton.*

Twenty-five years ago, after having had tea one pleasant afternoon in May with the family at Cherryburn, the late Mr. William Bewick [1] accompanied me to Wylam, and pointed out the locality where his uncle John so ardently desired to live alone and in peace. The lines of Cowley come to mind—

> "Would I a house for happiness erect,
> Nature alone should be the architect."

It is reported of Sir Francis Blake Delaval that, on having his attention called to the fragrance of a May evening in the country, he replied, "This may be very well, but for my part I prefer the smell of a flambeau at the playhouse." How tastes differ! This brilliant and talented gentleman, when the end came, bitterly deplored the misspent past. It would be well if from such an abode of peace as young Bewick sighed for, when the close of life draws near, we could look forward without a thought for the morrow, and contemplate the shadows of the passing cloud, that

> "Imitate, on field and furrow,
> Life's chequered scene of joy and sorrow."

Incessant toil, serious illness, and the cares of this world were obstacles in the way of John Bewick's realising such a dream.

---

[1] William Bewick, third son of Mr. William Bewick of Cherryburn, died 13th April 1863, aged seventy-two years, and was interred at Ovingham. He had been in the employ of his uncle Thomas as copperplate printer. He had a brother named John, who was apprenticed to his uncle also. This talented youth died at the age of nineteen, before he was out of his time. Several clever examples of his pencil are at Cherryburn.

ROBERT ELLIOT BEWICK was born on the 26th of August 1788. No father could be more delighted at the birth of a son and heir than was Mr. Bewick on this happy event. Through the years of childhood and youth he displayed toward this loved object of his hopes the most tender care and affection. Shortly after the child was vaccinated his eyes became inflamed, and his parents saw with sorrow that impure matter had been received into his system, threatening to entail deplorable consequences on their offspring at the very threshold of life. In course of time, however, a strong constitution enabled the little sufferer in a great measure to overcome its ill effects, whilst good country air and sea-bathing in after years contributed much towards restoring his health. In a letter dated 9th July 1799, written from Ovingham to his sister Jane, who was then staying at South Shields, he relates in boyish glee that "he had

never had such fun in his life. He had learned how to walk on stilts, and he believed he could cross the Tyne on them, and looked forward to the time when he should have a grand pledge with them at home, in the Forth, when the wet weather should set in. Jemmy Maffin (Maughan) had taught him many new tunes, which he had jingled away at Ovingham, Eltringham, and Hooly Hill. His father liked best the tune, 'What can a young lassie do with an auld man?' He wished he could get down to Shields, but his father would not let him out of his sight, and he would let Jane hear how he would jingle away on Bessy Skipsey's birthday." The above is written in a bold round hand, the letters being well formed and distinct.

He was now eleven years old, and a tolerable performer on the Northumberland small pipes. At the house of Mr. Dobson, who farmed at Mount Hooley, near Ovington, and whose son married Bewick's sister Ann, young Robert and his sisters were always at home. Here he was accustomed whilst a boy to enliven and amuse the company with the strains of his favourite instrument, on which he afterwards became such a proficient. In course of time he possessed a valuable collection

From the *History of a Fly* (Hodgson's Edition).

of pipe music. As he grew in years he took tolerably well to his father's profession, and could engrave respectably both on copper and wood, but did not manifest much enthusiasm or greatly endeavour to excel in either. He was fond of isometrical drawing, and wished to become an architect. Many excellent examples of his ability might be named. Fidelity to Nature and minuteness of detail distinguish his performances.

On 1st January 1812 Mr. Bewick admitted his son into partnership, and the business was continued in all its branches as before, under the style of "Thomas Bewick & Son." The late Rev. John F. Bigge, vicar of Stamfordham, had three drawings by Mr. R. E. Bewick, presented to him by Miss Isabella Bewick. These were interesting views of Seaton Delaval Hall, before the fire, the old house at the Forth in which Richard Wingate's father lived, and a sketch of cattle.

Robert Bewick died, unmarried, on the 27th July 1849, aged 61, and was buried at Ovingham. As an engraver he was not successful in maintaining the renown of his father.

The Earth-Worm—From *Tales for Youth*, 1794.

There certainly was latent talent, and I am persuaded that, if only the necessary effort had been made, his natural ability would have shown itself; but he was wanting in energy, somewhat listless, and of a retiring and diffident disposition, qualities not calculated to make their owner famous among artists. Through life he displayed a kindly feeling towards birds and animals and every living creature. Whilst taking a walk in the country, he would go before his sisters and remove out of the way the lowly palmer-worm, lest it should be trod upon. His pockets were usually filled with bread crumbs, to strew

2 H

on the road for pigeons and sparrows to pick up. His sensitive nature shrank from giving pain, and he passed from this life without having provoked a single enemy.

He was more at home with copper than with wood. The most notable of his performances are the following, viz. :—A Lobster, engraved for the late Isaac Cookson, Esq., to ornament lobster-pots. The Rev. Canon Raine of York owns one of these pots, probably the only perfect example in existence. A few proof impressions from the plate were struck

The Benighted Traveller—From *Tales for Youth.*

off and printed in red ink before it was delivered. These are now very rare. I possess the original pencil drawing,[1] with one of those proofs, both obtained from Miss Bewick. It is an admirable work of art. There is also a very pretty view on the Tyne, with Bywell Hall; the "Maigre," included amongst the woodcuts of fishes at the end of Bewick's Memoir; a View of Ryton Church, in the County of Durham, engraved in 1822 for the late Venerable Archdeacon Thorp,

---

[1] The finished drawing, a perfect gem, may be seen in the Museum of the Natural History Society, Newcastle.

FIEDWORTH MILLS

Bought of James Bone

and deservedly prized by that gentleman—it is a beautiful little plate; a Masonic Arch, with emblems (14 inches by 9 inches), engraved for the Northumberland Provincial Lodge of Freemasons in the same year, with others. These, though stated to be executed by T. Bewick & Son, are almost exclusively the work of the latter. In the last edition of the "Birds," 1847, will be found a cut of the Bewick "Swan." This is the most favourable example of his skill as a wood-engraver. In Fox's "Synopsis of the Newcastle Museum" there are also two plates by him. The superintendence of the seventh and eighth editions of the "Birds," in their passage through the press, devolved on Mr. R. E. Bewick and Mr. John Hancock, a very old friend of the family, and owe much of their excellence to the care and attention of both. His sisters would occasionally visit the printing office whilst the work was in progress, examine the proof-sheets, and, as Miss Jane told me, remove with a fine bodkin any particles of ink lodged in the interstices of the cuts and likely to affect the printing.

BOOK
IV

EWICK had many pupils in the course of his long career, but none who united in themselves those high and rare qualities found in their great master—that of being both draughtsman and engraver of unsurpassed excellence in the province his genius had created.

Johnson could design well, and express his artistic conceptions in colour with readiness and effect, but did not engrave, beyond a few trifles unworthy of mention, either on wood or copper.

Charlton Nesbit, though deficient in those intellectual powers which constitute a master mind, excelled as a wood-engraver.

The natural talents of Luke Clennell were of the highest order. He was essentially a man of genius, and an artist of Nature's own making. These justly entitle him to our homage, whilst that dire calamity, the loss of reason through so many years, will ever enlist the sympathy of every feeling heart.

William Harvey's talents as a designer and engraver on wood are too well known and understood to need particular mention. The same remark will apply to John Jackson.

ROBERT JOHNSON was born at Shotley, in Northumberland, in 1770, where his father followed the trade of a joiner and cabinetmaker. His mother being a great favourite with Mrs. Bewick, she besought her son, whilst on her deathbed, to take Robert, then in his eighteenth year, as an apprentice, which was accordingly done in or about 1788. This date does not agree with a remark Miss Bewick once made, that Johnson was bound on the day her father was married. His parents afterwards removed to Gateshead. Few masters would have felt disposed to take an apprentice at such an age, but Mr. Bewick had regard to the request of his mother. Young Johnson's fondness for drawing would thus be encouraged under the guidance of one who was himself self-taught, and well fitted to develop natural talent in others. Miss Bewick said that her father took uncommon pains with Johnson. She remembered him well. Miss Isabella told me that he had often carried her in his arms whilst a child, and spoke of him kindly. He used to bring flowers to the Forth on a Sunday afternoon from the garden of a relative. Miss Harvey (sister of William Harvey, Bewick's pupil) informed me that Johnson lodged with the father of the late Mr. John Bell, land surveyor, without the Westgate, near to where the Tyne Theatre now stands. At the expiration of his apprenticeship he engaged

R. Johnson, del.   T. Bewick, sculp.

THE DEPARTURE.

Published, March 1887, by Robert Robinson, 21 Pilgrim Street,
Newcastle-upon-Tyne.

rooms for awhile at the head of Dean Street, where he intended to follow the business of a copperplate engraver, but was seemingly unsuccessful. Towards the close of the last century, Mr. Joseph Whitfield, bookseller, at the north end of Tyne Bridge, well known for his ultra-Tory principles, published an Annual Ladies' Pocket-Book, with an engraved frontispiece. For one of these Johnson executed on copper a reduced view of his fine large drawing of St. Nicholas' Church. Subsequently Whitfield, having obtained a sight of the architect's design for intended alterations on the north front of the Exchange, Newcastle, employed Johnson to engrave the same, of a suitable size, to illustrate his next year's Pocket-Book. This was the origin of an amusing feud between the bookseller and the engraver. Johnson closely copied the drawing; but when finished Whitfield raised an objection, viz., that it wanted a foreground, although there was none in the original drawing, and refused to pay what he had bargained for unless there were figures introduced in front. Johnson, to get his money, added figures, placing Whitfield, who unfortunately had one leg much shorter than the other, conspicuously amongst them.

This proceeding exasperated the bookseller so much that at length he refused to pay anything, making use of the engraving nevertheless. Johnson, to be revenged, designed and etched a clever coloured caricature of Whitfield (which he sold for one shilling), who then took counsel's opinion as to prosecuting Johnson, but was advised to laugh it off. To retaliate on the artist, he had a pirated copy of the caricature done, which he sold at sixpence. This again roused the burin of Johnson, who published a second and a third caricature of Whitfield. These are now of extreme rarity. The first was entitled "A Real Friend to his Country Begs." This represented Mr. Whitfield standing, with his short leg raised, holding a declaration headed, "An Antidote against the Black Demon of Discord." He is attired in a light blue coat, striped pink and white vest, yellow breeches, white stockings, and shoes with buckles. A scroll proceeds from his mouth, on which is written, "Britons stand forward, and sacrafice a part to save the whole." Whitfield was an Irishman. These caricatures resembled him both in features and general appearance. The others were "The Asses in Danger" and "The Overthrow."

The Vain Sparrow and Cruel Judge—From *Tales for Youth*, 1794.

Whilst in Newcastle Johnson made a drawing of Sunderland Bridge, then in course of erection, which was afterwards engraved by himself and Mr. Abraham Hunter. It was Mr. Bewick's opinion that had Johnson lived, he would have obtained distinction as an engraver on copper; but engraving was not his *forte*, and I am persuaded that he never would have attained fame in that department of art. In his youth he studied Nature by Shotley Burn and the banks of the Derwent, or the more wild and romantic scenery about Allansford and Shotley Bridge. He possessed an elegant and refined taste, displaying much originality in his designs, and could portray the human form with grace and truth.

Mr. Bewick acknowledged that Robert Johnson could not draw out of perspective. It is on his skill as a painter in water-colours that his fame as an artist must depend. Dying so young and uncared for, fine examples of his pencil are, unfortunately, but few.

The Earl of Bute, in passing through Newcastle, called at Mr. Bewick's, where he was shown a portfolio of drawings by

The Spider and the Chieftain—From *Tales for Youth*, 1794.

Johnson, with which he was so much pleased that he purchased as many as amounted to £30. This sum Messrs. Beilby & Bewick retained, on the ground that they were the work of an apprentice, and that the making of such drawings was a part of his business. Johnson's friends took a different view of the matter, which ended in litigation. At the trial the case for the defendants broke down, it being proved by Charlton Nesbit, another apprentice, that they had never received any instruction from their masters in the art of painting in water-colours, and that it formed no part of the teaching necessary for an engraver.

The action was tried in the Sheriff's Court, Newcastle, April 29, 1795. The bill of costs against Beilby & Bewick amounted to £9, 10s. 11d.

Mr. Ralph Heron, an attorney, who was consulted by Johnson's friends, was informed by an anonymous correspondent that he had seen a caricature of him in Bewick's office, in which the bird of that name was represented holding a pen in its bill, and guiding the hand of a dying man in signing his will. Mr. Heron was recommended to secure the drawing before it was published, as it was likely to do him much harm. Some years after, that gentleman gave Mr. Bewick this note, when the latter assured him that such a drawing was never made or seen by him, and that he never caricatured any man, be he friend or foe.

In the summer of 1796, Mr. Johnson was recommended to Messrs. Morison, publishers, Perth, to make drawings of portraits by Jameson, the Scottish Vandyke, at Taymouth Castle, Kenmore, the seat of the Earl of Breadalbane, for Pinkerton's " Iconographia Scotica." Mr. Johnson was very anxious that his drawings should be well engraved, "as much as possible in the manner of ' Houbraken's Heads of Illustrious Persons.' Except the engravings are done with judicious exactness from these drawings," he remarks in a letter to Mr. Pinkerton, " I beg you will not put my name to them, as I think it a laudable precaution which every young artist should take and abide by who has only his hands and his little name to depend on." Mr. Johnson had probably seen some of the portraits already engraved which two years before had been so contemptuously spoken of by Horace Walpole.

The following letter details the sad circumstances attending the death of this unfortunate youth, " to fortune and to fame unknown :"—

Messrs. MORISON & SON *to* Mr. PINKERTON.

"PERTH, *November* 18, 1796.

"You no doubt will be surprised when we inform you that the purpose of this letter is to announce to you the death of poor Johnson. We have seldom met with an occurrence in which we have felt more interested than the latter end of that deserving young man.

"The very day after we last wrote you, we received a letter from Kenmore, from the man in whose house he lodged, desiring us to send for him, as he was quite delirious; and by express the day following we were informed of his death. Some weeks before this Lord Breadalbane and family had left Taymouth House, and he had continued his business in a large parlour, *without fire*. Anxious to get through with his job, and the hours of daylight but few, he frequently sat six and seven hours on a stretch, and contracted a terrible cold. A fever was the consequence; no person to take a charge of him, he neglected himself; it flew to his brain; and, terrible to relate, he was bound with ropes, beat, and treated like a *madman*. It is a subject too painful to be dwelt minutely on. Fortunately, the day before his death, a Dr. M'Lagan, passing through Kenmore, visited him, ordered him to be unbound, applied blisters, &c. The day following the delirium abated; he became calm, and died in peace and composure. As none of us could go from home, we sent an acquaintance to see him decently interred; and so entirely were we strangers to him, that we know not more about his relations than that they lived at Newcastle. Mr. Kirkwood, of Edinburgh, who recommended him to us, advised his friends of his death, and a young gentleman went up to Kenmore and investigated his little matters. There are two finished portraits among his drawings which will doubtless be sent you; but the young gentleman's instructions were to seal up everything and send them to Newcastle. We stated to him the circumstances concerning these portraits, and cannot for a moment doubt their being immediately ordered back.

"We have been informed of several anecdotes about him which are interesting. He was bound apprentice to the famous Bewick of Newcastle (who cuts figures on wood in so dexterous a manner) by his father. We should have set out with mentioning that he was the only son of an aged man, a carpenter, in Gateshead, near Newcastle. His master, observing his uncommon genius for drawing, employed him to trace the figures on the wood. This accustomed him to drawing, and the figures in Bewick's 'History of Quadrupeds' will be lasting monuments of his genius and abilities. A lady in Newcastle, observing his taste and abilities, was at the expense of keeping him at an academy for drawing; and by the time his apprenticeship was finished, he was considered as almost fit for London. He determined, however, to work at home till he could work more to his mind, and had been employed for about six months on his own account when he agreed to go to Kenmore. He had been so successful that he made his aged father give up his tools, for which he was now too infirm, and took upon himself his support. In this and several other respects his private character was most exemplary; and such of his drawings as can be had will bring great prices, and it is expected will raise a little fund to support the inconsolable parents, who have now no child left. His funeral charges came exorbitantly high, from eleven to twelve pounds. We have a great inclination to subscribe a little towards them : perhaps you may feel so disposed also. Excuse my freedom."

With respect to the assertion herein made that Mr. Johnson had rendered considerable help to his master in tracing on the wood the figures in the " History of Quadrupeds," Miss Bewick favoured me with a sight of the original draft of her father's vindication of himself from the erroneous statement of Mr. Pinkerton. Bewick affirms that the whole of the cuts in the " Quadrupeds " were designed, drawn, and engraved by himself; that he received no help or assistance from any one, except that some of the trifling ornaments or tailpieces were left to be cut by the pupils. He speaks in a friendly tone of Mr. Johnson, and of himself as the victim of " associated malice and envy."

Fifteen drawings had been finished, and there remained four to copy when Johnson died. His parents presented to his relatives and friends a memorial card with the following inscription :—

ROBERT JOHNSON, OF GATESHEAD,

Painter and Engraver,

Died at Kenmore, in Perthshire, 29th October 1796,

In the 26th year of his age.

The Works of his Pencil speak for themselves. His other Valuable and Pleasing Qualifications can be justly appreciated by those only who knew him.

———

This Memorial was executed from one of his own designs by his Friend and Fellow Apprentice, Mr. C. NESBIT.

An impression from the original woodcut is given below.

The following drawings by Johnson are in the collection of Joseph Crawhall, Esq., Newcastle :—

SAINT NICHOLAS' CHURCH, NEWCASTLE—The original drawing; afterwards engraved on wood by C. Nesbit. A work of great local interest.

LANDSCAPE WITH FIGURES—A drawing of remarkable beauty.

OVINGHAM CHURCHYARD—Signed R. J., on a stone in the foreground.

THE FRIARS—Newcastle-on-Tyne.

TANFIELD ARCH—County of Durham.

WARKWORTH CASTLE—Northumberland.

WARKWORTH CASTLE—Another view.

A lovely drawing, "Lavinia," is in the possession of James Leathart, Esq., Bracken Dene, Gateshead. John Hancock, Esq., Newcastle, has also several interesting examples.

In addition to the drawings made by this talented young artist to embellish Bulmer's fine edition of Goldsmith's "Deserted

Village," and the " Hermit," by Parnell, I have the pleasure to make known a little discovery of my own, viz., that a charming vignette, engraved by Charles Warren from what must have been an exquisite drawing of poor Johnson's, will be found on the engraved title of the second volume of Cooke's edition of Gay's Poems, 1804, and illustrates a line in the forty-fifth Fable, " The Poet and the Rose "—" A rose he plucked, he gazed, admired " (vol. i. p. 78).　Mr. Warren probably received the drawing from his son-in-law, L. Clennell.

JOHN JOHNSON, a cousin of Robert Johnson, was born at Stanhope, in Weardale.　He also was a pupil of Bewick's, but did not live to finish his apprenticeship.　The beautiful woodcut of the " Hermit at his Devotions," engraved in Poems by Goldsmith and Parnell (4to, 1795), was from a drawing by this talented young artist.

J. Johnson, del.

T. Bewick, sculp.

THE HERMIT AT HIS MORNING DEVOTION.

Published, March 1887, by Robert Robinson, 21 Pilgrim Street, Newcastle-upon-Tyne.

face page 256.

HARLTON NESBIT was born in 1775 at Swalwell, a village on the banks of the Derwent, near its influx with the Tyne, about four miles south-west from Gateshead, County Durham. His father was a keelman, who, perceiving the bent of his son's genius, had the good sense to apprentice him to Mr. Bewick about 1789. The kindliness of his heart was early shown, for on the sad death of his fellow apprentice, Robert Johnson, he engraved in memory of his friend the beautiful cut already given, which will ever remain not only a touching memorial of the strength of his friendship, but a charming example of the mastery he had attained in the art of wood-engraving. Whilst Johnson was in Scotland, Nesbit supplied the trade with his caricatures of Whitfield, and also with one of his own, representing Stephen Kemble as "Hamlet," wearing the Order of the "Elephant and Castle." Beneath are the words, "O that this *too, too* solid flesh would melt." The likeness was admirable. It is etched on copper, quarto size, and is very rare. An old lady, a relative, saw him busy with it; he then resided in Drury Lane, Newcastle. Nesbit's goodwill towards Johnson was still further manifested in that not long after the expiration of his apprenticeship, he engraved on twelve blocks of boxwood, firmly clamped together and mounted on an iron plate to prevent warping, a View of St. Nicholas' Church, for the benefit of Johnson's parents. The following is a copy of the Prospectus :—

"In January 1798 will be published an Engraving on Wood representing a North View of St. Nicholas' Church in Newcastle-upon-Tyne, from a highly finished Drawing of the late Robt. Johnson, Painter, and engraved by C. Nesbit, late pupil to Mr. T. Bewick. Size of the Print, Fifteen inches by Twelve: being the largest Engraving on Wood ever attempted in the present Mode. The patronage of the Public is earnestly solicited to the above, being undertaken solely for the Emolument of the aged Parents of the deceased artist.

"To be printed by Mr. Bulmer at the Shakespeare Press, London. Price five shillings."

Subscribers' names were received by the printer, and by the booksellers in Edinburgh, Perth, York, Newcastle, and surrounding towns, and by the father of the artist, Thomas Johnson, Gateshead.

For the execution of this large cut the Society of Arts presented Nesbit with the lesser silver palette, and in 1802 he received the Society's silver medal. About 1799 Mr. Nesbit removed to London, where he remained till 1815. During his residence there he engraved, from the designs of John Thurston, a number of cuts for various works. His cuts for Northcote's Fables are esteemed very highly, and considered amongst the best he lived to execute. At the latter date he returned to his native place, where he took up his abode until 1830, when he again left the North for London, and continued to reside there until his death on the 11th of November 1838, aged sixty-three. His large cut of Rinaldo and Armida, engraved in 1818 for Savage's "Hints on Decorative Painting," is unquestionably a fine work of art, and well adapted to display Nesbit's merits as an engraver. The subject was designed by Thurston, whose talents were so often called into requisition by the engravers of that day.

There is an elegant edition of "Hudibras," with Dr. Grey's Notes, plates engraved by Ridley after Hogarth, and woodcuts by Nesbit. This was printed by Bensley for Vernor & Hood in 1801, in 2 vols. super royal 8vo.

William Shield, the eminent musical composer, was also a native of Swalwell. In early life he became the friend of John

Cunningham, several of whose pieces he set to music. The charming melody of "The Thorn" will never cease to delight the most fastidious critic, together with "The Wolf" and "The Heaving of the Lead." The remains of the son of the Swalwell singing-master now rest with the illustrious dead, poets, statesmen, and dramatists, in the great Abbey of Westminster.

LUKE CLENNELL, the most brilliant offshoot of the Bewick school, was born at Ulgham, a small hamlet near Morpeth, in Northumberland, on the 8th of April 1781. When young he was placed under the protection of an uncle, a grocer at Morpeth, with whom he continued until he was sixteen. Evincing a strong liking for drawing, his friends seconded his inclination by sending him to Mr. Bewick, to whom he was apprenticed on the anniversary of his birthday, 1797. His genius, elegant taste, and fine imagination were soon manifest, for he was equally at home in depicting Nature in the recesses of woodland or village life, by the mountain stream or the wild ocean shore. He more than equalled Nesbit or Nicholson as a wood-engraver, and might claim the palm of excellence with Johnson as a painter in water-colours. After the termination of his apprenticeship he continued to work for Mr. Bewick, who employed him in engraving several of the cuts for an edition of Hume and Smollett's "History of England" (Scholey's edition), with historical woodcuts from Thurston's designs. For engraving those cuts Mr. Bewick paid him two pounds each, whilst he charged the publisher five pounds. On this being known to Clennell, he sent to the firm a proof of one of them—Alfred

in the Danish Camp—stating that it was his work.   This led
to an engagement in the Metropolis, where he arrived towards
the close of 1804.   Jackson, in his " Treatise on Wood-Engraving," observes that between the expiration of his apprenticeship and his departure for London he appears to have engraved
several excellent cuts for a school-book entitled " The Hive of
Ancient and Modern Literature," printed by S. Hodgson, Newcastle.   In boyhood he had watched the gathering storm and
tempest from the far-stretching coast that skirts Druridge Bay

DIONYSIUS the Tyrant—From *The Hive*, 1806.

to Cresswell, and wandered, " when summer days were prime,"
by the gentle windings of the Wansbeck to where that river
seeks the sea at Camboise.   His poetic soul in after years
mused upon those early remembrances heaped up in the store-
house of memory.   In an octavo edition of Falconer's " Shipwreck," published by Cadell & Davis, 1808, is an extremely
beautiful cut of a ship running before the wind in a gale,
engraved by Clennell, though the drawing on the block was
done by Thurston — no doubt a vivid recollection of what

he had frequently beheld off Northumbrian shores. The fine
large cut which he engraved for the diploma of the Highland
Society, from a design by Benjamin West, President of the
Royal Academy, obtained much praise. "The original drawing was made on paper; and Clennell gave Thurston fifteen
pounds for copying on the block the figures within the circle;
the supporters—a Highland soldier and a fisherman—he copied
himself. The block on which he first began to engrave this
cut consisted of several pieces of box veneered upon beech;

ALCANDER and SEPTIMIUS—From *The Hive*, 1806.

and after he had been employed upon it for about two months,
it one afternoon suddenly split when he was at tea. Clennell,
hearing it crack, immediately suspected the cause, and on finding it rent in such a manner that there was no chance of repair-
ing it, he, in a passion that the labour already bestowed on it
should be lost, threw all the tea-things into the fire. A new
block was made; Thurston was paid another sum of fifteen
pounds for redrawing the figures as before. For this cut
Clennell received one hundred pounds, and the Society for

the Encouragement of Arts presented him with their gold
medal, May 30, 1809."[1] In 1814 he received a commission
from the Earl of Bridgewater to paint a large picture of the
grand banquet given to the Allied Sovereigns in the Guildhall
by the City of London. After overcoming many difficulties,
and enduring much worry and anxiety in obtaining portraits
and sketches of the illustrious personages who were present,
he unfortunately became insane, a malady from which he was
never afterwards entirely free. Lucid intervals there were,

The Northumberland Lifeboat—From *The Hive*, 1806.

when reason seemed again to assert her former power, but
these were only transitory; the material organ of that faculty
of the soul had become fatally impaired, and the great work
on which he had been employed was left to be finished by
another hand (E. Bird, R.A.), who in his turn also became
insane. Not long after, Mrs. Clennell[2] was deprived of reason,
and died, leaving three young children destitute. Such a

---

[1] Jackson's "Treatise on Wood-Engraving," p. 617 (1839).
[2] Mrs. Clennell was the daughter of C. Warren, an excellent copperplate engraver.

calamity awakened the generous sympathy of several noblemen and gentlemen, patrons of the Fine Arts. It was resolved
to publish by subscription an engraving from his picture of
" The Decisive Charge of the Life Guards at Waterloo" for
the benefit of Clennell's helpless children, and to aid in pro-
viding for the future wants of himself. I possess Mr. Bewick's
superb proof impression of the plate, obtained from his daughters.
The following is a copy of the receipt attached :—

CLENNELL SUBSCRIPTION, MAY 22, 1819.

BY AUTHORITY OF THE LONDON COMMITTEE.

I hereby acknowledge the Receipt of Three Pounds, being the Deposit Sub-
scription for a Proof of a Plate, engraved by WM. BROMLEY, *after a Picture*
by LUKE CLENNELL, *representing* " The Decisive Charge of the Life Guards at
Waterloo," *from Mr. T. Bewick.*

N.B.—The whole Receipts arising from this Print to be appropriated towards
the Support and Education of three infant parentless Children of the Painter,
under the Direction of a Committee.

J. BRITTON, F.S.A., *Hon. Sec.*

This picture formed part of the collection of the late Mrs.
George Vaughan, and was sold by Messrs. Christie, Manson,
& Woods on February 23, 1885, for £89, 5s., and bought by
Mr. Vokins. It measures about 24 inches by 36 inches.

Whilst living in the neighbourhood he was accustomed to
call on Mr. Bewick. He was then quite harmless, and had
no misgiving but that he could both draw and cut on wood as
well as in past days, and longed to be put to the test. Bewick,
to amuse him, put a piece of wood into his hands. He went
away happy, and returned some time after with the finished
cut ; but how unlike his former work ! the contrast was pitiable
indeed. No more melancholy or painful spectacle could be

presented than to contemplate the wreck of such a mind. His
wild and pure and beautiful thoughts he took pleasure in com-
mitting to paper. The following specimen of his poetry is now
published for the first time :—

THE COTTAGER.

Written in October 1827.

In my Cabin of aubour
i took my wine
twas mine lot
to be Steward ! of an cot,
to dress the flowing Vine ?

Mine Hind, was at my door
did the forest range
for the green leafs change
Soft was the gale
over ! the Cottage of the vale :

My lute i woud sound
in soft simphoni abound
and my dear mate
my loveli Kate
each flower so rare
did in her bosom wear.

During the latter part of his life he had spent not less than
twenty-two years in lunatic asylums in London and Newcastle.
He lived several years with a relative at St. Peter's Quay,
Newcastle, beguiling the weary days in drawing, music, and
writing poetry. Becoming violent, it was thought prudent in
1831 to place him again under restraint, in which state he
remained until death kindly released him from all his troubles
on the 9th February 1840. In 1844 a handsome marble tablet
was placed in the north transept of St. Andrew's Church, Newcastle, to perpetuate his memory. Many excellent drawings

by this artist are to be found in the collections of local connoisseurs, including Mr. Joseph Crawhall and Mr. Thomas Gow of Cambo. This gentleman has several of Clennell's best drawings of monastic and castellated ruins in Northumberland, made for Sir Walter Scott's "Border Antiquities." Not less than sixty-four engravings in this important work are from drawings by Clennell. Mr. M. Lambert of Newcastle owns a very interesting little picture representing a scene on the Town Moor, Newcastle, on the day after the Cowhill Fair. Alderman Cail, of the Low Fell, Gateshead, has

The Grateful Turk—From *The Hive*, 1806.

several choice examples by the same artist. A few pleasing specimens, obtained from Miss Bewick, I have the pleasure to possess.

Mr. Austin Dobson, in his elegant monograph, "Thomas Bewick and his Pupils," speaking of Clennell, observes that his "last work of any moment as a wood-engraver is the series of cuts which illustrate Rogers' 'Pleasures of Memory, with Other Poems.' This little volume has an established reputation with collectors, and the excellence of the cuts as enlightened renderings of pen-and-ink sketches can scarcely be exaggerated."[1]

[1] The engravings are from pen-and-ink drawings by T. Stothard, R.A., Bensley, 1810–12–14.

2 L

ILLIAM HARVEY was born at Newcastle-upon-Tyne on the 13th of July 1796, his father being keeper of the Public Baths at the Westgate, and at the age of fourteen he was apprenticed to Thomas Bewick for the usual term of seven years to learn the art of engraving on wood. In 1817 he went to London, where he became a pupil of the unfortunate Benjamin R. Haydon, and studied anatomy under Sir Charles Bell along with those distinguished artists, Sir Charles Eastlake, George Lance, and Sir Edwin Landseer. His elaborate engraving of the Assassination of Dentatus, from a painting by Haydon, will ever remain as a witness of his skill and perseverance. His illustrations to Lane's translation of the "Arabian Nights," Henderson's "History of Wines," and the designs supplied to Northcote's Fables, mainly engraved by Nesbit and John Jackson, attest the versatility of his genius.

From about the age of thirty he gave up the practice of wood-engraving, and, like Thurston, confined himself to that of designing book illustrations for the trade.

I cannot here forego the pleasure of placing on record the following extract from a letter I had the honour to receive from Mr. Harvey, who was Bewick's favourite pupil. Fifty years had then passed since he worked as an apprentice under the eye of his distinguished master.

VINEYARD, RICHMOND, SURREY,
18th October 1860.

MY DEAR SIR,—I am really ashamed at having suffered your kind and flattering letter of the 22d of August to remain so long without an answer; but I trust to a charitable view of my case when I assure you the real delinquent has been your enthusiastic friend. . . . I shall feel great pleasure in forwarding you the impressions of Dentatus as soon as I can find an hour to look them

over, and delighted to be of any use to you in illustrating, by any little knowledge I may possess, the works of our great townsman, and in assisting you to
avoid the mistakes of many of his well-intentioned friends in attributing to him
the execution of engravings in which he had no share. I consider him so
superior to any one of his followers, that a careful "weeding" is more calculated
to serve than detract from his transcendent merit. The designs by Thurston for
Burns, I believe, were entirely engraved by Harry White. I merely mention
this as a case in point. Pray ask me, without reserve, anything in which I can
be of service to you in this matter, and believe me, yours very truly,

WILLIAM HARVEY.

To R. Robinson, Esq.

Mr. Harvey, esteemed by all who knew him, died at Prospect
Lodge, Richmond, on the 13th of January 1866.

THE OLD COACH OFFICE, NEWCASTLE.

OHN JACKSON was born at Ovingham, Bewick's native parish, on the 19th of April 1801. His youthful attempts at drawing attracted notice, for the fame of Bewick had awakened an interest in art previously unknown in the locality. It was the old story. When it was found that a boy of the village, without help or encouragement, was trying to express the power that was within him by chalking horses and dogs on barn doors, for want of better material, it was determined to extend a helping hand to the young artist. As Bewick had achieved success by becoming a wood-engraver, it was thought that was the best line for John Jackson to pursue, and through the interest of some gentlemen of the neighbourhood, he was apprenticed to Messrs. Armstrong & Walker, engravers and printers in Newcastle.

Armstrong & Walker having become bankrupt, Jackson was transferred to the workshop of Thomas Bewick, where he finished his apprenticeship. He then came to London, but there was so little apparent prospect of making a living, that Jackson seriously entertained a proposal that was made to him to go to Paris. He, however, had the good fortune to please Northcote, who was then preparing his Fables, and he was largely employed on that work, his name appearing to as many as one hundred and fifty in the index of engravings in the first series. The conscientious care he bestowed upon his work began to tell, and employment flowed in upon him from other quarters. When the Society for the Diffusion of Useful Knowledge began its operations, the art of wood-engraving received a powerful impetus under the directing influence of Mr. Charles Knight, who placed the chief part of the engravings for the *Penny Magazine* in Jackson's hands.

ST. MARY'S CHAPEL, TYNEMOUTH PRIORY.

John Jackson drew and painted domestic subjects with much originality of feeling, and he always had a strong desire to be a painter. He might have realised that ambition under more favourable circumstances, but he had all his life to contend against the depressing influence of bad health, and he was never able to do more in drawing and painting than amuse himself occasionally to relieve the tedium of his profession as an engraver. With the exception of a few weeks in the summer, he was compelled to take his recreation indoors, and among other amusements he collected materials for a history of wood-engraving, which, with the assistance of his friend, the late Mr. W. A. Chatto, resulted in the publication of the well-known work on that subject. Some good examples of Jackson's work both as a draughtsman and an engraver will be found in the latter part of "The Treatise on Wood-Engraving."

John Jackson died in London, March 27, 1848.

PORTRAITS

OF

THOMAS BEWICK,

Several of which have been Engraved.

———•———

The following is a list of them :—

1. Mr. Thos. Bewick, the celebrated Engraver on Wood, Miss Kirkley Pinxt., T. A. Kidd Sculpt.   Published as the Act directs, Jan. 4, 1798, by G. G. and J. Robinson, Paternoster Row, and W. Lubbock, Newcastle-upon-Tyne.

> This engraving, of which early impressions are extremely rare, was inserted in the *Gentleman's Magazine* for January 1829.

2. Mr. Thos. Bewick, restorer of the art of engraving on wood.   From an original miniature by Murphy, in the possession of Mr. Bewick, with whose permission this plate is engraved and published by J. Summerfield, November 1, 1815.

> The following year this plate was again published by T. M'Lean, Sackville Street, Piccadilly, February 1, 1816 ; but this also is now of considerable rarity.   Mr. Joseph Crawhall and Mr. J. W. Barnes of Durham, the executors of the late Miss Isabella Bewick, presented to the Museum of the Natural History Society, Newcastle, the beautiful drawing by Miss Kirkley, fresh as when first painted, and the equally beautiful miniatures on ivory by Murphy and Plymer.   The latter was much prized by the Misses Bewick.

3. Thomas Bewick, the celebrated Engraver on Wood. London, published by T. Ranson,[1] Judd Place West, New Road, and Messrs. Boydell, Cheapside, Jan. 1816.

> This print was engraved by subscription, and deemed the best portrait of Bewick which had then been executed. Falling into the hands of a local bookseller, he had it cut down to an octavo size, and used it as a frontispiece to several of Bewick's works. Both are now rarely to be met with. The original painting by William Nicholson is in the collection of the Right Hon. Earl Ravensworth, Ravensworth Castle. Mr. Charnley's fine dog "Don" is introduced by the side of the artist.

4. Mr. Thos. Bewick, Engraver on Wood, painted by Jas. Ramsey, engraved by Jno. Burnett, Pub. Oct. 25, 1817, for the Proprietor, at Molteno's, Pall Mall, and Colnaghi's, Cockspur Street.

> Original impressions of this beautiful portrait are now extremely rare. Bewick considered it by far the best likeness of himself. It was originally published at 21s. The artist made a present of the picture to Mrs. Bewick. Through the liberality of the executors it was also sent to the Museum.

5. Thomas Bewick, pencilled on the block by William Nicholson, and engraved by Charlton Nesbit, 1820.

> This portrait appeared as the frontispiece to Charnley's edition of the Select Fables, and was afterwards printed with a View of the Old Exchange, in Newcastle, on 4to, with large Cuts of a Tiger, Elephant,

---

[1] Thomas Fryer Ranson was born at Sunderland in 1784, and served his apprenticeship as an engraver with J. A. Kidd of Newcastle, after which he removed to London, and in 1814 received the silver medal of the Society of Arts for engraving a portrait of Sir Thomas Gresham. In 1818 he entered warmly into the controversy respecting the forgery of bank notes, on which the Bank authorities commenced proceedings against him, and he was confined in Coldbath-Fields Prison, where he engraved "An interior view of Cold-Bath-Fields Prison, in which "Thomas Ranson was unlawfully confined by the Bank of England, for holding an alledged "forged One Pound Note (that he paid forty shillings for), which was proved to be genuine by "a Court of Justice. Dedicated, without permission, to the Governor and Company of the "Threadneedle Street Paper Establishment." In 1821 he received from the Society of Arts a gold medal for his line engraving from a portrait of the Duke of Northumberland; and in 1822 another gold medal for his engraving from Wilkie's picture "Duncan Gray."

and Zebra, all by Nicholson. The Lion in this set was drawn on the wood by Bewick, and engraved by W. W. Temple. This fine woodcut was executed for the late Mr. Charnley a considerable time before the others. When finished it gave little satisfaction, for the skin had a wavy appearance, more like marble than hair. It was returned to Mr. Bewick, at his own request, who went three times over the work before it was brought to perfection. Impressions of this beautiful cut on vellum in the first, second, and third states are in my collection. Besides this portrait, Charnley gave in his Select Fables reduced facsimiles of the portraits engraved by Kidd, Ranson, Summerfield, and Burnett.

6. Thomas Bewick, drawn and engraved on wood by John Jackson, probably when a pupil with Bewick.

This Cut was inserted, with the account of Bewick's death, in the Local Historian's Table Book, published at Newcastle by Mr. M. A. Richardson. Mr. Jackson engraved on wood from recollection another portrait of Bewick which appeared in his History of Wood-Engraving.

7. Thomas Bewick, drawn and engraved by Edward Train, from a bust by Baily.

This portrait illustrated a memoir of Bewick and his works, by George Clayton Atkinson, Esq., of Newcastle, which was published in the Transactions of the Natural History Society of Newcastle for 1830.

8. Thomas Bewick, engraved on wood by Heaviside, after the picture by Nicholson.

This portrait, with a short memoir by William Howitt, appeared in Howitt's Journal, No. 38, vol. ii., Sept. 18, 1846.

9. A Portrait of Thomas Bewick was published as frontispiece to vol. v. of Jardine's Naturalist's Library.

10. Thomas Bewick, engraved on steel by F. Bacon, and published by Robert Turner, Newcastle, in 1852, from a highly-finished full length painting on panel by Jas. Ramsey in 1823, in the collection of Mr. R. S. Newall, Fern Dene, Gateshead.

TYNEMOUTH PRIORY AND LIGHTHOUSE.

11. Thomas Bewick, etched by Leopold Flameng (1880) from a beautiful drawing by William Nicholson, the property of Mr. Thomas Crawhall, Condercum, Newcastle. This fine work of art was painted for the late Mr. Emerson Charnley, Bewick's local publisher. R. E. Bewick was accustomed to bring friends to see it, he considered the likeness so faithful.

12. Thomas Bewick, a full-length painting in oil, by T. S. Good of Berwick, well drawn and highly finished, as Audubon remarks. This was the picture so much coveted by Dr. Dibdin to adorn his " Northern Tour," and which, by special resolution of the Committee of the Newcastle Natural History Society, is now engraved for the first time as a frontispiece to this volume.

This admirable work of art was presented to the Museum of the Society by the executors of the late Miss Isabella Bewick.

In addition to the portraits enumerated, there is one at Cherryburn by George Gray, a present to Bewick's mother. A fine miniature by W. Nicholson (John Trotter Brockett's) is now in my collection.

CATALOGUE

OF THE

PRINCIPAL WORKS ILLUSTRATED

BY

THOMAS AND JOHN BEWICK.

———•———

(1.) A Treatise on Mensuration, both in Theory and Practice, by Charles Hutton, Newcastle-upon-Tyne, printed by T. Saint, for the author, and for John Wilkie, St. Paul's Churchyard, and Richard Baldwin in Paternoster Row, London.   1770.

> This work, which is in 4to, was published by subscription, and in numbers. It was commenced in 1768, and completed in 1770, and is dedicated to Hugh Percy, Duke and Earl of Northumberland: the armorial bearings which embellish the dedication are understood to have been engraved by Beilby.   It contains 648 pages, besides 26 of preface, and list of subscribers.   The diagrams are plain, but neatly executed, and are exceedingly numerous.   The copperplate at page 600 is also by Beilby.   At page 42 there is a view (diagram) of the Tower and Steeple of St. Nicholas' Cathedral, Newcastle, Bewick's earliest known woodcut.

(2.) The Youth's Instructive and Entertaining Story Teller. 12mo.   Printed by Saint, Newcastle, 1774.

> Many of the cuts of this work, considering them as Bewick's earliest productions, are beautiful, and show the wonderful progress he had made in the art in so short a period.   A second edition of it was published in 1775;[1] the third edition, with 37 cuts, in 1778.   All are of great rarity.

---

[1] Some of the cuts of this work are introduced as vignettes in Charnley's edition of the Select Fables, as also various other cuts which occur in the juvenile publications of T. Saint at this period.

(3.) Moral Instructions of a Father to his Son, comprehending the Whole System of Morality, &c., and Select Fables on the most important occasions of Life, extracted from Dodsley and others. Adorned with Emblematical Cuts. Third Edition. Newcastle, printed by and for T. Saint. MDCCLXXV. 12mo, pp. 168. With 34 Woodcuts.

> Many of these woodcuts were the work of Thomas Bewick during the early years of his apprenticeship, and on this account interesting. Nearly the whole of the cuts appear in the rare edition of Select Fables, published by Saint in 1776. My copy has John Bewick's autograph (1775) on first leaf, and the autograph of Thomas Bewick (1776) on the last. It was bought of Miss Bewick.

(4.) Fables by the late Mr. Gay, in one volume complete, with cuts by Thomas and John Bewick. 18mo. Newcastle, printed by and for T. Saint, W. Charnley, and J. Whitfield and Co. 1779. Pp. viii. 252.

> In the advertisement announcing the publication of this book Saint terms it " A new and elegant edition of Gay's Fables in 8vo, on fine writing foolscap, adorned with very curious cuts and a finely engraved frontispiece ; some of these cuts have gained the premium of the Royal Society," —alluding to the five prints, for the execution of which the Society of Arts presented Bewick with the sum of seven guineas. It contains 67 cuts and 33 vignettes by Bewick, and an engraved frontispiece by Beilby, and was published at 3s., but is now rarely to be met with. A good copy is worth 50s., the price paid for my choice copy at the sale of Mr. Hugo's collection. It has the autograph, " Jno. Bell, Novo Castro," on fly-leaf. Other editions of this work were printed in Newcastle by Saint, and his successors Hall and Elliot, and afterwards at York by Wilson and Spence, all having the same cuts. Nearly the whole of the last edition printed in Newcastle was sold to an Edinburgh bookseller, who printed a new title-page, with the following imprint—" Edinburgh, printed for W. Coke, Leith, 1792."

(5.) A Pretty Book of Pictures for Little Masters and Misses, or Tommy Trip's History of Beasts and Birds, with a familiar description of each, in verse and prose; to which is prefixed the History of Little Tom Trip himself and his Dog Jouler, and of Woglog, the Great Giant. Newcastle, Saint, square 24mo, 1779.

> Though this little work went through several editions, it is rarely to be met with. It contains 62 woodcuts. Mr. Clayton Atkinson states that we are indebted to this little book for Bewick's more celebrated productions, the Histories of Quadrupeds and of British Birds. Several of these cuts were afterwards introduced as tailpieces in Charnley's edition of the Select Fables: see that work, pages 66, 144, 152, 214, 226, 244, 262, 276, and 290. The 12th edition, though also from a Newcastle press, is stated to be printed in London for the booksellers in town and country.

(6.) A Curious Hieroglyphick Bible, or Select Passages in the Old and New Testaments, represented with emblematical figures, for the amusement of youth; designed chiefly to familiarize tender age, in a pleasing and diverting manner, with early ideas of the Holy Scriptures; to which are subjoined, a Short Account of the lives of the Evangelists, and other pieces, illustrated with cuts.

> This little book, which was published in London by T. Hodgson about 1780, contains several cuts by Bewick, though the whole of the cuts are not by him. It passed through many editions. The third edition is dated 1785, the thirteenth being published by Robert Bassam, by assignment from the executors of T. Hodgson, in 1796, price 1s. plain, 2s. coloured. The frontispiece, representing Adam and Eve in Paradise, the Last Judgment, and that at p. 134, are by Bewick.

(7.) Select Fables, in three parts. Part I., Fables extracted from Dodsley's; Part II., Fables with Reflections, in prose and verse; Part III., Fables in Verse, to which are prefixed the life of Æsop and an Essay upon Fable.[1] A new edition, improved. 12mo. Newcastle, printed by and for T. Saint. 1784.

A book, with nearly a similar title, was printed in Newcastle in 1776, illustrated by 114 small cuts, poorly executed, with two or three exceptions. Part III., Fables in Verse, is embellished with 14 large cuts, executed in a very superior style, 13 of them being introduced in the above. The cut heading Fable IX. is omitted. For this new edition a new set of cuts was engraved by Thomas and John Bewick, assisted by David Martin, an apprentice of Beilby's when Bewick first entered his service. After Saint's death the cuts became (as before mentioned) the property of Hall and Elliott, his successors, who sold them to Wilson and Spence of York, and they afterwards sold them to Charnley of Newcastle, who had them retouched by Nesbit, and part of the ornamental borders removed, and published them uniform with Bewick's other works (see Select Fables, 1820). Mr. Charnley in turn parted with his collection to Mr. Henry George Bohn of York Street, Covent Garden, who published an inferior edition of Charnley's reprint (in demy 8vo only); he, in 1865–6, disposed of them to Mr. Edwin Pearson of London, and are now the property of the Rev. E. Pearson of Cheltenham.

The same year another impression of this work was printed with precisely the same title-page, but with considerable variations in the body of the work; for instance, vignettes occur at pages 122, 125, and 152, which are not in the first edition; the letterpress varies at pages 123, 143, 147, 151, and 164. The parts in verse are shorter, while the Reflections are longer; it also has an index of two pages at the end, which the other has not, and an elegant frontispiece, drawn and engraved on copper by Ra. Beilby. The Misses Bewick presented the writer with a copy of this rare book. Above the title is written, " The Gift of T. Bewick to his little daughter Elizabeth, April 2, 1801 ; " and on the fly-leaf, " Presented by I. and E. Bewick to Mr. R. Robinson, May 15, 1877."

(8.) Choice Emblems, Natural, Historical, Fabulous, Moral, and Divine; for the Improvement and Pastime of Youth; displaying the beauties and Morals of the Antient Fabulists, &c.

---

[1] The first part contains 48 Fables, the second 67 Fables, and the third part 26 Fables ; in all, 141 Fables. The arrangement given in Charnley's edition in 1820 is quite different, and contains 166 Fables. Some of the cuts engraved for Saint's edition of Gay's Fables are also given by Charnley ; but none of the Fables in his edition are in verse. Copies of the work as printed in 1784 are now exceedingly scarce.

London: printed by J. Chapman for E. Newbery, St. Paul's Churchyard, MDCCLXXXI.

> This little work was one of the first productions of John Bewick after his removal to London. It is in 12mo, and contains 69 wood-engravings and a frontispiece on copper. The sixth edition bears date 1788, and was published at 2s.

(9.) The Chillingham Wild Bull, with a beautiful ornamental border; size of the cut 9½ inches by 7½ inches. Newcastle, 1789.

> Every attention was paid by Bewick to this cut. The border, which was of a highly ornamental character, was about three-quarters of an inch in breadth. From the block, which was finished and sent to the printer's on a Saturday, four beautiful impressions were taken on thin drawing vellum, at the suggestion of Mr. John Bell of Newcastle, land surveyor, who was aware that the beauty of the cut would appear much finer on vellum than on paper. These four copies were appropriated, one to Mr. Tunstall,[1] another to Mr. Beilby (Mr. Bewick's partner), the third to Mr. Hodgson the printer, and the fourth to Mr. John Bell. It is understood that Mrs. Hodgson sold the copy belonging to her to Earl Spencer, and Mr. Beilby's copy has also been disposed of. The price obtained for one, if not both of these copies, is stated to be twenty guineas. The block, after these impressions were taken, was cleaned, and heedlessly laid in a window, where it remained until the Monday morning, and when the workmen arrived at the printing office they found it split into two pieces, apparently by the heat of the sun during the Sunday. Immediate attempts were made to repair the accident, and the block was screwed together, and impressions were eventually taken for sale, but these impressions showed a deficiency in the cut by a ragged white line running across it, hardly the breadth of a hair; afterwards it was found necessary to remove the ornamental border, so as to endeavour to screw the pieces of the block tighter together, which

---

[1] See a Memoir of Tunstall, in the Synopsis of the Newcastle Museum, by G. T. Fox, and a particular account of his Museum, which was sold soon after his death to George Allan, Esq., and on the death of the latter gentleman (principally through the interest excited in reference to it by Bewick and a few friends) became the property of the Literary and Philosophical Society of Newcastle.

was done so as to remove the white line. The later impressions, therefore, are found wanting the border. Repairs were made about the year
1817, and more lately in 1876, after my purchase of the block from the
Misses Bewick. I then took it out of the old iron frame in which it
had so long been clamped up, removed the mahogany wedges, and inserted others of boxwood, carefully wedging the precious woodcut in a
new frame of gun metal. For this my best thanks are due to Mr. Henry
Watson of the High Bridge Brass Works, Newcastle. *Vide* pp. 78–80 of
this work.

(10.) Emblems of Mortality; representing, in upwards of
fifty cuts, Death seizing all Ranks and Degrees of People,
imitated from a painting in the cemetery of the Dominican
Church at Basil in Switzerland; with an Apostrophe to each,
translated from the Latin and French. Intended as well for
the information of the curious as the instruction and entertain-
ment of youth. To which is prefixed a copious Preface, containing an Historical Account of the above, and other paintings
on this subject, now or lately existing in divers parts of Europe.
(12mo.) London: printed for T. Hodgson, in George's Court,
St. John's Lane, Clerkenwell, 1789. Pp. xxviii. 51.

> The cuts to this book were engraved by John Bewick, and display con-
> siderable talent. The work went through only three editions, the blocks
> being destroyed by fire in London. The third edition is much inferior
> to the two first. Charnley of Newcastle at a subsequent time reprinted
> the title, inserting his own name in lieu of Hodgson's, but retaining the
> original date. Another edition of this work, with woodcuts imitating
> those of Bewick, but much inferior, was published in London at a sub-
> sequent period, but has the same number of cuts, and is also of great
> rarity. My copy of the first edition of this rare work has on the title the
> autograph, "Thomas Bewick, Newcastle." The original drawings are in
> my collection. The Preface was written by John Sidney Hawkins, Esq.

(11.) The Whitley Large Ox, belonging to Mr. Edward
Hall of Whitley, in Northumberland. Rising seven years
when killed at Newcastle by Mr. Thomas Horsley; weighed

187 st. at the public weigh-house, March 21, 1789. Drawn and engraved by Thomas Bewick. Newcastle : published and sold by Beilby and Bewick, Newcastle, April 10, 1789.

> This is a copperplate, measuring 10¾ inches by 7¾ inches. In the background is a view of the celebrated ruin of Tynemouth Abbey.

(12). A Tour through Sweden, Swedish Lapland, Finland, and Denmark. In a series of letters ; illustrated with copper plates, designed and engraved by Ralph Beilby and Thomas Bewick. By Matthew Consett, Esq., who accompanied Sir H. G. Liddell, Bart., and Mr. Bowes, in his Tour. Stockton : printed by R. Christopher, 1789. (Demy 4to.)

> The birds in this work were engraved from drawings sent to the artist. The fine plate of the Reindeer, and that representing Sighre and Aniea, were designed and engraved by Mr. Bewick. Beilby, as a partner, insisted on having his name introduced on the copperplates. My authority is Miss Bewick : "I have heard my father say," she remarked, "that Beilby had no hand whatever in any of these plates." See pp. 80, 81 of this work.
>
> A second edition was published in 12mo, Stockton, 1815.
>
> An interesting notice of Consett's Tour will be found in Fox's Synopsis of the Newcastle Museum, pp. 289, 292. This work also contains a variety of other matter relating to Bewick and his works.

(13.) Proverbs Exemplified, and Illustrated, by pictures from real life, teaching morality and a knowledge of the world, with prints ; designed as a succession book to Æsop's Fables, after the manner, and by the author of Hogarth Moralised. Printed for and published by the Rev. J. Trusler, and sold at the Literary Press, No. 62 Wardour Street, Soho, and by all booksellers. Entered at Stationers' Hall. Price three shillings, half-bound. London, May 1, 1790.

> This work consists of 196 pages, 12mo, and contains 50 woodcuts from the graver of John Bewick, most of them bearing tokens of considerable

ability. Those at pp. 13 and 97 are amongst the best. My copy has the autograph, "Thomas Bewick, Newcastle," on the title, and was bought of Miss Bewick.

(14.) Proverbs in Verse, or Moral Instruction conveyed in Pictures, for the use of schools, on the plan of Hogarth Moralised, by the same author, with fifty-six cuts; to which are prefixed rules for reading verse. London: sold by J. Souter, 1 Paternoster Row.

> The illustrations to this book, which is in 12mo, pp. 124, are also by John Bewick. It has no date, but was published about the same time as the preceding work.

(15.) Harrison's Nursery Picture Book, containing seventy interesting engravings. Devizes: printed and published by J. Harrison, and sold by the booksellers and stationers.

> A pretty little book, illustrated by John Bewick. It has two cuts on a page, and is without letterpress, save a short inscription to each cut.

(16.) A General History of Quadrupeds. The figures engraved on wood by T. Bewick. Newcastle-upon-Tyne: printed by & for S. Hodgson, R. Beilby, & T. Bewick. Newcastle: sold by them, by G. G. J. and J. Robinson, and C. Dilly, London, 1790.

> Of this, the first edition, fifteen hundred copies were printed on demy, and one hundred on royal 8vo, the former being sold for 8s., and the latter for 12s. It contains 456 pages, and is illustrated by 200 figures and 104 tail-pieces, and was published on the 27th of April.[1]

---

[1] In Mr. John Bell's (of Newcastle) Catalogue of Books, printed in 1795, occur the following interesting copies of the first edition of the Quadrupeds :—

"A copy of Bewick's Quadrupeds, printed on Whatman's fine wove atlas vellum paper, on which only two copies were printed." The late E. B. Jupp's copy brought £50 at the sale of his fine collection in 1878. It was bought of R. Robinson.

"Another copy, the cuts only (above 130) taken off upon strong writing paper, music 4to size, one on a leaf, for colouring."

"Another copy, the cuts only, proof impressions, on wove demy paper; two, three, and four of the animals on a leaf, interleaved with writing paper. This is a unique book."

2 N

The second edition appeared the following year, the same number of demy copies being printed and sold at 9s. each, and three hundred on royal, which were sold at 12s. The work was increased to 483 pages, containing 212 figures and 108 tail-pieces, many of the latter in both this and the first edition being reprinted, or given in duplicate. The principal addition to this edition was the Bats. The impressions of the cuts in the royal paper copies are brilliant.

The third edition in 1792 was nearly a reprint of the second, the number of pages and illustrations being the same; the only alterations occurring are the addition of a note at page 392 respecting the application of mole-skins in the manufacture of hats, and the variation of several of the tail-pieces, different ones occurring in the third edition at pages 16, 80, 87, 94, 192, 194, 207, 236, 290, 344, 351, 357, 386, 391, 398, and 419, from those in the second edition, by which means the repetition of the cuts of this nature, which occurred in the two first editions, was avoided. The impression was of like number, and the price similar, and the edition was printed in demy and royal octavo.

The fourth edition, which was published in 1800, shows a considerable improvement. It contains 525 pages, and has 225 figures and 100 tail-pieces, and the Linnæan names of the animals are introduced. This is the first edition of which imperial paper copies were taken. The impression was as follows:—Two hundred and thirty on imperial 8vo, which sold at 21s.; three hundred on royal 8vo, at 15s.; and one thousand on demy 8vo, at 10s. 6d. On the publication of this edition some difference arose between Messrs. Beilby, Bewick, and Hodgson as to the disposal of the copies, and it was finally arranged that each party should have a third share of the edition, and dispose of it as he should think fit. Beilby, having then retired from business, sold his share to Mr. John Bell, book-seller, of Newcastle, in consequence of which his name is introduced into the title of a portion of this edition. Mr. Beilby soon after sold his interest in the copyright and engravings of the work to Mr. Bewick, between whom and Mrs. Hodgson[1] the altercation became so violent, that both parties appealed to the public (see the Annual Review for 1804, Monthly Magazine, August 1805, &c.)

The fifth edition was not published until 1807, and was then printed by

---

[1] Mr. Solomon Hodgson died April 4, 1800, in the fortieth year of his age, and was interred in St. John's Churchyard, Newcastle. Mr. Bewick executed a very beautiful wood-engraving to his memory, which, through the kindness of his grandson, James Hodgson, Esq., of Newcastle, has been inserted at page 218 of the present volume.

Edward Walker of Newcastle. In it there appears an addition of one figure and one tail-piece on the same number of pages. None of this edition was printed on royal paper. The price of the book was now advanced to 13s. for the demy, and £1, 11s. 6d. for the imperial copies. Bewick sold his share of this edition to Messrs. Longmans & Co., of London.

The sixth edition is again similar to the fifth, consisting of the same number of pages and illustrations. It appeared in 1811, and was only printed on demy paper, the price being further raised to 21s.

In 1818 twenty-five copies of the figures to the Quadrupeds were printed on demy 4to paper, without letterpress, and were sold for 2 guineas in sheets.

The seventh edition was issued in 1820, and an eighth in 1824, but they are both very similar to that done in 1811. Of both editions copies were printed on imperial, royal, and demy paper, the prices being £1, 1s. for the demy, £1, 11s. 6d. for the royal, and £2, 2s. for the imperial paper.

Shortly before her death, Miss Isabella Bewick sold me a demy copy, with additions in MS. by Mr. Bewick, giving an enlarged and minute account of the Wombach, intended for insertion in a subsequent edition, with corrections of the text. This last impression, published in the author's lifetime, contains 226 figures of animals, 76 vignettes, and 29 of an inferior class.

A second edition of the figures to the Quadrupeds without letterpress was printed in 1824, both on octavo and quarto paper; and the vignettes (or tail-pieces) were also done in the same manner as a supplement. The impression was very small (250), and copies are rarely to be met with.

The descriptive part of the History of Quadrupeds was written by Mr. Beilby,[1] at that time partner with Bewick. The work was favourably received by the public, and highly praised by the critics of the day (see the Critical, English, Monthly, Analytical, and Annual Reviews),[2] par-

---

[1] Ralph Beilby died 4th January 1817, in his seventy-fourth year.

[2] From a long and highly commendatory article in the last-mentioned Review (vol. iii. p. 729), the following is taken:—"It was reserved for Mr. Bewick to restore to its original dignity a nearly forgotten art. Educated for the profession of an engraver, but endowed with a painter's eye, he could not confine his attention to the mechanical operations of his regular business, and, though placed by the accident of his birth in a provincial town, at a great distance from the capital and from extensive patronage, his native genius burst through every impediment, and pointed out to him the way to celebrity and honour. His particular turn of mind led him to observe and to delineate the form and manners of the animal creation, and he soon found that the yielding consistence of wood is better fitted to express the ease, freedom,

ticularly on account of the correctness of the drawing and superiority of the wood-engravings to any that had previously appeared, and the taste and care bestowed on the subordinate parts of the subject. The tail-pieces to many of the chapters are full of interest and pathos, though some are rather tinged by a want of delicacy, occasionally indulged in by the artist.

In January 1828 a short memoir of Mr. Bewick appeared in the *Gentleman's Magazine*, in which, speaking of the History of Quadrupeds, the writer says: "Perhaps there never was a work to which the rising generation of the day was, and no doubt the rising generation for many years to come will be, under such obligations for exciting in them a taste for the natural history of animals. The representations which are given of the various tribes possess a boldness of design, a correctness of outline, an exactness of attitude, and a discrimination of general character which convey at the first glance a just and lively idea of each different animal."

(17.) The remarkable Kyloe Ox, bred in the Mull, Argyleshire, by Donald Campbell, Esq., and fed by Mr. Robert Spearman, of Rotheley Park, Northumberland. Six years old, killed July 22d, 1790. Drawn and engraved by Thomas Bewick, 1790.

This copperplate was engraved for Mr. Spearman, and measures 13 inches by 10. Copies in the first state are now of great rarity. The drawing is in the Museum of the Natural History Society, Newcastle.

and spirit which ought to characterise portraits of animated beings, than the stubborn surface of a metallic substance. He accordingly engraved wooden blocks of all the domestic and most of the wild British Quadrupeds, and neglected no opportunity of drawing such foreign animals as were exhibited in the itinerant collections which visited Newcastle-upon-Tyne. These universally show the hand of a master. There is in them a boldness of design, a correctness of outline, an exactness of attitude, and a discrimination of general character, conveying at the first glance a just and lively idea of each different animal, to which nothing in modern times has ever aspired, and which the most eminent old artists have not surpassed. But Mr. Bewick's merits as an artist extend far beyond the simple delineation of the animal. The landscapes which he sometimes introduces as a background and relief to his principal figures, as well as the greater part of his numerous vignettes, have a similar excellence; and though the parts of which they consist are extremely minute, there is in them a truth to nature whioh admits of strictest examination, and will be admired in proportion as they are more attentively observed and better understood. Many of them are adapted to the work, and exhibit several of our domestic animals in various situations and modes of action."

(18.) Pieces of Antient Popular Poetry, from authentic manuscripts and old printed copies, adorned with cuts (post 8vo). London: printed by C. Clark, &c., 1791.

> This interesting volume (compiled by Ritson) contains 14 cuts by Thomas and John Bewick, partly facsimiles of the cuts occurring in the original poems. A second edition, with the same cuts, was published by Pickering in 1833.

(19.) The Progress of Man and Society, illustrated by upwards of one hundred and twenty cuts, opening the eyes and unfolding the mind of youth gradually. By the Rev. Dr. Trusler, author of Hogarth Moralised, Proverbs Exemplified, &c. &c. The best knowledge of Man is Man. London: printed for the Author, John Trusler, at the Literary Press, No. 62, Wardour Street, Soho. Entered at Stationers' Hall, July 1791. (12mo.) Price 5s. bound; picked impressions, 7s. MDCCXCI.

> My fine paper copy, with picked impressions, has the autograph, "Thomas Bewick, Newcastle," on the title. It was purchased of Miss Bewick, who has written above the imprint, "The cuts designed and engraved by John Bewick."
>
> The second edition, which appeared in 1810 (but bears no date), was much altered by a rearrangement of the cuts, and the addition of some fresh ones; the title also varies a little.

(20.) The Poetical Works of Oliver Goldsmith, M.B., Complete in one volume, with the Life of the Author. The Vignettes Designed and Engraved on Wood by T. Bewick. Hereford: printed by D. Walker, at the Office of the Hereford Journal, in the High-Town. 1794.

> This work, which is printed in 18mo, and was published at 2s. 6d. sewed, contains six beautiful cuts. Walker published another edition, the same

size, and containing the same cuts, in 1809, at Gloucester. The charming vignette on the title is one of Bewick's happiest efforts. The title and imprint was afterwards adapted to suit the London sale. The publisher was J. Parsons, Paternoster Row.

(21.) Tales for Youth, in thirty poems; to which are annexed Historical Remarks and Moral Applications in Prose, by the author of "Choice Emblems for the Improvement of Youth, &c.," ornamented with cuts, neatly designed and engraved on wood by Bewick. London : printed by J. Crowder, for E. Newbery, the corner of St. Paul's Churchyard. 1794.

This little work is in 12mo. It contains 30 beautiful cuts by John Bewick, many of them equal to the highest efforts of his genius : that of a prowling cat at page 55 has been pronounced the most natural likeness of that animal ever engraved. The work is written by Mr. J. H. Wynne. I possess the whole of the wood blocks. My copy of this work was bought of Miss Bewick, and has her autograph on the fly-leaf, "Isabella Bewick, 1798." In 1815 another edition of it was published in 18mo by J. Harris, St. Paul's Churchyard, with the addition of 24 new cuts, making in the whole 54 cuts; but the additional cuts are understood not to have been engraved by Bewick.

(22.) The Looking-Glass for the Mind, or Intellectual Mirror, being an elegant collection of the most delightful stories and interesting tales, chiefly translated from that much admired work, L'Amie des Enfans. A new edition, with seventy-four cuts, designed and engraved on wood by John Bewick. London : printed by J. Crowder, for E. Newbery, the corner of St. Paul's Churchyard. 1794.

> This work went through a great number of editions, but all were mere reprints of their predecessors. The seventh edition appeared in 1798, the ninth in 1803, the fifteenth was published in 1821. In the early editions is a copperplate frontispiece, which does not occur in the latter ones, representing a lady, attended by Virtue and Prudence, presenting her children to Minerva, from whom they are receiving the " Looking Glass." All editions consist of 271 pages 12mo.

(23.) The Blossoms of Morality, intended for the Amusement and Instruction of Young Ladies and Gentlemen, by the Editor of the "Looking Glass for the Mind," with forty-seven cuts, designed and engraved by J. Bewick. London : printed for E. Newbery, the corner of St. Paul's Churchyard. MDCCXCVI. 12mo, pp. x. 221.

> This is the first edition with cuts by John Bewick. The publisher, in his advertisement, observes : " Much time has elapsed since the commencement of this edition, owing to a severe indisposition with which the artist was long afflicted, and which unfortunately terminated in his death. And sorry, very sorry, are we compelled to state that this is the last effort of his incomparable genius.—Oct. 6, 1796." The work passed through several editions ; the third is dated 1801, the fifth 1810, and the sixth 1814.

(24.) Poems by Goldsmith and Parnell, London : printed by W. Bulmer and Co., Shakespeare Printing Office, Cleveland Row, 1795.

The original edition was in royal 4to in 1795, which was followed by another impression in 1796 in royal 8vo. Another edition, called the second, appeared in 1802 in royal 8vo, and was followed in 1804 by another impression on the same sized paper. Of the original, one copy was printed on white satin for a gentleman of Altona, and three were done on fine vellum, at twelve guineas each; one went to the Royal Library, the second to that of Mr. Hoare, and the third was bought by Mr. Edwards the bookseller, and was in 1804 sold by auction, when Sir M. M. Sykes bought it for 14 guineas. Such was the success of the work that, after paying all expenses, Bulmer [1] realised a profit of £1500.

(25.) Robin Hood, a collection of all the Antient Poems, Songs, and Ballads now extant, relative to that celebrated English Outlaw; to which are prefixed Historical Anecdotes of his Life. 2 vols. post 8vo. London: printed for T. Egerton, Whitehall, and J. Johnson, St. Paul's Churchyard. 1795.

I have the pleasure to possess Miss Isabella Bewick's copy of this interesting work of the late Joseph Ritson, which contains 58 woodcuts by Thomas and John Bewick. In it that lady has noted the passages omitted by Mr. Pickering in the second edition, published in 1832. These occur in the Life of Robin Hood, and in the notes and illustrations which follow. The fine cut at p. 1, vol. i., is by Thomas Bewick. The above was bought of Miss Bewick, and contains her autograph, "*Isabella Bewick, Gateshead,*" in both vols., and R. E. Bewick's autograph and book-plate.

A collection of poems relative to Robin Hood, under the title of " Robin Hood's Garland, being a complete History of all the notable exploits performed by him and his men," &c., was printed by Saint in Newcastle, at a very early period, with cuts by Thomas Bewick. Many editions of the work were printed, and the cuts being sold, with others, to Wilson and Spence of York, they afterwards printed various editions of it.

---

[1] William Bulmer was a native of Newcastle, where he was born in 1757. He learned the printing business under Isaac Thompson, in the Burnt House Entry, in the Side. He left Newcastle for London, visited Paris, returned to London, where in 1787 he established the Shakespeare Press, forming a valuable connection with Mr. Nichols, bookseller to George III. He retired in 1819 with an ample fortune. From this time he resided at Clapham Rise, Surrey, where he died in 1830, aged seventy-three.

(26.) The Chase, a Poem, by William Somervile, Esq., with woodcuts engraved by Thomas Bewick, after designs by John Bewick. London : printed by W. Bulmer and Co., Shakespeare Printing Office, Cleveland Row. 1796.

> The first edition of this beautiful book was printed in the above year in royal 4to, three copies being done on vellum.
>
> The second edition appeared in 1802, and was printed in super royal 8vo. This work contains the best specimens of John Bewick's abilities as a designer. All the cuts were drawn by him except one, but none of them were engraved by him. Shortly after he had finished the drawings on the blocks, he returned to the North, in consequence of ill-health. They were engraved by Thomas Bewick, with the exception of the tail-piece at the end of the volume, which was engraved by Nesbit. Speaking of the death of John Bewick, a writer in the *Gentleman's Magazine* says—" The works of this young artist will be held in estimation, and the engravings to Somervile's Chase will be a monument of Fame of more celebrity than marble can bestow."

(27.) Fabliaux, or Tales abridged from French Manuscripts of the XIIth and XIIIth Centuries, by M. le Grand ; selected and translated into English Verse (by the late Gregory Lewis Way, Esq.) ; with a Preface, Notes (and Appendix, by G. Ellis,

2 O

Esq.) London: printed by W. Bulmer and Co., Shakspeare Press (Cleveland Row, St. James's, and) sold by R. Faulder, New Bond Street. 1796–1800.

> This work is in two volumes, super royal 8vo. The first volume was published in 1796, and the second in 1800. This edition is now scarce. In the above transcript of the title, what is within the parentheses does not occur on the title of the first volume, but does on the second. The first volume contains twenty-five, and the second twenty-seven illustrations.
>
> A second edition appeared in 1815, in 3 volumes small 8vo, published by J. Rodwell, New Bond Street, but was only a reprint of the first.
>
> The cuts in the first volume by Thomas Bewick are "The Priest," p. 49; Vignette, p. 173. "The Lay of Sir Gruelan," p. 177, was finished by him. "The Canonesses," p. 51, is engraved by John Bewick. In the second volume, "The Lay of Narcissus," p. 31, is by Thomas Bewick, who partly engraved the cuts at pp. 14 and 109. The "Three Knights," p. 17, was drawn on the wood by John Bewick. The "Lay of Sir Gugemer," p. 3, was designed by Thurston. Those at pp. 128, 131, 155, 163, 167, 174, are by Luke Clennell.

(28.) History of British Birds. The Figures engraved on wood by T. Bewick. Newcastle: printed by Sol. Hodgson, for Beilby & Bewick: sold by them, and G. G. & J. Robinson, London. 1797, 1804.

> The first edition of the first volume of the History of British Birds (containing 335 pages, exclusive of introduction, &c., illustrated by 117 figures of Birds and 91 tail-pieces) appeared in 1797, and consisted of one thousand copies on demy 8vo, which were published at 10s. 6d., and eight hundred and fifty on thin, and the like number on thick royal, at 13s. and 15s. each, and twenty-four on imperial paper, at 21s. each; and the following year, 1798, a further impression, also bearing date 1797, was printed as follows :—Seven hundred and fifty on demy, six hundred and sixty-nine on royal, and two hundred and seven on imperial. The first edition of volume ii. (consisting of 400 pages, exclusive of introduction, &c., illustrated by 101 figures and 139 vignettes) appeared in 1804, and a similar number was printed on demy paper at 12s. each, on thin royal paper at 15s. each, thick royal paper at 18s. each, and on imperial paper at 24s. The text of volume i. was written by Mr. Beilby, that of volume ii. by

Mr. Bewick, assisted by the Rev. H. Cotes, then vicar of Bedlington, county Northumberland.

The figures of the Land Birds with the tail-pieces were taken off in 8vo in 1800 without the letterpress. Of this edition 500 were printed at 12s.

The second edition of both volumes was published in 1805, volume i. containing 346 pages (exclusive of introduction, &c.), illustrated by 118 figures and 117 vignettes or tail-pieces; and volume ii. consisting of 400 pages (exclusive of introduction, &c.), with 103 figures and 133 tail-pieces. No copies were printed on demy of this edition.

The third edition, published in 1809, was printed on demy paper only.

The fourth edition was also printed only on demy 8vo in 1816; it contains 729 pages, viz., vol. i. 329 pages, and vol. ii. 400 pages.

In 1817 twenty-five copies of the Figures of the Land and Water Birds were taken off on 4to, without letterpress, at £2, 2s. each. These are rarely to be met with. The impressions of the cuts are very fine.

The fifth edition appeared in 1821, to which was added the Supplement.

In 1825 an edition of one hundred copies of the Land and Water Birds and 14 Foreign Birds was taken on quarto paper, without letterpress, at £3, 3s. in sheets. This contains all his Birds, excepting the King Duck, Harlequin Duck, Vulture, Blue-breasted Robin, Reed Wren, and Cream-coloured Plover, which he engraved subsequently.

The sixth edition, printed in 1826, was the last superintended in its passage through the press by Bewick. Copies were printed on imperial, royal, and demy paper. Vol. i. contains 394 pages, with 157 figures; and vol. ii. 432 pages, with 143 figures, besides the 14 figures of foreign birds. The Supplement is incorporated with this edition.

A seventh edition was printed in 1832, and an eighth in 1847.

A Memorial Edition of the works of Thomas Bewick, in five volumes, royal 8vo, is now in course of publication. The "Memoir" will be prefaced and annotated by Mr. Austin Dobson. This edition of 750 copies will be issued to Subscribers only at £10, 10s. the set. Newcastle: R. Ward & Sons. London: Bernard Quaritch.

It is said that "in after years Bewick advanced an opinion that light, or rather grey, impressions were the best; but the key to the matter was, he was always afraid of too great a pressure injuring the blocks, and to a very serious extent his fears were justifiable, as may be inferred from the fact that, among a multitude of other and constant renovations, the Blackbird has had six bills!"

Bewick's British Birds have so often and so fully received the praise of critics, that it is unnecessary in this place to dwell upon their beauties, save by the insertion of the opinions of judges of known ability.

" Have we forgotten," says a writer in *Blackwood's Magazine* for June 1828 (generally supposed to be Professor Wilson), " in our hurried and imperfect enumeration of wise worthies—have we forgotten ' The Genius that dwells on the banks of the Tyne?' the matchless, inimitable Bewick? No. His books lie on our parlour, bedroom, dining-room, drawing-room, and study table, and are never out of place or time. Happy old man! The delight of childhood, manhood, decaying age! A moral in every tail-piece—a sermon in every vignette. Not as if from one fountain flows the stream of his inspired spirit, gurgling from the Crawley Spring so many thousand gallons of the element every minute, and feeding but one city, our own Edinburgh. But it rather oozes out from unnumbered springs—here from one scarcely perceptible but in the vivid green of the lonesome sward, from which it trickles away into a little mountain rill—here leaping into sudden life, as from the rock—here bubbling from a silver pool, overshadowed by a birch-tree—here like a well asleep in a moss-grown cell, built by some thoughtful recluse in the old monastic days, with a few words from Scripture, or some rude engraving, religious as Scripture, *Omne bonum desuper — Opera Dei mirifica.*"

Our distinguished townsman, Thomas Doubleday, in an eloquent article in the *British Quarterly Review* for November 1845, observes—"In addition to the figures of the birds, which are beautifully executed, the artist had adorned the work with a profusion of those exquisite tail-pieces which, whether we contemplate their admirable design, their nature, their truth, or the humour and keen satire, or powerful morality, which are so often superadded and transfused, certainly divide our admiration with the principal objects of the work. As a whole, the publication was universally admired, and the hold which it eventually took of the public attention has been equalled by few works which have appeared either before or since." " Of the marvellous correctness of Bewick's eye, and of the wonderful precision with which he seized and transferred the form and lineaments of whatever in nature, animate or inanimate, he chose to depict, it is almost superfluous to speak. In that extraordinary power resides the great charm of all he has done. The sheer truth of Bewick's drawing was, perhaps, hardly ever matched, certainly never exceeded. Whether his subject be animated or lifeless, in motion or at rest, he at once seizes and impresses its form and character. Verisimilitude is too weak a word for some of his most finished portraitures. They are not like the truth, they are the truth itself. In some of his Quadrupeds and Birds, we have not only the form and action of the animal, but its very air and physiognomy." The same writer, speaking of the continued attraction of his works, says—"The scholars of the scholars of Bewick can cut lines on wood as finely as their master. In this sense, engravings on wood equal to those of Thomas Bewick may be met with at every turn and every corner. It is only requisite to repeat the names of Branston, Vasey, Landells, and Williams, to bring this undoubted truth before the mind. The difference between these engravings and those of Bewick resides, not in the nature of the lines cut, but in the nature of the souls of those that cut them. It is not because their hands are dissimilar that their works are dissimilar, but because their minds are dissimilar. Had distinction rested in handicraft only, distinction would have been confounded. Samson would have been shorn of his locks, and have become only as other men. Hence, to solve the problem of the continued attraction of these celebrated specimens of art, we must look to causes very different from mere mechanical improvement. That solution is to be found in the higher and more intellectual feelings associated with that art, in the *vivida vis* of the mind, in the truth and beauty of the conception which they embody, and not in the craft of hand or delicacy of touch which they exhibit. The charm of these would soon have been outrivalled and soon have passed away."

The distinguished ornithologist, Audubon, writes of Bewick—"He was purely a son of nature, to whom alone we owe all that characterised him as an artist and as a man. Warm in his affections, of deep feeling, and possessed of vigorous imagination, with correct and penetrating observation, he needed little extraneous aid to make him, what he became, the first engraver on wood that England has produced. Look at his tail-pieces, reader, and say if you ever saw so much life represented before, from the Glutton, who precedes the Great Black-backed Gull, to the youngsters flying their kite; the disappointed sportsman, who, by killing a magpie, has lost a woodcock; the horse endeavouring to reach the water; the bull roaring near the stile; or the poor beggar attacked by the rich man's mastiff. As you turn each successive leaf, from beginning to end of his admirable books, scenes calculated to excite your admiration everywhere present themselves. Assuredly you will agree with me in thinking that in his peculiar path none has equalled him. There may be men now, or some may in after years appear, whose works may in some respects rival or even excel his, but not the less must Thomas Bewick, of Newcastle-upon-Tyne, be considered in the art of engraving on wood, what Linnæus will ever be in Natural History, though not the founder, yet the enlightened improver and illustrious promoter."

"Of Bewick's powers," says a writer in *Blackwood's Edinburgh Magazine* for July 1825, "the most extraordinary is the perfect and undeviating accuracy with which he seizes and transfers to paper the natural objects which it is his delight to draw. His landscapes are absolute *fac-similes ;* his animals are whole-length portraits. It needs only to glance at his works, to convince ourselves with what wonderful felicity the very countenance and air of his animals are marked and distinguished. There is the grave owl, the silly wavering lapwing, the pert jay, the impudent over-fed sparrow, the airy lark, the sleepy-headed gourmand duck, the restless titmouse, the insignificant wren, the clean harmless gull, the keen rapacious kite—every one has character. This is far beyond the mere pencilling of fur or feathers. It is the seizure and transfusion of countenance. In this, Bewick's skill seems unapproached and unapproach-able by any other artist who has ever attempted this line. His vignettes are just as remarkable. Take his British Birds, and in the tail-pieces to these two volumes you shall find the most touching presentation of Nature in all her forms, animate and inanimate. There are the poachers tracking a hare in the snow, and the urchins who have accomplished the creation of a 'snow man.' In the humorous, there are the disappointed beggar leaving the gate open for the pigs and poultry to march over the good dame's linen which she is laying out to dry, or, what a Methodist would call profane, the cat stealing the old man's dinner whilst he is devoutly saying grace, or the thief who sees devils in every bush and stump of a tree—a sketch that Hogarth himself might envy. Then, in another strain, there is the strayed infant standing at the horse's heels and pulling its tail, the mother in an agony flying over the stile, the sportsman who has slipped into the torrent, and the blind man and boy unconscious of 'keep on this side.' In the satiric there is that best of burlesques upon military pomp, the four urchins astride of gravestones for horses, the first blowing a glass trumpet, and the others bedizened in tatters, with rush caps and wooden swords.

"Nor must we pass over his seaside sketches—all inimitable. The cutter chasing the smuggler—is it not evident they are going at least ten knots an hour? The tired gulls sitting on the waves, every curled head of which seems big with mischief. What pruning of plumage, what stalkings and flappings, and scratchings of the sand, are not depicted in that collection of sea-birds on the shore? What desolation is there in that sketch of coast after a storm, with the solitary rock, the ebb tide, the crab just venturing out, and the mast of the sunken vessel standing up through the treacherous waters? What truth and minute nature is in that tide coming in, each wave rolling higher than its predecessor, like a line of conquerors, and pouring in amidst the rocks with increasing aggression? And last and best—there are his fishing scenes. What angler's heart but beats when he sees the pool fisher deep in the water, his rod bending almost double with the rush of some tremendous trout or heavy salmon? Who does not recognise his boyish days in the fellow with the 'set rods,' sheltering himself from the soaking rain behind an old tree? What fisher has not seen yon 'old codger' sitting by the river side, peering over his tackle, and putting on a brandling? It is needless to recapitulate. Bewick's landscapes, in short, are upon the same principle with his animals. They are, for the most part, portraits. They are the result of the keenest and most accurate observation. You perceive every stone and bunch of grass has had actual existence. His moors are north-country moors, neither Scotch nor English. They are the progeny of Cheviot, of Rimside, of Simonside, and of the Carter. The tail-piece of the old man pointing out to his boy an ancient monumental stone, reminds one of the Milfield Plain and Flodden Field. Having only delineated that in which he himself had taken delight, we may deduce his character from his pictures. His warm-hearted love of his native country, its scenery, its manners, its airs, its men and women; his propensity

> 'by himself to wander
> Adown some trolling burn's meander,
> An' no think lang;'

his intense observation of nature and human life; his satirical and somewhat coarse humour; his fondness for maxims and old saws; his views of worldly prudence now and then 'cropping out,' as miners call it, into daylight; his passion for the seaside, and his delight in the angler's 'solitary trade'—all this, and more, the admirer of Bewick may deduce from his sketches."

Mr. Jackson, who was a pupil of Bewick's, and gained considerable celebrity as a wood-engraver, speaking of the illustrations, says :—"Nothing of the same kind that wood-engraving has produced since the time of Bewick can for a moment bear a comparison with these cuts. They are not to be equalled till a designer and engraver shall arise possessed of Bewick's knowledge of Nature, and endowed with his happy talent of expressing it. Bewick has, in this respect, effected more by himself than has been produced by one of our best wood-engravers when working from drawings made by a professional designer, but who knows nothing of birds, of their habits, or the places which they frequent, and has not the slightest feeling for natural incident and picturesque beauty. No mere *fac-simile* engraver of a drawing ready made to his hand should venture to speak lightly of Bewick's talents until he has both drawn and engraved a cut which may justly challenge a comparison with the Kyloe Ox, the Yellow-hammer, the Partridge, the Woodcock, or the Tame Duck. Bewick's style of engraving, as displayed in the Birds, is exclusively his own. He adopts no conventional mode of representing texture or producing an effect, but skilfully avails himself of the most simple and effective means which his art affords of faithfully and efficiently representing his subject. He never wastes his time in laborious trifling to display his skill in execution ;—he works with a higher aim to represent Nature ; and consequently he never bestows his pains except to express a meaning. The manner in which he has represented the feathers in many of his birds is as admirable as it is perfectly original. His feeling for his subject and his knowledge of his art suggested the best means of effecting his end ; and the manner in which he has employed them entitle him to rank as a wood-engraver, without reference to his merits as a designer, among the very best that have practised the art."

It has been stated that some of the illustrations to the Birds were executed by Bewick's pupils, and both Robert Johnson and Luke Clennell are particularly mentioned as having done so. It is certain, however, that, with one or two exceptions, the figures of the Birds and the great majority of the tail-pieces are exclusively Bewick's work. On this subject, Mr. Bewick's own testimony is thus related by Mr. Atkinson :—"Talking of his art, I inquired if he permitted the assistance of his apprentices in many cases? He said, 'No ; it had seldom happened, and then they had injured the cuts very much.' I inquired if he could remember any of them in which he had received assistance? He said, 'Ay, I can soon tell you them ;' and after a few minutes' consideration he made out, with

his daughter's assistance, 'the Whimbrel, Tufted Duck, and Lesser Tern.'
He tried to recollect more, and, turning to his daughter, said, 'Jane,
honey, dost thou remember any more?' She considered a little, and
said, 'No, she did not, but that certainly there were not half a dozen in
all.' These we both pressed him to do over again. 'He intended it,'
he said. But, alas! this intention was prevented."

A very important collection of upwards of one thousand five hundred woodcuts, formed for the most part by Bewick himself for a friend, is well
worthy of special mention. The first volume consists of proofs of the
Quadrupeds and Birds in various states. The second volume contains
proofs of the cuts in Poems by Goldsmith and Parnell; the "Blossoms
of Morality;" miscellaneous subjects, including tradesmen's cards, rare
book-plates, ball and theatre tickets, funeral cards, book illustrations,
unfinished proofs, and proofs on yellow India paper, &c. To such of
the woodcuts as have been engraved by pupils their names have been
added in pencil. These precious volumes grace the splendid library of
J. W. Pease, Esq., Pendower, Newcastle. The correspondence which led
to the formation of this unique collection is given at pp. 109–114 of this
work. Choice uncut presentation copies of the early editions of Bewick's
works, of the largest paper, are owned by J. W. Barnes, Esq., Durham;
Thomas W. U. Robinson, Esq., Hardwick Hall; and Edward Mounsey,
Esq., Darlington.

(29.) The Hive of Ancient and Modern Literature, a Collection of Essays, Narratives, Allegories, and Instructive Compositions. Newcastle: printed for S. Hodgson and G. G. and J. Robinson, Pater Noster Row. London. 1799.

This work was a selection made by the late Solomon Hodgson, Newcastle.
The first had only three cuts by Bewick, but the subsequent editions had
an increased number of wood-engravings, that printed in 1806 having
fourteen cuts by Thomas Bewick, and ten (besides several vignettes) by
Luke Clennell. It was republished in 1812.

(30.) Four large Woodcuts, a Zebra, an Elephant, a Tiger, and a Lion.

These were engraved in 1799 for Mr. Gilbert Pidcock, the proprietor of a
celebrated menagerie then in Newcastle. Previous to the blocks being

delivered to him, by arrangement, 150 copies of the Zebra, the same number of the Lion, 200 copies of the Tiger, and 250 copies of the Elephant, were taken off on drawing paper. These are now of extreme rarity. Choice proofs are in my collection, that of the Tiger being coloured by Bewick himself.

(31.) A Short Treatise on that Useful Invention called the Sportsman's Friend, or the Farmer's Footman, by a Gentleman Farmer of Northumberland, with Figures of the Instrument and its use, engraved on wood by Thomas Bewick, from the paintings of Joseph Atkinson, Cattle Painter, in Newcastle, etc. Newcastle : printed by Edward Walker.

This work was written by Henry Utrick Reay, Esq. of Killingworth, Newcastle, and published in 1801. It has two engravings on wood, and an etching on copper, all by Thomas Bewick. The beautiful cut of the Bay Pony has been lent for this work by the owner, Thomas W. U. Robinson, Esq., Hardwick Hall, Durham.

(32.) The Sportsman's Cabinet ; or a correct delineation of the Canine Race. London : printed for the Proprietors. 1803.

This splendid work, in two volumes 4to, contains numerous fine plates by Scott,[1] and woodcut vignettes by Thomas Bewick, Austin, &c. A second edition was published in 1820.

---

[1] John Scott, the celebrated animal engraver, was the son of a journeyman brewer in Newcastle, where he was born in March 1773. At the age of nine years he was sent to be an errand boy to Mr. Greenwell, tallow-chandler, in the Old Fleshmarket, to whom he afterwards became an apprentice, but his evenings were devoted to the pencil. His earliest efforts in engraving were made on smooth halfpennies by the light of the fire. Mr. Fisher, who kept a circulating library, and was also clerk to St. Nicholas' Church, encouraged his taste for drawing and engraving, and exhibited his specimens to the gentlemen who frequented his library, who confirmed him in the estimate he had formed of the talents of the untaught artist. He removed to London, where he was kindly received by Mr. Robert Pollard, who waived his claim to a fee, and immediately gave him instruction and employment. Soon after he engraved " Breaking Cover " and the " Death of the Fox," in the line manner after Gilpin and Reinagle, for which the Society of Arts honoured him with the most distinguished approbation. The Duke of Sussex presented him with a large and elegant gold medal. He died in March 1828, aged fifty-four years, leaving one son and eight daughters.

THE BAY PONY.

(33.) The Seasons, by James Thomson, with his Life by Samuel Johnson, LL.D., and a Complete Glossary and Index, embellished with engravings on wood by Bewick, from Thurston's designs. London : printed for James Wallis, Paternoster Row. 1805.

It is in 8vo, but an edition in 12mo was printed the same year.

(34.) The Hermit of Warkworth, a Northumberland Ballad, in three fits, by Dr. Thos. Percy, Bishop of Dromore, with engravings on wood by Mr. Bewick, after designs by Mr. Craig. Alnwick : printed and sold by J. Catnach. 1806.

A second edition of this work was published in 1807.

(35.) The Poetical Works of Robert Burns, with his Life, ornamented with engravings by Mr. Bewick, from original designs by Mr. Thurston, in two volumes. Alnwick : printed by Catnach and Davison ; sold by the Booksellers in England, Scotland, and Ireland. 1808.

12mo, containing 32 cuts in the first, and 29 cuts in the second volume, all engraved by Henry White.

(36.) The Poetical Works of Robert Fergusson, with his Life, in two volumes, ornamented with engravings on wood by Mr. Bewick, from original designs ; with a number of characteristic tail-pieces, etc. Alnwick : printed by W. Davison. 1814.

From *Fergusson's Poems,* 1814.

(37.) A History of England, in a Series of Letters from a Nobleman to his Son. London: printed for J. Brambles, A. Meggitt, and J. Waters, by H. Mozley, Gainsborough. 1807.

GEORGE I.

GEORGE II.

GEORGE III.

Two vols. 12mo. The large woodcut portraits are admirably executed by Thomas Bewick. The entire series is introduced in this work, and given to me by my old and much respected agents, Messrs. Mozley of Derby. When first published the portraits were of oval form; afterwards the tints were removed.

(38.) Newcastle Typographical Society Publications.

This valuable series was commenced in 1817, and continued till 1845.
They were uniformly printed in crown 8vo. Mr. John Adamson,
Thomas Hodgson, John Trotter Brockett, Mr. Straker, William Garret,
John Fenwick, and other local gentlemen, edited the several reprints.
Each publication had one or more cuts by Thomas Bewick. That done
for Mr. Thomas Hodgson is given at p. 180, and Mr. Adamson's at p.
243 of this volume. The above, by Bewick, is an excellent *fac-simile* of
the original portrait prefixed to " The Life and Death of Robert, Earle of
Salisbury," 1612, reprinted by J. T. Brockett, 1818.

(39.) The Fables of Æsop, and others, with designs on wood by Thomas Bewick. Newcastle: printed by E. Walker

" The wisest of the ancients delivered their conceptions of the Deity and
their Lessons of Morality in Fables and Parables."

for T. Bewick and Son; sold by them, Longman & Co., London, and all Booksellers. 1818.

> A second edition was published in 1823. A few proofs on India paper were taken of the cuts, but they are extremely rare. A third impression in royal 8vo is now in the press, forming the fourth volume of the Memorial Edition.

(40.) Bibliotheca Lusitana, or Catalogue of Books and Tracts relating to the History, Literature, &c., of Portugal, in the library of John Adamson, Esq., F.S.A. Newcastle, 1818.

> This work, which is now rarely to be met with, was printed in two parts for private circulation by Mr. Adamson, and contains some beautiful wood-cuts by Thomas Bewick.

(41.) Memoirs of the Life and Writings of Luis de Camoens, by John Adamson, F.S.A. London, Edinburgh, and New-castle-upon-Tyne. London : printed for Longman, Hurst, Rees, Orme, and Brown. 1820.

> This work, which is in two volumes, and of which two editions were printed, viz., one in crown 8vo, and the other in royal 8vo, is illustrated with several wood-engravings by Thomas Bewick, as also some copperplates by Skelton. The blocks, including the beautiful cut of the Grotto of Camoens, were destroyed by fire at the burning of Mr. Adamson's library,

April 21, 1849.[1] For the cuts in this work Mr. Adamson paid Bewick for Davidson's Arms, 15s.; the Grotto of Camoens, £4, 4s.; Two Viceroys, £2, 2s.; Faria Sousa, £2, 12s. 6d.; Camoens, £2, 12s. 6d.; portrait, whole length, £9, 9s.; Camoens, head and reverse, first and second medals, £5, 5s.

(42.) Select Fables, with cuts designed and engraved by Thomas and John Bewick, and others, previous to the year 1784; together with a Memoir and a Descriptive Catalogue of the Works of Messrs. Bewick. Newcastle: printed by S. Hodgson for Emerson Charnley, and Baldwin, Craddock, and Joy. London, 1820.

> This work contains a Memoir of Thomas and John Bewick, as well as a Descriptive Catalogue of their various publications, by Mr. John Trotter Brockett. This edition was printed on imperial paper at £1, 11s. 6d., on royal at £1, 1s., and on demy at 15s. each. Twelve copies of the imperial size had India proofs of the cuts, and were sold at £5, 5s.

(43.) A Supplement to the History of Birds, the Figures engraved on wood by Thomas Bewick. Newcastle: printed by Edward Walker, Pilgrim Street, for T. Bewick, &c. 1821.

---

[1] John Adamson was the son of Lieut. Cuthbert Adamson, R.N., of Gateshead, where he was born, September 13, 1787. Having ultimately chosen the law as his profession, he was articled to Messrs. Davidson of Newcastle, who, from their social position and the important offices they held, might be considered the leading firm of solicitors at that period. After being admitted to practise himself, he was fortunate in succeeding at an early age, on the death of Mr. Walter Heron, to the office of Under Sheriff, and continued to act in that capacity until the passing of the Municipal Reform Act. During a residence in Lisbon, where an elder brother was long settled as a merchant, he acquired a knowledge of Portuguese, and imbibed a taste for the literature of the country which bore fruit in after years. He translated the play of Donna Inez de Castro from the original of Nicola Luis, and wrote Memoirs of the Life and Writings of Camoens. The Queen of Portugal recognised his services by conferring upon him the Orders of Christ and of the Tower and Sword. He was member of various societies both at home and abroad. For many years he was Secretary of the Literary and Philosophical Society of Newcastle, and took a prominent part in the formation of the Society of Antiquaries, and of the Natural History Society in the same town. He was a collector of coins, medals, books, and prints; of plants, fossils, minerals, and shells. His collection of shells was always much admired, and of great value. His correspondence with men of letters and science, and other distinguished persons in various parts of the world, extends over nearly half a century. Mr. Adamson died, after a short illness, September 27, 1855, in his sixty-eighth year.

This Supplement consists of two parts, illustrated by forty-two figures and forty-one tail-pieces, on imperial, royal, and demy paper. A few copies of the figures were printed in 4to without letterpress. The Foreign Birds were mostly done from preserved figures in the Wycliffe Museum.

(44.) Vignettes by Thomas Bewick. Newcastle-upon-Tyne: printed by Edward Walker, Pilgrim Street. 1827.

These embrace the tail-pieces to the Histories of Quadrupeds and Birds, and were printed in octavo and quarto without the letterpress, and are now scarce.

(45.) A Memoir of Thomas Bewick, written by himself. Embellished by Numerous Wood-Engravings, designed and engraved by the author for a work on British Fishes, and never before published. Newcastle-on-Tyne: printed by Robert Ward, Dean Street, for Jane Bewick, Gateshead. Sold by Robert Robinson, Pilgrim Street. London: Longman & Co. 1862.

Demy 8vo, cloth, price 18s. My first order was for 100 copies. The vignettes do not call for particular remark. Ten shillings for a single copy of the Prospectus of the History of British Fishes (1825), with the cut of the John Dory or the Lump Sucker, was the ordinary price I paid Miss Bewick, and glad to purchase at that sum. At the head of the Preface is a View of Bywell; to the left is the deep pool below the rock where the Rev. H. P. Dwarris, curate of Bywell, was drowned whilst crossing the Tyne in a boat, May 3, 1855; to the right is the mill dam, destroyed by Mr. Beaumont. At the end of the personal narrative a woodcut is given representing a funeral procession wending its way through the meadows which lie between Cherryburn and the Ford at Eltringham, where a boat is observed, ready moored, to convey the departed to his last resting-place in Ovingham Churchyard, on the opposite bank of the Tyne. This appears from the date of the block to be the last tail-piece ever cut by Thomas Bewick. The original pencil drawing is in my collection.

A FEW OF THE MISCELLANEOUS CUTS EXECUTED BY BEWICK.

Cherryburn Cottage, the birthplace of Thomas Bewick.

This was drawn by John Bewick in 1781, and partly engraved by him, but being left unfinished at his death, it lay for many years, and was eventually finished by Thomas Bewick. The beautiful drawing in Indian ink is in the possession of the family at Cherryburn.

The then Spire of the Exchange in Newcastle.

This was engraved in 1783, and drawn from nature, to insert in the large old watch-cases then in fashion. It shows the rook's nest above the vane, in which situation a pair of rooks built in despite of all interruptions for many years; and what was remarkable, the iron rod to which the vane was fixed went through the centre of the nest, which turned with every change of wind.

Ticket of Admission to a Ball, for the benefit of the family of the late Mr. Clagget.

This beautiful cut now adorns the title of this work. It was engraved by Thos. Bewick in 1795. The inscription was erased many years afterwards.

Book Plates with Armorial Bearings.

Some of the happiest efforts of Thomas Bewick's genius were displayed in book plates, which he engraved on wood for various gentlemen. The above is one he did for John Murray, Esq., M.D., of Newcastle.

The Fleece.

This most beautiful and rare woodcut of a Heath Ram suspended by the middle, was engraved by Thomas Bewick for Mr. William Frood, Rochdale, in May 1812, and charged only £1, 18s. A proof on yellow China paper is in my collection—size, $7\frac{1}{4}$ inches by 5 inches.

Mail Coach, Hull, York, and Newcastle, drawn by four horses at full gallop.

This fine rare cut was "drawn and mostly engraved by me, Thomas Bewick, and given this 24th February 1826 to my dear son, T. B."— inscribed on an impression of the print. The cut is $14\frac{1}{2}$ inches by 5 inches, and engraved on five wood-blocks. My impression was obtained from Miss Bewick.

The Theban Harp.

Engraved on copper by Thomas Bewick, and the first job of the kind he received after his return from London (1777). It was done for the Rev. James Murray, and appears in No. 5 of the "Magazine of the Arts." The drawing from which it was made was the work of James Bruce, Esq., the celebrated traveller.

An Oak Tree.

This beautiful cut belonged to the Rev. J. F. Bigge. After his lamented death it was given to me at Stamfordham Vicarage by his widow and sons in memory of a friendship of more than forty years. It was engraved for Mr. Falla in 1815.

Thomas Coulson's Cut.

The fine cut given below was engraved by T. Bewick as a business card for Mr. Coulson, an eminent decorative painter, a native of Newcastle. Since then it has been ingeniously manipulated—Coulson's name erased, and "Walker" inserted. The letter *a* in painter being covered by the boy's hand, it would stand for *printer* without alteration. There is no date in the first state of the cut. I am indebted to the kindness of J. W. Barnes, Esq., Durham, for the use of this cut and the two vignettes to Fergusson's Poems.

S.AM.ᴸ BEARDSLEY,

FERRY-HILL.

	L	S	D
Breakfast			
Dinner			
Tea & Coffee			
Supper			
Wine			
Brandy			
Rum			
Gin			
Cyder			
Beer & Porter			
Hay & Corn			
Servants Eating			

The name of Joseph Garnett will ever rank amongst the most worthy of old Newcastle tradesmen. This gentleman was born at Alnwick, in 1772, of humble parentage. When quite young he obtained a post in the Royal Observatory, Greenwich; but owing to an affection of the eyes he was compelled to resign, and towards the close of the last century commenced business as a chemist and druggist on the Quayside, Newcastle. In the month of February 1803, he removed to a shop at the "*Foot of the Side*, near the *Scale-Cross;*" he lived in the house above his place of business for the long period of sixty years. When Mr. Garnett died, he had attained the patriarchal age of ninety years. He was an accomplished musician, and rarely absent from his accustomed seat in the organ box at St. Nicholas' Church. The charitable institutions of the town were liberally remembered in his will; his acts of private charity were unstinted. His valuable library, cabinet of rare coins, paintings, articles in gold and silver, diamond rings, antique seals, and cameos, were sold in Newcastle in the months of February, March, and April 1862. The sale occupied seventeen days. Amongst the books, one excessively rare little volume I was fortunate enough to secure, viz., Lot 889—"The Psalter of David, in Englishe, purely and faithfully translated after the Texte of Feline (Martin Bucer). *Argentine, by me Francis Foye*, 1530." But two or three perfect copies of the first edition of the Psalter in English are known. The above was imperfect. In antique silver, a couple of Apostle spoons, very fine, with figures of St. Peter and Paul, 1562, and others, were knocked down to me. These are now in the collection at Hardwick Hall. The series of exquisite old Wedgwood cameos went to enrich the keramic treasures of Robert Spence, Esq., North Shields.

Mr. Garnett's executors were fortunate in securing the services of W. H. D. Longstaffe, Esq., an accomplished numismatist and able antiquary, to compile the coin catalogue. That gentleman told me he might say "*fine*" to every lot, the examples were so choice, comprising Greek and Roman coins in gold, silver, and brass, highly preserved English, Scotch, and foreign coins in gold, silver, and copper. The coins and medals relative to Charles I. and Cromwell were particularly choice and interesting. A Hadrian in gold cost me £4. The heavy English gold sold cheap. For the use of the beautiful cut engraved for Mr. Garnett by Thomas Bewick in 1805, I have to thank Mr. Councillor Dobson, who had the conduct of Mr. Garnett's business for so many years before his death, and has continued the same ever since on the old lines, without change.

THE HOWDY

AND

THE UPGETTING.

TWO NORTHUMBRIAN TALES

OF

ONE HUNDRED YEARS SIN SEYNE,

AS RELATED BY THE LATE

THOMAS BEWICK, OF NEWCASTLE,

IN THE TYNESIDE DIALECT.

THE ORIGINAL MANUSCRIPTS

OF THE TWO FOLLOWING TALES RELATED BY THE LATE

THOMAS BEWICK,

The celebrated Engraver on Wood,

WERE FORMERLY IN THE POSSESSION OF

MR. JOHN BELL OF GATESHEAD,

TO WHOSE MEMORY THEY ARE NOW DEDICATED.

THE HOWDY

IN THE TEYNE SEYDE DIALECT.

ONE HUNDRED YEARS SEYNE.

AE-HY, AE-HY, kih she, yeh may say what yeh leyke, but Aze suer aws reet, aw ken weel eneugh when he was bwoarn, fir aw meynd, aw was up at the Mistrisses suon ee mworning, ith th' howl oh wounter, when in cam little Jenny runnin—Muther! Muther! sez she, here cums little Andra Karr, plishplash throw the clarts, thockin and blowin, wiv his heels poppin out ov his Clogs every step, leyke twe little reed Tatees—wiv a Hares bum on his Hat and the crown ov his head and teheyteed hair stannin up throw't—poor fellow, sez the Mistriss, aws warn a keahm hesint been int this twe months— Andra! Andra! whats the mayteer, sez the Mistriss—is thee Muther shoutin out—eyeh that she is—ayrms aye by George! for aw heard her o th' way fra our Hoose te Roaffies Staggarth Deyke—whees there (sez th' Mistriss) wey theres our Dehyim an Isbil an Barbary—an aw so oad Mary commin tappy lappy owr the Stob-Cross-Hill—an Jack Gorfoot galloppin by Antys Garth neuk on the oad Gray Meer, wiv Mragery the Howdy behint him fit te brik their neeks—aeyh (sez the Mistriss) an aw mun away tee—whares thee Fayther, Andra (sez the Mistriss) wey sez Andra, aw so him stannin at th' lown end oh the Byer, wouv his Jasay Neet cap on, an his hands in his kwoat pockets, beayth thrimpt owr his Thees—an glowrin about, but aw so nowse he wis leukin at—sit doon Andra—oh the Trou Steahyn—see doon sat Andra an weypt his nwoase on ov his kwoat kuff—meayk heayst lass an bring him (poor fella) a shive oh Butter an Breed—cut him a good counge an strenkle a leapyt ov sugar ont for aw warnt he hesint brokken his fast to day.—Jack Roe was sittin o the teyme, leanin on the hud steahyn, wiv his braid shouthers an his leg pletted oure his Yek Pleught, warmin his sel—Aehy, sez Jack, an as aw cum owre the Bwoat-Hill—aw so Jenny the Gardner with Teagnhey-bed, an sum mare sic leyke Fwoak, cummin as hard as they cud drive—By George!

2 R

sez Jack, what a rummin theyres meayhd, at sic a teyme, spechelly whare
thair's ne occasion fort, amang a House-fuh of Bayrnes an Mebbies but a
tehuhm cubbard for them — How monny Bayrnes hes thee Muther now,
Andra, sez Jack, aw dar say this is the seevent or eight—aw think if thee
Muther gans on this way, yeel hev as monny seughn as the Boucher ov
Bawwell—aw wonder how thee Fayther gets yeh o fed, sayrey man, aw dar
say he hes eneough to de to get it o deughn—Boucher o Bywell (sez the
Mistriss) how monny bayrnes had he—wey, sez Jack, they had twoalve, an
brout them o up to men and women, an tho' they never gat owse better than
thaaf keahyk, crowdie an milk, or tatees an soat—they war as reed cheekt an
thriven, an leuked better than the Swires bayrnes, or ony Gentlemens on
Teynesyde.   Bliss us ! (sed the Mistriss) how did they find neayhms for them
o—weel eneugh (sez Jack)—there wis Will, an Mat, an Jack, an Tom—an
Raney, an Gwoardy, an Roger, an Fenwick, an Jerry—an Nanny, an——an
Peggy.

History of a Foundling (Mozley's Edition).

THE UPGETTING

IN THE TEYNE SEYDE DIALECT.

ONE HUNDRED YEARS SEYNE.

OH! Mawlee! Oh Maw-aw-aw-lee!—how way hehaym wouth th'—thou theayks a vast oh caaling on—what do's th' want! yammering and shouting as kin yen was deef—thous neahn deef but was ower bissey tiggen on woh Jemmy Grame the theaker lad behint the staggarth Deyke—awze sure of thee impidence! whe dos thou tig on wee Thee sell aw wonder!—wey, wey ne mare oh that, or Muther wants th' directly to gan to Peggy Hivers upgettin, meayke heayst, shes waitin.—What de yeh want Muther yer aye fashin yen wh' somethin or other—aw want th' to be sharp an dress thee sell, smartly, an gang to the upgettin at Micklee. Houts Muther cannit ye gang yoursell,—aw was gannin to th' Madam's at Apperly, wh' the Young Chickins—an ye ken weel eneugh whatever present ye give to her, she aye gives ye tweyce as gude aghayn— aw dinnit leyke te gang amang a heep oh weyves o dresset up at seckin a pleace—Come Come maw hinney, thou mun gang, for maw shoun hes been mendin at the Coblers this Month an mare, and thou can get on thee sisters shoun and ony thing else of her claiths—and mheyk thee sell leuk varra sprunt wouth them—an aw warnt thoul leuk as weel as the best oh them— and when thous there, meynde what their o toakin about and put in thee word leyke a woman and dinna sit there leyke steuke and sit and say nowse— Varra weel Muther A'll try what aw can de.

THE RETURN.

Wey hinney thous gettin heayhm aghin and dis na leuk varva pleasd come tells o whe was there and what passet amang them and how ye fared—Aw hardly know where to begin, Muther, for there was sic clatterin and sic din when they o gat fairly startet—There was the skeul Maisters Weyfe—the Howdy—Tibby Bell—Jenny the Gardner, an Betty Kell—an Mary Nicholson

—an some aw dident ken—an there was Posset—a good speyce suet keayk— an honey an bacon collops an frummety—aw langed for some oh the Collops, but aw gat neahyn—an what did they toak about—wey they spak about Weylam Engine—The Lairds oh Ryton—an of the great Swires Deeth ith th nwoarth the other day and the number oh fwoak that went to his Dhael— monny oh them keept crakin oh the Bayrn an tippin its cheeks wouth the're fingers th meayk it smeyle—the Howdy never gav ower cryin Gwoardy, Gwoardy, Gwoardy, wheres the Bayrne hah lad gittsey, gittsey, gittsey,—an praising its Beauty—mouny oh them thrimped in to dih the sheym and aw thout aw wad dih see tee—see aw stept up an begun ih maw turn—but L—d forgih mih for leeing, for aw thout it the *ugliest, ilfardest* Bayrne aw ever so— it was blutherin and slverin leyke a drownin whelp—Betty Kell was the wisest body there sheed seen a vast o' the warld, and is an oad farvent body she spack a deal about the deeth of the Swire and his Dhael—and tell'd how after o the grandeur oh this warld it mhead ne mater, how hee Fwoak leyke him held up their heeds and thout themsels of sic consequence—a bit of spurt was mhead about them for a whyle after they deed—deeth cam to them at last an they leyke other fwoak were seun forgotten—Aye, Aye, kih Mary Nicholson thats true for the varra mwoarning after the Dhael—Nickel Urn was driving away and whistlin in his kayrt leyke a Nightengal and mheakin a' ring aghaym as kin nowse had happend—an Aws sur his Muther grat mair at the Dhael than ony body that was there an Gwoardy the Thaleur said their Christan was thare an she thout she grat as much as was decent but as for Nanny Urn she blaired out for a greet while an teuk the lead of o' the rest— The Skeul Maisters Weyfe said it was melancholly when you leukd about them, to see such numbers of yens freends constantly droppin off when they were never thinkin about it—Its varra true, sed Jenny the Gardner, for theres aw swoart of fwoak deed this year that was never deed afwore. Betty Kell gav her sic a gleyme and see did the Skeul Mistriss—Then up spake Tibby Bell and said that she knew little mare about Weylam Engine than that when she peeped into it she thout she wad ha' been skumfeesht wi' the steyth an then she set on a telling about a vast of Bayrnas that had deed without knowing ony thing about this wicked warld—aw then thout it teyme to put in maw word—an sez aw tiv her "prey ye if ye please" had your muther ever any Bayrnes, yes yeh feul ye (wi' sec a Glower) ti' be sure, or else how wad aw heh been heer, oh kiv aw, but aw was meanin your Grandmuther— aw thout she was gannin to spit at me—Confound her for beheavin se to maw Bayrne—if aw had her heer aw wad let her find how aw wad clout her lugs for her for her impidence.

INDEX.

ADAMSON, JOHN, 222, 302, 303, 304 note.

Æsop, Croxall's, 128.

"Æsop's Fables," offer by London publisher for cuts of, 128; Miss Bewick's indignation at offer, 128.

Agriculture in Northumberland, Report concerning state of, in 1800, 109.

Allan, George, 71, 103, 107.

Alpine Vulture, cut of, 158.

Anderson, Major, 19.

Anderson, Robert, 19.

Angus, Thomas, 48, 89.

Annual Review on Bewick, 283.

Apprentices' assistance, Atkinson's relation of Bewick's testimony as to, 296.

Apprenticeship, Bewick's story of his, 14.

Atkinson, George Clayton, 57, 71.

Atkinson, Joseph, cattle-painter, 298.

Audubon, the ornithologist, his opinion of Bewick, 293.

BAILEY, Mr., of Chillingham, 108.

Baily, Mr., sculptor, 155.

Ballantyne & Robertson of Edinburgh and Bewick's only attempt at lithography, 148.

Barber, George, 115.

Barber, Joseph, 104, 105, 107.

Barber, Martin, 107.

Barber's Circulating Library, catalogue of, 106.

Barker, Robert, 21.

Barnes, J. W., 80, 297, 308.

Barnes, Mr., of Whitburn, 187.

Bayles, Serjeant, 104 and note.

Bedingfeld, Thomas, 81 and note.

Beilby and the illustrations of "Tour through Sweden," 280.

Beilby & Bewick, firm of, 53; bill of costs against, *in re* Johnson's drawings, 252.

Beilby, Bewick, and Hodgson, difference between, in reference to fourth edition of Quadrupeds, 282.

Beilby, Ralph, 104, 283 note; settlement between, and Bewick, 117.

Beilby, Mr., his work on the Land Birds, 101; curious handbill, 102.

Beilby, William and Ralph, 14, 44.

"Beilby's wild lad," 19.

Bell, John, 312.

Bell, John Gray, 221, 235.

Bell, Joseph, portrait-painter, 115.

Bell, Sir Isaac Lowthian, 62 note.

Bell, William, 63.

Bell's, John, catalogue of books, 281 note.

Benwell, 17.

Berghem, 206.

Bewick, Agnes, and Cherryburn, 2.

"Bewick Collector," Thomas Hugo's, 126.

Bewick, Elizabeth, 224 and note.

Bewick family, the, 1, 2.

Bewick family (Thomas), habits of, 176 *et seq.*

Bewick, Isabella, and Cherryburn, 2.

Bewick, Isabella, her father's companion, 77; Carey's projected life of Summerfield and, 136, 138; Dibdin's "Tour," her opinion of, 197 ; jealous of father's fame, 198 ; a visit to, in 1881, 213 ; last interview with, 215 ; death, 216 ; funeral, 217.

Bewick, John, brother, 2 ; apprenticed to Thomas, 53 ; drawings for Somerville's Chase made on wood by, 98 ; genius and characteristics, 220, 236, 237; contributions to Saint's publications, 221 ; works for Dr. Trusler, 223 ; character of his work, 226, 234; "The Sad Historian," 230 ; death, 235 ; marble tablet to memory of, 236; acquirements, 236 ; Miss Jane Bewick's opinion of, 236 ; best specimens of work, 289.

Bewick, John, father of Thos. Bewick, 1.

Bewick, Miss, on publication of father's manuscript, 203 ; her remarks on printer's proof-sheets, 204 ; opinion of printers, 204.

Bewick, Misses, the, and their father's first drawing, 16 ; a visit to, 115 ; author's first acquaintance with, 203 ; pleasant society, 203.

Bewick, Miss Jane, 19 ; rare intelligence of, 205 ; knowledge of world, 206 ; acquaintance with Shakespeare, 206 ; death, 206.

Bewick, Mrs., and "Gentle Shepherd," 168 ; pleasure in seeing her children attending Parish Church, 173.

Bewick, Mrs., artist's mother, death of, 69.

Bewick, R. E., son of Thomas, birth, 239; health and disposition, 239 ; musical talent, 240 ; character as an artist, 240 ; admitted to partnership by father, 241 ; death, 241 ; mental characteristics, 241 ; sensitive nature, 241 ; example of his work, 242.

Bewick, Robert, Bulmer's condolence with, on father's death, 163.

Bewick's father, likeness of, 103.

Bewick's house, description of, 207 *et seq.*

Bewick's, Miss, executors, 80 ; her gift to author, 120.

Bewick's pupils, 247 *et seq.*

Bewick, Thomas : birth, 1 ; childhood, 2 ; school life, 2, 3 ; hopeful spirit, 7 ; early essays in Art, 11 ; recollections of home, 12 ; love of Nature, 12 ; his parents' anxiety regarding his safety, 14 ; apprenticeship, 14 ; his earliest known design, 16 ; how leisure time spent, 19 ; love of literature, 20, 21 ; how he passed his winter evenings, 32 ; proficiency in cudgel-playing, 34 ; his services at the fall of Tyne Bridge, 36 ; evening visits to Cherryburn, 41 ; "flights up the Tyne," 42 ; first employment as an apprentice, 43 ; his first book with pictorial woodcuts, 45 ; bar bills, 45 ; end of apprenticeship, 45 ; honoured by Society for Promoting Fine Arts, 47; his appreciation of neighbourly congratulations, 48 ; works as a journeyman, 48 ; his favourite amusement, 48 ; purposes " seeing more of the world," 48 ; sets out on his travels, 49 ; his dog Witch, 49 ; experiences, 49 ; goes to London, 50 ; London life and manners distasteful to him, 50 ; last night in London, 52 ; fits up bench at Hatfield's, 52 ; partnership with Beilby, 53 ; weekly visits to Cherryburn, 53, 54 ; work in connection with " Select Fables " and " Gay's Fables," 56, 59 ; how far assisted in this work by his brother, 57 ; illustrates Tommy Trip's History of Birds, &c., 58 ; style of wood-cutting, 60 ; elected member of social clubs, 60 ; first grief, 69 ; father's death, 69 ; marriage, 70 ; first important work, 70 ; philanthropy, 75 ; abhorrence of war, 77 ; detestation of Pitt, 77 ; diligence in business, 78 ; an important commission, 78 ; his *chef-d'œuvre*, 79 ; copperplate, 80, 82 ; narrative concerning his " History of Quadrupeds," 82 ; domestic character, 92 ; issue of first volume of " British

Birds," 99; visit to Wycliffe-on-the Tees, 99; public interest in his work, 99; his workshop in St. Nicholas' Churchyard, 104; removes from, 104; independent mind, 108; writes description of cuts, 117; dissolution of partnership with Beilby, 117; works for several publishers, 118; occupied in devising means to prevent the forgery of bank notes, 119; a *nom-de-plume*, 124; serious illness, 126; knowledge of Northumbrian phraseology, 132; allusion to his portrait, 134, 135; his generous disposition, 138; unpleasant business experiences, 147; pays second visit to Edinburgh, 147; well received, 147; his only attempt at lithography, 148; publication of eighth and last edition of Quadrupeds, 148; views with regard to regulation of salmon fisheries, 151; sixth edition of "Birds"—a retrospect, 157; his last and largest woodcut, 159, 160; the last bird drawn and engraved, 161; his last vignette, 161; his governing passion strong to the end, 161; death, 162; personal characteristics, 166; once only known to dance, 166; and sing, 167; as paterfamilias, 168; friendship with Kemble the actor, 170; simple in all his habits, 171; where he commenced housekeeping, 171; Sunday spent in quiet meditation, 172; his favourite poet, 173; his home, 173; choice of Nature, 181; fertile imagination, 181; his winter scenes, 182; endeavour to purchase land, 192; instance of his gratitude, 192; a long day's work, 193; his dependence on St. Nicholas' clock, 193; never possessed a watch, 193; a morning practice, 194, 206; incident with his two apprentices, 194; habits of work, 194; methodical in his home, 195; encounter with journalist, 195; supper-beer, 195; his

dog Cheviot, 196; the manuscript he left, 203; his pupils, 247 *et seq.;* opinion of Johnson, 250; his favourite pupil, 268; portraits of, 270 *et seq.;* principal works illustrated by, 274 *et seq.;* earliest known woodcut, 274; compared to Linnæus, 294; love of native country, 295; Jackson's opinion of, 296; assistance received from apprentices, 296; miscellaneous cuts executed by, 306 *et seq.*

Bewick, Thomas, list of Portraits of :—
By Miss Kirkley and T. A. Kidd, 270.
Drawing and Engraving on wood by John Jackson, 272.
Drawing and Engraving by Edward Train, 272.
Engraving on steel by F. Bacon, 272.
Engraving on wood by Heaviside, 272.
Engraving on wood by C. Nesbit, 271.
Engraving published by T. Ranson, 271.
Etching by Leopold Flameng, 273.
Full-length Painting in oil by T. S. Good, 273.
Miniature by Murphy, 270.
Miniature by W. Nicholson, 273.
Painting by Jas. Ramsay, 271.
Portrait by Geo. Gray, 273.
Portrait published as frontispiece to Jardine's Naturalists' Library, 272.

Bewick, William, brother of Thomas, 1.
Bewick, William, nephew of Thomas, 238 and note.
Bible, Hieroglyphick, frontispiece of, 276.
Bibliographer, letter of Bewick's in, 83.
Bigge, Rev. John F., 2, 125, 217, 241, 308.
Bigge, Thomas Charles, 15 note.
"Birds and Beasts, Tommy Trip's History of," 57, 58, 275.
"Birds, Beasts, and Fishes, History of," Conrad Gesner's, 21.
"Birds, British," sketch of owl for, 19; text of vol. i. written by Beilby, 290.

"Birds, British," vol. ii., letterpress the work of Bewick and Rev. H. Cotes, 116, 291.

"Birds, History of," Edwards', 21.

Bird's Nest and Eggs, cut of, 181.

Birds, The, assertion as to Johnson and Clennell executing illustrations for, 296.

Birds, The, last edition of, published in artist's lifetime, 157; the Misses Bewick and, 243.

Blackett, Sir Walter, 45, 52.

Blackett, Sir William, 19.

"Black Fleet," the, 180.

Blue Bell Inn and Bewick, 196.

Bohn, Henry George, 277.

Book of Pictures for Little Masters, Clayton Atkinson's statement regarding, 276.

Books, absence of good, 3, 9.

Booksellers' shops, situation of, 21.

"Border Antiquities," Walter Scott's, 265.

Bourne's Newcastle, 31.

Bowes, Andrew Robinson, 52, 80, 280.

Bridgewater, Earl of, and Clennell, 262.

"British Birds, History of," various editions, 290 et seq.

British Quarterly Review, and bust of Bewick, 155.

Brockett, John Trotter, correspondence with Bewick, 129 and note; editorial work of, 302, 304.

Brown, Thomas, 65 note.

Bruce, James, the celebrated traveller, and the Theban Harp, 308.

Bryson, Martin, Allan Ramsay's address to, 22.

Bryson & Charnley, 32.

"Buffon, Smellie's Abridgment of," 82.

Bulkley, Stephen, 21.

Bulmer, William, 41, 94, 95; his edition of Goldsmith's Poems, 230; death of, 288 note.

Bulmer's suggestions regarding Allan Ramsay's and Burns's Poems, 120.

"Burglar Disturbed, The," vignette, 185.

"Burns's Poems, Alnwick Edition of," 109.

Burnt House Entry, 288 note.

Busby, Mrs., 6.

Bute, Earl of, and Johnson's drawings, 251.

Button, Sarah, 21, 23.

Bywell, 1, 4, 14.

"CADGER'S TROT," the, 148.

Cail, Alderman, 265.

Camoens, Luis de, Memoirs of Life of, 303.

Campbell the poet, and his landlady, story of, 126.

Cant, William, 196.

Carey, William, author, 136.

Carlele, John, knight, 26.

Carlisle, See of, Church of Newcastle and, 24.

Carmichael, 65.

Carr, George, 184, 185 note.

Castle Garth, the, 19.

Castle, Lumley, 6.

Catnach and Davison, the Alnwick Press, 109, 300.

Changes, beneficial, 7.

Charlton, William Oswald, 6.

Charlton, Dr. E., 8.

Charlton, John, 62 note.

Charnley, Emerson, bookseller, 139; his "Select Fables," 144.

Chase, Somervile's, Bewick's payment for illustrating, 120; originality and elegance of illustrations in, 234.

Chatto, W. A., 269.

Cherryburn, 1, 2, 14 note, 16, 48.

Cherryburn House, 14.

Cheviot, Bewick's dog, anecdote of, 197.

Chillingham Wild Bull, 78, 79; Sir Walter Scott's suppositions regarding, 79; rarity of impressions of, 79; description of cut, 278, 279.

Choice Emblems, 221.

Chronicle, Newcastle, extract from, 55.

Chronicle Office, titles of Æsop's Fables printed at, 145.

Church, St. Andrew's, 264.

Church, St. John's, 72, 173.

Church, St. Nicholas', 47, 52, 72, 73, 193, 249, 257, 309.

Churchyard, Ovingham, marble tablet to memory of John Bewick in, 236.

Churchyard, St. John's, 39.

Churchyard, St. Nicholas', 21, 53, 104, 107.

Clagget, Mr., 306.

Clennell, Luke, 119, 247, 259 *et seq.;* subscription in behalf of, 263 ; references to his work, 290, 297.

Clennell, Mrs., 262.

Colliers, improvement amongst, 10 ; cultivation of music by, 11.

Collingwood, Lady, and family, 190.

Collinson, Rev. John, 197, 199.

" Comfortables," the, 188.

" Commonwealth, the Spensonian," 35.

Congreve, Sir William, 119.

Consett, Matt., 80, 81, 280.

Copperplate engraving, the first done in Newcastle, 105.

Coquetdale Fishing Songs, the, 215.

Corbridge, 3.

Correspondence—
    Between Bewick and Mr. T. Vernon, 109 *et seq.*
    Between Bewick and Mr. John T. Brockett, 130.
    Between Bewick and his local publisher, 139.
    With reference to bust of Bewick—
        A. Donkin to Mr. Brockett, 153 ;
        Thos. Crawhall to Mr. Brockett, 155.

Cotes, Rev. H., Bewick's obligations to, 116.

" Cottager, the," 264.

Coulson, Thomas, 66, 308.

Courant, Newcastle, establishment of, 139.

Cowen, Joseph, and stained glass window to memory of John Cunningham, 38.

Cowley, quotation from, 238.

Crawhall, Joseph, 80, 213, 255, 265.

Crew, Crowley's, 54 and note.

Critics' opinion of Bewick's work, 292 *et seq.*

Cross-hatching, 57.

Culley, George, 109.

Cunningham, John, 38 *et seq.*

Curthose, Robert, and the New Castle,

Cuts, miscellaneous, by Bewick—
    Book plates, 307.
    Cherryburn Cottage, 306.
    Fleece, the, 307.
    Mail Coach, 307.
    Spire of Exchange, 306.
    Thomas Coulson's Cut, 308.
    Ticket of admission to ball, 306.

DARLINGTON, Bewick's visit to, 108.

Davidson, John and Thomas, 81, 304 note.

Debord's tavern, 8, 10.

Defoe, Daniel, and his Newcastle correspondents, 21.

Delaval, Sir Francis, 10, 238.

Delaval, Thomas, 47.

Denton Burn, 17.

Dentatus, Assassination of, 266.

Denton Chare, 19.

Derwentwater, third earl of, 5 and note ; " Lament " for, 5.

" Deserted Village," Goldsmith's, and Bewick, 173.

Diaries, Dr. Charles Hutton's, 43.

Dibdin, Dr., 197 *et seq.*

Dilston Hall, 5 and note, 6, 7.

Dobson, Ann, 235.

Dobson, Austin, on Thomas Bewick and his pupils, 265 ; his Memorial Edition of Bewick's works, 291.

Dobson, Councillor, 309.

Dobson family, the, 185.

Dobson, Thomas, 184.

Domenico, the fire-eater, 10.

Donkin, Armorer, 153.

Donocht Head, 215.

Doubleday, Thomas, 129 note, 215; article in *British Quarterly Review* on Bewick's birds by, 292.

Dovaston's story, 70.

Duke of Northumberland, his Grace the, 125; treatise on mensuration dedicated to, 234.

Dwarris, Rev. H. P., 305.

"Dyers, the Ovingham," cut of, 184.

EDITION, Memorial, of works of Thomas Bewick, 291.

Editions, early, of Bewick's works, presentation copies, owners of, 297.

Elegy, Gray's, Spence's new version of, 35.

Elliot, Isabella, 70.

Elliot, Miss Esther, 115.

Elliot, Robert, 37, 70, 219.

Ellis, G., 289.

Ellis, James, 81 and note.

Ellison, Rev. John, hospitality of, 190.

Elswick, 17.

Eltringham, 4.

Engravings of varied character, 183.

Errington, Mr., of Capheaton, 7.

Ewbank's daughter, 67.

Ewbank, John Wilson, 63, 65 *et seq.*

Ewbank, Michael, of Gateshead, 66.

Ewbank, Miss, 67.

FABLES of Æsop, publication of illustrated edition of, 127; non-success, 127; second edition of, 127; revolution of opinion regarding the work, 128.

Fables, Select, number of parts, 277.

Fair, St. Luke's, 28.

Falla, Mr., 308.

Family Bible, Bewick's, 219.

Fenham, 41.

Fenwick, John, 4; his opinion of Bewick's memoir, 205; editorial work, 302.

Feudal feeling, strength of, 4.

Fisher, Mr., 298 note.

Fleming, John, 22.

Forster, Matthew, 215 note.

"Forth, cot in the," numerous attractions of, 191, 192.

Freehold Dwelling-House and Garden advertisement, 193 note.

GARNETT, JOSEPH, 309.

Garret, William, 302.

Garrick, David, 38.

Gay's Fables, and Edinburgh bookseller, 275.

General Magazine, Newcastle, 22, 43.

Gentleman's Magazine on "Quadrupeds," 285; memoir of Bewick in, 284.

"Gentle Shepherd, the," performed by Scotch regiment in Newcastle, 168.

George and Dragon, 45.

George III. and Bewick's woodcuts, 235.

Gibside, 18.

Gibson & Usher, Messrs., 65.

Gibson, William, town-clerk, 186.

Glossary of North-country words, Brockett's, 129 note, 132, 133; Jackson's projected, 134.

Goldsmith, Oliver, and Miss Bewick, 58.

Goldsmith's Poems, 230, 233.

Good's portrait of Bewick, 199, 208.

"Good times," 7.

Gossip, pleasant, 179.

Goulburn, Gabriel, 145 note.

Gow, Thomas, of Cambo, 16.

Grainger, Richard, 19.

Graphic, the, special number of, and woodcut portrait of Bewick, 214.

Gray, George, fruit-painter, 63, 121, 122; his portrait of John Bewick, 121, 122, 209.

Gray, Gilbert, 32.

Gray, William, 34, 50.

"Gray's Chorographia," 21.

Greencroft Park, 100.

Greenwell, Mr., 298 note.

Gregson, Christopher, 2, 15, and note 134.

Gregson, Christopher and Philip, 50.

Griffith, Moses, 103.

Groat Market, the, 6.

HALL, Edward, of Whitley, 279.

Hall and Elliot, 277.

Hall, Joseph, 21, 23.

Hall, Matthew, 45.

Hamilton, Lieutenant, 175 and note.

Hancock, John, 62 note, 243, 255.

Handbill, a curious, 102.

Hanover, House of, Jacobite gentry of North and, 7.

" Hart, the White," 8.

Harvey, Wllliam, apprentice and favourite pupil of Bewick, 266 ; pupil of Haydon's, 266 ; his fellow-artists, 266 ; illustrates Arabian Nights, etc., 266 ; death, 267.

Hawkins, John Sydney, and Emblems of Mortality, 279.

Haydon Bridge, 34.

Heaton, Breet Star o', 47.

Heddon-on-the-Wall, 41.

" Hermit, Angel, and Guide," instructions concerning, 97.

Hermit, the, at his Devotions, 233.

Heron, Ralph, 73, 252.

Heron, Walter, 304.

" History of British Birds," Bewick's, influence of, 11.

History of Durham, Hutchinson's, 70.

History of Quadrupeds, the several editions of, 281 *et seq.;* Miss Jane Bewick and, 179.

Hive of Ancient and Modern Literature, 118.

Hive, The, extract from, 75.

Hodgson, James and Thomas, 129 note.

Hodgson, James, 282 note.

Hodgson, John, of Elswick Hall, 177.

Hodgson, Rev. John, learned antiquary, 146 ; Bewick's connection with, 146.

Hodgson, Solomon, 82, 118 ; Bewick's wood-engraving to memory of, 218, 282 note.

Hodgson, Thomas, 50, 51.

Hogarth's monument, Garrick's inscription on, applicable to Bewick, 218.

Hole, Henry, pupil of Bewick, 110, 112.

Hole-in-the-Wall, the, 51 and note.

" Holinshed's Chronicles," 21.

Hornby, Miss, of Newcastle, 40.

Horsley, 41.

Horsley Lane, 42.

" Horsley Wood, Hermit of," 124.

Howard, John, visit to Newcastle, 74 ; Burke's estimate of, 74.

Howdy, the, 133, 313.

" Hudibras," 258.

Hugo, the Rev. Thomas, and the " Bewick Collector," 177.

Hunter, Abraham, 250.

" Huntsman and Old Hound," cut of the, 47.

Hunt, William, reference to drawings of, 181.

Hutton, Dr., 43 ; the instructor of Bewick, 44.

" ICONOGRAPHIA SCOTICA," Pinkerton's, 252.

" Impressions," Bewick's opinion as to the best, 291.

Ismay's, Mr., collection of pictures, 66.

JACOBITES and Catholics, 8.

Jacobitism in the North, 7.

Jackson, John, birth, 268; engravings for *Penny Magazine* by, 268 ; his projected Glossary, 133, 134 ; his opinion of Bewick as a wood-engraver, 296.

Jackson, Mason, 134.

Jameson and Wallace, Professors, and Bewick's second visit to Edinburgh, 147.

Jesmond Dene, stocking manufactory at, 123.

Johnson, John, 96, 233, 256.

Johnson, Robert, 96, 233, 247 *et seq.*

Johnson, Willy, playmate of Bewick, 182.

Johnson's caricatures, 249, 250.

Jonson, Ben, 181.

KAY, Thos., pressman, and Bewick, 149.

Kemble, Mrs, 189.

Kemble, Stephen George, 170 and note, 188.

Kenmure, Lord, 5 note.

Kingsley, Rev. William, his estimate of Bewick, 164 *et seq.*

Knight, Charles, and Jackson, 218.

Kyloe Ox, Mr. Spearman's, 82.

LADIES' dress, the Misses Bewick on, 174.

Laird, the, and his vow, 184.

" Lavinia," 255.

Law, William, of Littleborough, 40.

Lawson, Thomas, 219.

Leadbitter, Mr., 77.

Leathart, James, 255.

Leland's Chronicle, 23.

Letters—

    Bewick, John, to Thomas, 94, 224.

    Bewick, Thomas, to Hutchinson, 71; to *Bibliographer*, 83; to his brother John, 90; to Mrs. Bewick, 92; to George Allan, 107; to J. Payne, bookseller, London, 123; to his friend Wm. Carey, 136; to Messrs. Tipper & Fry, 138; to Mr. Charnley, 139, 143; to the printer, etc., 140; to London author and publisher, 145; to Mr. Hopper anent salmon fishing regulations, 151.

    Bulmer, William, to Thomas Bewick, 120.

    Charnley, Mr., to Mr. Bewick, 142.

    From Mrs. Bewick's executors to Mr. Robinson, 212.

    Harvey, William, to Mr. Robinson, 266.

    Morrison, Messrs., of Perth, to Mr. Pinkerton, 253.

Liddell, Anthony, 182.

Liddell, Sir Henry George, 8.

Lightfoot, Joseph Barber, Lord Bishop of Durham, 107.

Linn, John, 22.

Liston the comedian, anecdotes concerning, 189.

Literary coterie and Mr. Charnley, 129 note.

Lloyd, Rev. John, 103.

Locke's head, 22.

London, William, 21.

Longman & Co., fifth edition of Quadrupeds sold to, 238.

Longstaffe, W. H. D., 301.

" Looking Glass for the Mind," 225.

Lushington, Rev. James, 190.

Magazine, Blackwood's, on Bewick, 292, 294.

Magazine Gate, the, 20.

Magazine, Gentleman's, extract from, 56; on death of John Bewick, 289.

Magazine, Newcastle, letter in, respecting the Brothers Beilby, 43.

Magazine, Penny, 268.

Maiden's Walk, the, 17.

Maplisden, Peter, 21.

Marble bust of Bewick, proposal with reference to, 153; circular regarding, 154; extract from article in *British Quarterly Review* on, 154.

Marley, Sir John, 4.

Martin, David, 57, 60; Bewick's opinion of, 142.

Martin, John, 63, 64.

Mary, Charlotte, Countess of Newburgh, 5 note.

Memoir, Bewick's : early essays in Art, 11, 12; chapter treating of religion and politics, 204.

Mensuration, Treatise on, Dr. Hutton's, 43; instruction of Bewick as to cutting and squaring blocks, 44.

Merry Monarch, the, statue of, at Newcastle, 30.

Mickley Bank Colliery and Bewick's father, 1.

Milton, quotation from, 238.

Mitford, Admiral Robert, 222.

Montagu, Mrs. Elizabeth 38, 52, and note.

Morality, Blossoms of, 228.

Morrison, Messrs., Perth, and death of Johnson, 252.

Mortality, Emblems of, 89, 222.

Mounsey, Edward B., 81, 297.

Mozley, Messrs., of Derby, 301.

Murphy's miniature of Bewick, 134 ; engraved by Summerfield, 135.

Murray, John, M.D., 307.

Murray, Rev. James, Bewick's engraving on copper for, 308.

Museum, Wycliffe, 99, 305.

Muss, Charles, 63.

NASMYTH, the landscape-painter, and Bewick, 147.

" Natural History," Goldsmith's, 11.

Naturalist's Library, Jardine's, 156.

Nesbit, Charlton, 247, 251, 257 *et seq.*

Nevill's Cross, 70, 71.

Newburn, 17, 24.

Newburn Church tower, 4.

" Newe House," the, 19.

Newcastle : market days, 3 ; exempt from Royalist and Roundhead loans, 4 ; Bull and Crown Inn, 6 ; Groat Market, 6, 38, 77 ; Literary and Philosophical Society, 8 ; gaiety of, 8 ; the races, 8, 168, 169 ; gentlemen of the Hunt, 8 ; Bewick indentured at, 16 ; natural features of the town, 17 ; monastery of Grey Friars, 18 ; apartments occupied by King Charles I., 18 ; Westgate, 17, 77 ; Pilgrim Street, 17, 169 ; Castle Garth, 19 ; Black Gate, 19 ; Tyne Bridge, 20 ; shops on, 20 *et seq.;* derivation of name, 24 ; the Quayside, 34 ; fall of Tyne Bridge, 35, 36 ; a familiar figure in streets of, 38 ; first mail coach from, 45 ; contested election in, 45, 52 ; natives of, in London, 51 ; picture of the times, 55 ; Saints' Press in, 57 ; social clubs in, 60 ; liquor traffic in, 61 ; fine arts in, 62 ; Lunardi's balloon, first ascent of, in, 72 ; deplorable accident at, 73 ; John Howard's visit to, 74 ; Baillie's History of, 75 note ; state of prison accommodation in, 75 ; club of wits in, 81 ; local songs, 92 ; improvements in, 104 ; Circulating Library in, 106 ; Museum of Natural History, portrait of John Bewick in, 121 ; Literary and Philosophical Society, marble bust of Bewick in, 153 ; " Gentle Shepherd," performed by Scotch regiment in, 168 ; Theatre-Royal at, 170 ; summer attire of fair sex, 174 ; price of tea in, sixty years ago, 179 ; early rising in, 187 ; spinning a principal industry, 187 ; Kemble in, 188 ; claims of, for Bewick treasures, 211 ; itinerant collection of wild and domestic quadrupeds in, 285 note ; spire of the Exchange in, 306 ; worthy tradesmen of, 307.

Newcastle, royal visits, &c., to—Princess Margaret, 23 ; Robert Curthose, son of William the Conqueror, 24 ; Henry I., 24 ; King David of Scotland, 24 ; King Stephen, 24 ; mint of Henry II. at, 24 ; King John and William, king of Scotland, 24 ; Henry III. and his Queen, 24 ; Queen of Scotland, 24 ; Edward I., 26 ; John Baliol pays homage to Edward I. at, 26 ; Edward II. 26 ; Edward III., 26 ; Edward Baliol, 26 ; Henry IV. separates town from county of Northumberland, 26 ; Henry VI., 26 ; Edward IV., 28 ; Richard III., 28 ; Henry VII., 28 ; Henry VIII.'s grant of the Black Friars, 28 ; Edward VI.'s grant to Corporation, 28 ; Queen Mary's do., 28 ; James I., 28 ; presentation to, 28 ; Charles I., 30 ; Charles II. confirms charter to town, &c., 30 ; James II., magnificent statue of at, 30.

Newcastle and the Fine Arts, 62.

Newcastle, contested election at, 45.

Newcastle, Corporation of, grants to, 28.

Newcastle, first mail coach from, to London, 45.

Newcastle General Magazine, 22.

Newcastle Hunt, the, 10.

Newcastle Literary and Philosophical Society, 8.

Newcastle, old inns in, 61.

Newcastle Races, 8 ; the old squires and the, 9.

"Newcastle Reprints," 37.

Newcastle-upon-Tyne, "the county of the town of," 26.

Newspapers in Newcastle, references to— *Chronicle*, 10 note, 32, 38 and note, 55, 82, 129 note, 139, 145 ; *Courant*, 43 note, 50, 81, 139, 178.

Nichols, Mr., bookseller to George III., 235, 288 note.

Nicholson, William, engraver, 147.

Northumberland, domestic annals of, 3, 4 ; society, 8 ; habits of gentry, 8 ; neglect of music and painting in, 10.

"Northumberland, History of," 146.

Northumberland, prison for county of, 75.

Nun's Moor, the, 41.

"Nuremberg Chronicle," the, 21.

OVINGHAM, 1, 2, 3, 4, 11, 15, 37, 42, 54.

Ovingham Bridge Company, the, 125.

Ovingham Church, 216.

Oracles, the, 237.

"Ornaments, Copeland's," 43.

"Ornithologia Nova," 72.

PARTNERSHIP, dissolution of, with Beilby discussed, 93 ; recommended, 117.

Pastime, a cruel, example of, in "British Birds," 185.

Pearson, Edwin, 277.

Pearson, Rev. E., 277.

Pease, J. W., 89, 114 note, 136, 297.

Peltro, J., 89.

Pennant, Thomas, 102.

Phipps, Hon. Constantine John, 45.

Pickering, George, 81 and note, 215.

Picture, a saddening, 75.

Pidcock, Gilbert, 297.

Pintado, sketch for cut, 177.

Pocket-Book, Annual Ladies', 249.

Poems, Goldsmith's, Bulmer's edition of, 95 ; John Bewick's work in connection with, 95 ; unique copy of, 96.

Pollard, Robert, 50, 89, 298 note.

Pope, quotation from, 181.

Preface, an interesting, 157.

Printers, self-sufficiency of, 204.

Prospectus of "History of Quadrupeds," 84.

"Proverbs Exemplified," 223.

Prowling Cat, the, 227.

Prudhoe and Ovingham, bridge between, 124, 125.

QUADRUPEDS, History of, narrative concerning, 82, 281 *et seq.*

RACE Week at Newcastle, Bewick's custom during, 168.

Races, Newcastle, a thing of the past, 169.

Radcliffe, Charles, 5 note ; his assumed name, 6 ; at Durham, 6, 7.

Ramsay, Allan, 23, 32.

Randell, Richard, 21.

Ravensworth, 18.

Ravensworth Castle, 80, 81.

Ranson, Thomas Fryer, 271 and note.

Reay, Henry Utrick, 298.

Receipt, a curious, 127.

Red Brick House, the, 185 note.

"Reedwater Minstrel," the, 215 and note.

Relic, an early, of Bewick's, 195.

Rents, house, on Tyne Bridge, 22.

Review, Annual, on Bewick, 283 note.

Richardson, Thomas Miles, 63, 65.

Richardson, children of, 66.

Ridley, the house of, 47.

Ridley, Sir Matthew White, 45.

"Rob, Little," 116.

Robin Hood, Isabella Bewick's copy of, 288.

"Robin Hood's Garland," 288.

Robinson, Thomas W. U., 297, 298.

Rogers' "Pleasures of Memory," 265.

Roxby, Robert, 215 and note.

"Rubens and his Wife," engraving, 136.

Ruskin, John, his opinion of Bewick's Memoir, 205.

SABOURN'S Latin Grammar, 21.

" Sad Historian, The," 230, 234.

" Seasons," Thomson's, 118 ; Bewick and, 173.

Saint, Thomas, 45, 47, 56.

Scott, David, R.S.A., Memoirs of, 126.

Scott, John, animal painter, 298 note.

Scotus, Duns, the Subtle Doctor, 18.

Shakespeare Press, the, 98, 233, 289, 290.

Sheep, the, and the Bramble-bush, 40.

Shenstone, quotation from, 67.

Shield, William, 258.

" Shipwreck," Falconer's, 260.

Sighre and Aniea, 280.

Slack, Mr., 38.

Society for Diffusion of Useful Knowledge and wood-engraving, 268.

Somervile's Chase, 120, 234.

Song, Lapland, 81.

Speed's Map, 19.

Spence, Robert, 309.

Spence, Thomas, 34, 35.

Spinning at the Forth, 187.

Spital Field, 19.

Squires, old, habits of the, 9.

St. Nicholas' Churchyard, Bewick's workshop in, 104.

Stamfordham, Vicar of, 2.

Stephenson, George, centenary of, 214.

Strathmore, Lady, 52.

Stuart, Prince Charles Edward, 5 note ; favour towards, in North, 7.

Sugar-basin, Bewick's, 212.

Summerfield, J., 135, 136.

Sunderland Bridge, 250.

" Synopsis of the Newcastle Museum," Fox's, 243, 278, 280.

" TABLE Book, Local Historian's," 39.

Tailpiece, Bewick's last, 305.

Tale-pieces full of meaning, 184.

Tales Abridged from French Manuscripts, cuts by T. and J. Bewick in, 290.

" Tales for Youth," 227.

Tam o' Shanter, suggested illustrated edition of, 109, 111.

Taylor, Isaac, 40, 50, 51.

Temple, William, 127.

Thompson, Isaac, 288 note.

Thomson, quotation from, 173.

Thornton's Family Herbal, 145.

Thurston, John, 96 note.

Town watch, the, 193.

Tower, Gunnerton, 171.

Tower, Westgate, 41.

Tower, West Spital, 171.

" Traveller, The," 233.

Travels of Imagination, Rev. James Murray and, 180.

Treasures, Bewick, 211 ; value of, 211.

Trevelyan, Sir John, 52.

Trevelyan, W. C., 158 and note.

Trusler, Rev. Dr., his opinion of John Bewick, 223.

Tunstall, Marmaduke, 78, 99, 103, note.

Turk's Head Long Room, performance by Scotch regiment of " Gentle Shepherd " at, 168.

Turner, Rev. William, his memoir of Bewick, 156.

Tyne Bridge, 20 ; fall of, 35.

Tyne, River, 17.

Tyneside, pastoral loveliness of, 42, 43.

VAUGHAN, Mrs. George, 263.

Vignette, an interesting, 149.

" WAITING for Death," 16, 159 *et seq.*

Wallbottle, 41.

Walker, Edward, 149, 140, 158, 283.

Ward, Robert, 219, 305.

Warkworth, Hermitage at, engraving of, 89.

" Warkworth, Hermit of," 118.

Warren, Charles, 256.

Watson, Henry, 115.

Watson, Robert, 63.

" Wauking of the Fauld," Allan Ramsay's, 167.

Way, Gregory Lewis, 289.

Westall, Richard, 96 and note.

Wheatley, Mr., 83.

White, John, 139.

White, Robert, and Bewick's Memoir, 204.

Whitfield, Joseph, 249.

Whitley Large Ox, 82.

Willis, Edward, 185.

Willy Dean's Cottage, 116.

Wingate, Richard, 19, 100.

Winter-night amusements, 3.

Wood, Mr. H. Trueman, 83.

Wood-engraving prior to Bewick's time, 72.

Woodward, George, 36.

Woollett, William, 159.

Works, list and description of, illustrated by Thomas and John Bewick—

Blossoms of Morality, 287.

Burns's Poetical Works, 300.

Camoens, Luis de, Memoirs of, 303.

Chillingham Wild Bull, 278.

Choice Emblems, 277.

Curious Hieroglyphick Bible, 276.

Emblems of Mortality, 279.

Fables, Æsop's, 302.

Fables by Gay, 275.

Fables extracted from Dodsley's, 276.

Fables in Verse, 276.

Fables, Select, 304.

Fables, Select, 276.

Fabliaux, or Tales abridged from French MSS., 289.

Fergusson's Poetical Works, 300.

General History of Quadrupeds, 281.

Harrison's Nursery Picture Book, 281.

Hermit of Warkworth, the, 300.

History of British Birds, 290.

History of Birds, Supplement to, 304.

History of England, a, 301.

Hive of Ancient and Modern Literature, 297.

Large Woodcuts, Four—Zebra, Elephant, Tiger, and Lion, 297.

Looking-Glass for the Mind, 287.

Lusitana, Bibliotheca, 303.

Memoir of T. Bewick, 305.

Moral Instruction of a Father to his Son, 275.

Pieces of Antient Popular Poetry, 285.

Poems by Goldsmith and Parnell, 287.

Poetical Works of Oliver Goldsmith, 285.

Pretty Book of Pictures for Little Masters and Misses, 275.

Progress of Man and Society, 285.

Proverbs Exemplified and Illustrated, 280.

Proverbs in Verse, 281.

Remarkable Kyloe Ox, 284.

Robin Hood, 288.

Seasons, Thomson's, 300.

Short Treatise, a, on Useful Invention called Sportsman Friend, 298.

Somervile's Chase, 289.

Sportsman's Cabinet, the, 298.

Tales for Youth, 286.

Tour Through Sweden, &c., 280.

Treatise on Mensuration, 274.

Typographical Society Publications, Newcastle, 302.

Vignettes, 305.

Whitley Large Ox, 279.

Wray, William, M., 217.

Wren, Sir Christopher, 30.

Wrightson Family, the, 1.

Wynne, J. H., author of Tales for Youth, 286.

YOUTH'S INSTRUCTOR, cuts for, and other publications, 274.

Youth's Instructor, the, 45.

PRINTED BY BALLANTYNE, HANSON AND CO.
EDINBURGH AND LONDON.